Created and Directed by Hans Höfer

INSIGHT GUIDES
US★NATIONAL PARKS EAST→

Edited by John Gattuso
Managing Editor: Martha Ellen Zenfell

Editorial Director: Brian Bell

APA PUBLICATIONS

ABOUT THIS BOOK

Höfer

A US Senator once called the national parks "a great breathing place for the national lungs." The description is particularly apt in the eastern US, where the parks provide welcome islands of wilderness in an otherwise crowded land.

Insight Guide: US National Parks East is the second of two books dedicated to America's national parks, and part of the award-winning travel series created in 1970 by **Hans Höfer**, chairman of Apa Publications. One of the first guidebook companies to recognize the need for ecologically aware travel, each of Apa's 190 Insight titles encourages readers to celebrate the essence of a place rather than try to tailor it to their expectations, and is edited in the belief that, without insight, travel can narrow the mind rather than broaden it.

Gattuso

The present project was conceived and directed by **John Gattuso**, editor of Stone Creek Publications in Milford, New Jersey. An Apa veteran whose credits include *Insight Guide: US National Parks West*, *Insight Guide: Native America*, *Insight Guide: Wild West*, *Insight Guide: Philadelphia* and a half-dozen other titles, Gattuso attempts to present the parks not only as a travel destination but "a cornerstone of America's environmental conscience." He was aided in the overall direction of the book by Apa Publications' editor-in-chief of US titles, **Martha Ellen Zenfell**, whose own experience of growing up in Shenandoah National Park can be read on page 220.

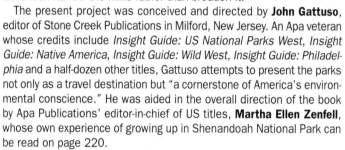

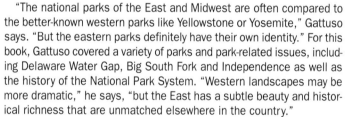

Zenfell

"The national parks of the East and Midwest are often compared to the better-known western parks like Yellowstone or Yosemite," Gattuso says. "But the eastern parks definitely have their own identity." For this book, Gattuso covered a variety of parks and park-related issues, including Delaware Water Gap, Big South Fork and Independence as well as the history of the National Park System. "Western landscapes may be more dramatic," he says, "but the East has a subtle beauty and historical richness that are unmatched elsewhere in the country."

Toops

W hen it came time to assemble a team of writers and photographers, Gattuso searched for people who combined detailed knowledge of the parks with the sort of lucid journalistic style that is the hallmark of Insight Guides. One of the first to be chosen was **Connie Toops**, a writer and photographer based in Martinsburg, West Virginia. A former park ranger, Toops has lived or worked in more than a half-dozen parks, including Everglades, Gulf Islands, Buffalo National River and Shenandoah. The author of five books and countless articles, Toops's interest in the outdoors started early. "I was always up in a tree," she says of her childhood. In addition to writing about several southern parks, her photographs appear throughout the book.

Rice

The Midwest was covered by **Larry Rice**, a writer and photographer living in Lacon, Illinois. A wildlife biologist and avid outdoorsman, Rice has written four books and more than 250 articles chronicling his adventures in the wilderness. In this book, he concentrates on the parks of the great North Woods. "This is one of the last and largest wilderness areas in the Midwest," Rice says. "It's quintessential canoe country, where a person can load up a canoe and travel for a few hours or a few weeks in the path of 18th-century missionaries and fur-traders."

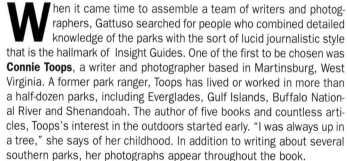

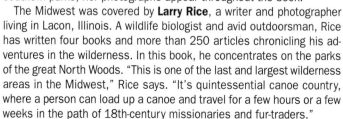

In New England, Gattuso found **Stephen Gorman**, who penned the chapters on Acadia, Cape Cod, the Appalachian Trail and radical outdoor recreation. A former Park Service planner, Gorman now works as a freelance writer and photographer from his home in Exeter, New Hampshire. "Diversity is the catchword for New England," Gorman says. "From the coast to the mountains, there may be more to do in this compact region than anywhere else in the country."

Gorman

Houk

Rounding out the text was **Rose Houk**, a writer, editor and former park ranger who covered the Great Smoky Mountains and eastern flora. Husband-and-wife team **Bill Sharp** and **Elaine Appleton** of Fresh Air Communications wrote about wildlife, geology and the Civil War parks. **Yvette LaPierre**, a frequent contributor to *National Parks Magazine*, covered a variety of historic sites, and **Michael McCormick** wrote about the New River Gorge.

T he book's vivid and exceptional photography is the work of many people. One of the premier landscape photographers in the US, **Tom Till** says his photographs "express my joy in being surrounded by nature." He's especially fond of shooting in the "special light" produced by "rough weather" and "often follows storms across the country to capitalize on the possibility of a special moment."

Till

Larry Ulrich in Trinidad, California, has been a professional photographer for more than 20 years. He is the author of five books and contributes to major magazines and calendars. **Lewis Kemper** is an outdoor photographer based in Sacramento, California.

Tom and **Pat Leeson**, a husband-and-wife team from Vancouver, Washington, have specialized in wildlife photography for many years. **Lyle Lawson** has shot over a dozen Insight Guides, from *Burgundy* to *Jordan*. **Robert Llewellyn** has produced more than 20 books of photography.

Photographic contributor **Bill Lea** claims to get "a thrill in experiencing nature firsthand." A member of the US Forest Service as well as a wildlife photographer, Lea says he "put down a fishing pole and picked up a camera" about 15 years ago, "and it's been all photography ever since." Based in Franklin, North Carolina, Lea specializes in the wilderness areas of the southeastern US. "From the snow-covered peaks of the Blue Ridge Mountains to the subtropical hardwood hammocks of the Everglades," he says, "no other place in America has a greater diversity of habitats."

Lea

Tom Stack & Associates, a stock agency based in Colorado Springs, Colorado provided an assortment of stunning images, while additional photographs were contributed by **Art Wolfe, Joseph Nettis, Steve Mulligan, Stephen Trimble, Arvilla Brewer, Robert Harrison, Judith Jango-Cohen, Catherine Karnow, Pat and Bob Momich, Stephen Shaluta, George Wuerthner** and **Pat Toops**.

In Insight Guides' London editorial office, the manuscript was proofread and indexed by **Pam Barrett**. In the United States, special thanks go to **Edward A. Jardim** for invaluable editorial help, and to the many park rangers and naturalists who answered what seemed like a million questions and subsequently reviewed the text.

CONTENTS

CONTENTS

TRAVEL TIPS

IN SEARCH OF WILDNESS

The question is invariably asked: How do the national parks of the eastern United States compare with those of the West?

Well, to begin with, the eastern parks tend to be smaller. There are exceptions, of course. The Everglades and Great Smoky Mountains, for example, are larger than most of their western counterparts. But most parks in the East don't rival the sweeping tracts of wilderness encompassed by the Grand Canyon, Yellowstone or the vast Alaskan preserves.

More important than actual size, however, the eastern parks *feel* smaller, more intimate. The mountains aren't quite as high in the East nor the canyons quite as deep. The landscapes seem gentler, rounder, less given to extremes of topography and weather. There are no glaciers or icebergs, no active volcanoes or searing deserts. And even in the most rugged places, the terrain is softened by a thick blanket of vegetation and an abundance of free-flowing water.

To be sure, there is plenty of gorgeous scenery in the eastern parks. What could be more stirring than the Blue Ridge Mountains cloaked in an early-morning mist, the New River Gorge ablaze with autumn color, the Atlantic Ocean raging against Acadia's rocky shore, the turquoise waters of Trunk Bay fringed with a crescent of sand and deep-green forest?

But the beauty of these places is more subtle than the western parks. They are less spectacular, less monumental, easier to relate to on a human scale. They draw us in, urge us to look closer, to see not only the great canyons and mountains and other natural wonders that have made the national parks famous but also the rocks at our feet, the flowers and leaves and wildlife that we might otherwise take for granted.

"The inevitable mark of wisdom," said Ralph Waldo Emerson, "is to see the miraculous in the common." The eastern parks encourage us to do exactly that, to understand the environment on its own terms, to see the miracle of nature in its humblest as well as its grandest manifestations. To borrow a phrase from E.F. Schumacher, "small is beautiful." And for those who make the effort to look closely, there is no end of wonders in the smallest objects – a fragile spring blossom, a pebble on the beach, a spider's web, a blade of grass.

"Nature will bear the closest inspection," Henry David Thoreau observed. "She invites us to lay our eye level with her smallest leaf, and take an insect view of its plain."

These "insect views" led Thoreau to powerful insights into the natural world and its importance to the human spirit. But of course he was ahead of his time. A hundred years before such notions became fashionable, he saw nature as a living thing, a source of

Preceding pages: petals and pine needles; white-tail buck; rafting guide and friends on the New River, West Virginia; sunset over the Great Smoky Mountains; Miners Beach on Lake Superior, Pictured Rocks National Lakeshore; eroded landscape of Providence Canyon in Georgia; a dazzling display of prairie wildflowers. **Left,** bald eagles perch on a snag.

spiritual renewal. "The earth I tread on is not a dead, inert mass; it is a body, has a spirit, is organic and fluid…"

For Thoreau, contact with the natural world was a deep-seated need. He made a ritual of his daily walks through the fields and forests around his Concord home, filling his journal with keen observations. "In wildness is the preservation of the world," he proclaimed, suggesting that an experience of nature – even in the humble woods and meadows around Concord – is a human necessity. And it's this search for wildness, this hunger for intimacy with the natural world, that makes the national parks such a valuable resource. Although less spectacular than their western cousins, the eastern national parks give us something that's difficult to find elsewhere, places where we can relate to nature on its own terms, where we can strap on a backpack or get into a canoe and be filled with wonder.

But nature isn't the only focus here. The land also bears a human imprint. Unlike Denali or Yellowstone, which were preserved in a virtually pristine state, many eastern parks are pieced together from private lands that had been inhabited for generations. It's not uncommon to stumble upon the remains of an old cabin or tumbled-down chimney even in the most remote backwoods. The ghosts of the former residents are close at hand, and in parks such as Big South Fork and New River Gorge they occasionally come back in the flesh to spruce up gravesites, visit old homesteads, or wander about familiar woods. The lush forests that now stand in parks such as Shenandoah and Great Smoky Mountains are not only testimony to the healing powers of nature but to the fortitude and ingenuity of a people who, as Freeman Tilden put it, "fought and bled, pioneered and hungered, created homes, raised children, laughed and wept, and lived and died" in these very same mountains.

The old voices may also be heard at the many historic parks that are scattered throughout the East. These include places like Gettysburg, Independence Hall, Jamestown and Ellis Island where the American experience is brought to life. These parks are not only a link to the past, they're a source of identity. They tell the story of America's people from the ancient Mound Builders right up to the struggle for civil rights in the late 20th century. They chronicle the great leaders, artists, thinkers, events and institutions that continue to shape the nation. They relate the stories that tell Americans who they are and where they came from.

This is a crowded land. Wilderness – what little remains – is broken up by cities and suburbs, ribbons of highway and so-called "industrial parks." All the more reason that the national parks deserve our care. These precious slices of wilderness are more than overgrown playgrounds. They are a source of peace and renewal that is available to anyone who, in Rachel Carson's words, is willing to "place himself under the influence of earth, sea and sky."

Carson wrote: "Those who dwell… among the beauties and mysteries of the earth are never alone or weary of life. Whatever the vexations or concerns of their personal lives, their thoughts can find paths that lead to inner contentment and to renewed excitement in living. Those who contemplate the beauty of the earth find reserves of strength that will endure as long as life lasts."

Right, canoe country, Voyageurs National Park, Minnesota.

The idea was hatched in 1870 around a campfire in Yellowstone. The author was Cornelius Hedges, a member of the famous Washburn Expedition, who proposed that the geologic wonders of the Yellowstone country be withheld from private ownership. Two years later, Yellowstone became the world's first national park.

And that's how it all began. At least that's one version of how it happened. More likely, Hedges simply latched onto an idea that had been floating around for quite a while. In fact, a few reserves, such as the Yosemite Valley in California, had already been created, although none were quite as large as Yellowstone or under the direct control of the federal government.

Protect nature: Yellowstone may have been the first in name only, but that doesn't diminish its importance. Actually, it's quite amazing that it happened at all. Americans in the late 19th century weren't much in the mood for creating parks. Protect nature? Most people were more interested in profiting from it. In fact, Congress approved the park only after it was convinced that Yellowstone contained nothing but "valueless land."

The way a lot of Americans saw it, the nation had a legitimate right to exploit and "civilize" the wild territory west of the Mississippi River. Settlers rushed across the prairie to the goldfields and sawmills, farms and ranches that sprang up across the West. The settlers were called argonauts, saints, pioneers, nation-builders, and were regarded as the vanguard of an anointed people.

"Our manifest destiny is to overspread and to possess the whole of the continent," wrote editor John Lewis O'Sullivan, giving a purpose, and a name, to the great westward migration.

There were some people who worried that "progress" could also mean loss. In 1832, George Catlin, a painter from Pennsylvania

who chronicled the Indians of the West, realized that the wild country beyond the Mississippi River would soon be overrun by civilization. With uncanny foresight, he proposed that the Great Plains be preserved "by some great protecting policy of government… in a *magnificent park.*"

"What a beautiful and thrilling specimen for America to preserve and hold up to the view of her refined citizens and the world, in future ages!" he wrote. "A *nation's park*, containing man and beast, in all the wild[ness]

and freshness of their nature's beauty."

Catlin was a voice in the wilderness. Busy building a nation, most Americans weren't prepared to hear what he had to say. But there were a few exceptions, those who, like Catlin, found a deeper value in nature.

In the East, Ralph Waldo Emerson, Henry David Thoreau and other writers associated with the New England Transcendentalists looked to the natural world for spiritual renewal. As the guiding light of the movement, Emerson urged his devotees to eschew the example of the Old World and seek the invigorating spirit of the American earth.

"Embosomed for a season in nature, whose

floods of life stream around and through us… why should we grope among the dry bones of the past…?" he asked. "In the woods is perpetual youth…. In the woods, we return to reason and faith. There I feel that nothing can befall me in life – no disgrace, no calamity… which nature cannot repair…. The currents of the Universal Being circulate through me; I am part and parcel of God."

Thoreau was equally devoted to the "sublime revelations of nature," although, unlike Emerson, he actually possessed detailed knowledge of plants and animals. And though he rarely ventured far from home ("I have traveled broadly in Concord," he quipped), he saw what few others were able to see – that

far from the healing power of living things.

John of the Mountains: The baton was passed from east to west in 1871 when, during a sojourn in California, an elderly Ralph Waldo Emerson encountered an extraordinary, if rather odd, young man named John Muir, who was then living in a ramshackle "hangnest" in the mountains around Yosemite. The old philosopher spent a day with Muir taking in the wonders of the Sierra woods. "There is a young man from whom we shall hear," Emerson told friends. And indeed, the young naturalist would be heard by many.

John Muir had come to the Sierra Nevada two years earlier and immediately fell in love with the place. "We are now in the mountains

the best use of nature is to leave it as it is. "This curious world which we inhabit is more wonderful than it is convenient, more beautiful than it is useful; it is more to be admired than to be used."

Thoreau detested the intrusive designs of government, but he recognized the need for preservation before both men and beasts were "civilized off the face of the earth." "Every creature is better alive than dead, men and moose, and pine trees," he wrote; "and he who understands it aright will rather preserve its life than destroy it." He even suggested that small parks be set aside in every town so that residents would never be

and they are in us, kindling enthusiasm, making every nerve quiver," he wrote in 1869. Like Emerson and Thoreau, Muir felt a spiritual attachment to the land and regarded wilderness as a human necessity. "The trees, the mountains are not near or far," he wrote. "They are made one, unseparate, unclothed, open to the divine soul, dissolved in the mysterious, incomparable spirit of holy light."

A gifted and persuasive writer, Muir quickly became the voice and conscience of American conservationism. He wielded his pen against loggers, sheepherders and other "temple destroyers" who threatened his beloved Yosemite, and he campaigned for new parks dedicated to mountains and forests elsewhere in the West. "God has cared for these trees, saved them from drought, disease, avalanches and floods, but he cannot save them from fools. Only Uncle Sam can do that," he said.

Slowly, grudgingly, Uncle Sam acted. In 1890, after much campaigning and cajoling, Congress authorized the creation of Sequoia, General Grant (later incorporated into Kings Canyon) and Yosemite national parks in California, followed several years later by Mount Rainier in Washington. Then, in 1901, Muir and his fellow conservationists found a powerful ally in President Theodore

another several years before the idea was even seriously considered.

There were problems with establishing a park in the East. For one thing, the eastern states were much more populated than the West. For another, the wild country – what little still remained – was already owned by private citizens. There was something else, too: a certain flatness to the landscape, the East lacking the monumental canyons and mountains that one finds in the western parks.

The solution came in the person of John D. Rockefeller, Jr, who, together with a group of concerned (and wealthy) friends, donated 6,000 acres (2,400 hectares) of Mount Desert Island, an extremely rugged and picturesque

Roosevelt. An avid outdoorsman and a firm believer in the goals of conservationism, Roosevelt added more than 130 million acres (53 million hectares) to the national forests, launched a system of wildlife refuges, and created 18 national parks and monuments, including the Grand Canyon, Petrified Forest and Devils Tower.

Eastern parks: But there were still no parks east of the Mississippi River. In fact, it took

<u>Left</u>, John Muir (on left), and John Burroughs, among the most eminent naturalists of their day. <u>Above</u>, park rangers, wearing the signature Smoky Bear hat, regularly patrol the parks.

piece of real estate off the coast of Maine. Originally designated Sieur de Monts National Monument in 1916, the site was later expanded and renamed Acadia National Park.

Rockefeller came to the rescue again in the 1920s after Congress authorized two new parks in the southern Appalachians – Great Smoky Mountains and Shenandoah. He contributed $5 million to purchase land for the former and a lesser amount for the latter.

These new parks presented a number of difficulties. First, much of the land was already occupied, which meant that thousands of small parcels had to be acquired and the owners relocated – a slow and tedious process at best. Second, the parks had been badly damaged by farming and logging. The Park Service was not only required to preserve the natural features that already existed but to restore the park to an essentially primitive state, all the while building roads, exhibits and other visitor facilities.

Much of the work was done by the Civilian Conservation Corps. Formed during the Great Depression by President Franklin D. Roosevelt, the new organization was designed to rehabilitate both the economy and the land. Thousands of jobless men were recruited by the corps and dispatched to the nation's parks and forests to plant trees, control erosion and build much-needed facilities. By

the time the Civilian Conservation Corps was disbanded at the onset of World War II, many of its finest men and programs had been incorporated into the Park Service.

Still other changes were broadening the mission of the national parks. Starting in 1916, immediately after the creation of an independent National Park Service, the system underwent a long period of expansion, taking over a variety of national monuments and historic sites formerly administered by the Forest Service or War Department.

The most significant event in this period was the reorganization of 1933. With a stroke of the presidential pen, Franklin Roosevelt transferred more than 50 sites to the National Park Service, including important Civil War battlefields such as Gettysburg, Shiloh and Antietam. The transfer also covered the many monuments and memorials administered by the National Capital Parks in Washington, DC, as well as several significant natural areas such as Saguaro and Chiricahua national monuments in Arizona and Olympic National Park in Washington.

Much later, efforts were made to confer national park status on sites such as Voyageurs in Minnesota, Isle Royale in Michigan, Everglades and Biscayne Bay in Florida, and St John in the Virgin Islands that were more notable for their ecological than scenic value. This was a critical shift in philosophy. The national parks were no longer regarded simply as a catalog of natural wonders but as "vignettes of primitive America" dedicated to the protection of entire ecosystems. The mission of the Park Service was redefined. It was no longer enough simply to protect the parks; they should also be restored to an essentially primitive state. That effort continues. Among the most notable programs are the reintroduction of red wolves to Great Smoky Mountains and, in 1995, the return of gray wolves to Yellowstone after a 50-year absence.

The Park Service also developed entirely new categories of parks, including national recreation areas, lakeshores, seashores and rivers. Many are more recreation-oriented. Parks such as New River Gorge National Park, Cape Cod National Seashore and Delaware Water Gap National Recreation Area are intended to protect natural features while providing for a wide range of uses.

The national parks have been called the best idea America has ever had. An overstatement, perhaps, but it's certainly a measure of how precious the parks are in the hearts of those who visit them. These places are more than islands of nature. They are part of America's identity. And in the East, where wild places are few and far between, they provide a much-needed opportunity for people to see in nature what Thoreau and Catlin and Muir saw – a glimpse of the world "beyond the boundaries of human existence."

Left, ranger on duty. **Right**, an avid outdoorsman, President Theodore Roosevelt helped create more than a dozen national parks and monuments.

Pick up a rock and hold it in your hand. Ask yourself where it came from and how it was created. It may be hundreds of thousands, perhaps millions of years old. Was it blasted from a volcano, carried inside a glacier, crushed and baked in the bowels of the earth?

The eastern national parks are so rich in plant and animal life that many people forget about the rocky strata that lies beneath them. But the biosphere, the zone of life, is only a wisp of living matter layered over the crust of the planet. Wherever you look – from the glacier-carved shores of Acadia to the mangrove swamps of the Everglades – the character of living things is dependent upon the nurturing breast of the earth.

The backbone of the East: When life on our planet was exploding in the shallow seas of the Paleozoic Era 500 million years ago, the land masses that would later become Europe and Africa moved toward North America, forcing the sea floor under its plate and thrusting the mighty Appalachians skyward. From present-day Labrador to Alabama, the eroded roots of this ancient mountain range dominate the eastern landscape.

The slow-motion collision that created the Appalachians was a messy affair. It wrenched the earth's crust into a mountainous melange that author John McPhee describes as a "compressed, chaotic, ropy enigma 4,000 kilometres from end to apparent end, full of overturned strata and recycled rock, of steep faults and horizontal thrust sheets, of folds so tight that what had once stretched 20 miles might now fit into five."

Confusing the geologic record throughout the Appalachians are layers of older rock thrust atop younger, deep faults and highly metamorphosed rock. Was the creation of the Appalachians as simple as a collision of two tectonic plates? Geologists are not so sure. Some conjecture that a string of islands – so-called "suspect terrain" – may have been caught in the crash and pressed against

the rising mountains, creating a geologic hash whose origins are still being debated.

The rise of the Appalachians had profound effects far beyond the misty summits of the Blue Ridge and Great Smoky Mountains. Along its western ramparts, for example, are the Allegheny, Cumberland and Pocono plateaus – a long shelf of high country that rose up with the mountains and was later eroded into the dramatic river valleys of the New River Gorge, Big South Fork and Delaware Water Gap.

Less obvious, perhaps, is how the Appalachians helped create Mammoth Cave in Kentucky. Formation of this subterranean labyrinth began about 200 million years ago when water, made acidic by carbon dioxide in the air and soil, began trickling down to a thick layer of limestone, widening the joints and cracks created during the uplift of the mountains. As the water table dropped, it left behind a network of magnificent caverns and tortuous crawlways, many encrusted with bizarre mineral formations created by the slow accumulation of calcite crystals. More than 330 miles (530 km) of underground passages have been mapped at Mammoth

Preceding pages: rock formations inside Mammoth Cave, Kentucky, the longest explored cave in the world. **Left**, ice amphitheater, Ice Age National Scenic Trail, Wisconsin. **Right**, granite waterfall, White Mountains, New Hampshire.

Cave, making it the longest explored cave system in the world.

Legacy of ice: From the moment the Appalachians began to rise up, the process of tearing them down was underway. Ice and water worked on the mountains, carrying tons of silt and sand down its tumbling streams and giving the middle-aged Appalachians a mellower profile than younger ranges like the Rockies and Sierra Nevada.

At the onset of the Ice Age, or Pleistocene, about 1.8 million years ago, the first of several waves of glaciers barreled through the northern Appalachians. The great sheets of ice, some 2 miles (3.2 km) thick, broadened river valleys, smoothed jagged peaks, metamorphic and granitic rocks, gouging out the estuaries, coves, lakes and U-shaped valleys that characterize the Maine coast, most of which are oriented in the southeast-to-northeast direction of the glaciers' retreat.

Far to the west, glaciers widened the huge depressions that would later become the Great Lakes. When they retreated north about 10,000 years ago, they laid bare portions of the Canadian Shield, a huge platter of basement rock that underlies much of Canada and the northern United States. This is the oldest exposed rock in the country. Patches at Voyageurs National Park, in the Boundary Waters between Minnesota and Ontario, are some 2½ billion years old, about half the age

deposited huge mounds of debris, and plucked up house-sized boulders (known as erratics) and transported them miles from their origin.

The path of these icy juggernauts is particularly clear at Acadia National Park off the rugged Maine coast, which was overtaken by thousands of feet of glacial ice at least 20 times during the past few million years. Acadia's rocky foundation is perhaps 500 million years old; it was formed by marine sediments and volcanic ash that were successively buried and uplifted, shattered and baked by intrusions of molten rock that slowly hardened into granite. Glaciers scraped across this complex assemblage of of the earth. Some parts of Voyageurs were worn so smooth by the great mantles of ice that trees and other plants grew only where glacial grooves collected enough soil for seedlings to take root. At Isle Royale National Park, off the northwest shore of Lake Superior, retreating glaciers left behind a series of parallel ridges and valleys that run the entire length of the island.

Edge of the sea: Glaciers left their mark elsewhere in the Northeast, too. The flexed arm of Cape Cod, for example, is what geologists call a "terminal moraine," a great pile of boulders, gravel and silt that were dumped at the edge of a receding glacier.

Like massive footprints, the Cape's bowl-like "kettle ponds" were created by huge blocks of ice pressed into the morainal mound and left to melt about 10,000 years ago.

Glaciers also helped shape the shores to the south of Cape Cod, although they never advanced much beyond Long Island. As they melted, fast-moving streams and rivers carried pulverized rock to the sea, where waves and currents piled the sediments onto beaches. The release of glacial water caused sea level to rise, drowning the old coastline. The seashores are now among the most dynamic landscapes in the East. Barrier islands such as Cape Hatteras, Cape Lookout and Cumberland Island are constantly altered

is under water. Below the surface, limestone contains the massive acquifers that are the lifeblood of the Everglades, although diversions to cities and corporate farms threaten to choke off the supply of fresh water that keeps the "river of grass" flowing.

The rise in sea level inundated all but the very tops of Florida's coral islands, or keys, which arc across some 200 miles (320 km) from Biscayne National Park to the Dry Tortugas. The keys were built up over hundreds of thousands of years by the tiny, calcium-secreting polyps that form coral reefs. In fact, reef-building continues. Within the Park system, scuba divers and snorkelers can get a first-hand look at the rainbow world

by wind and waves and by the earth-shaping power of hurricanes and winter gales.

The sea swallowed up much of southern Florida, too, swamping the gently sloped bed of Miami limestone that underlies Everglades National Park. The Everglades are actually a wide, shallow river that moves slowly toward the brackish waters of Florida Bay, a vast marine nursery for shrimp, lobsters, sponges and a variety of fishes. During the rainy summer season, about 90 percent of the park

Left, Rugged shore of Newport Bay, Acadia National Park. **Above**, Place of One Thousand Drips, Great Smoky Mountains National Park.

of coral reefs at Biscayne Bay and Dry Tortugas national parks.

The Park Service also protects coral reefs in the Caribbean at Buck Island Reef National Monument off the island of St Croix and Virgin Islands National Park on St John, both volcanic islands fringed by living reefs.

From the azure waters of the Caribbean Sea to the windswept shores of the Great Lakes, the national parks are a vast repository of geologic treasures. There is history in the rocks, stories about creation, cataclysm and earth-shaping change. And although it may seem difficult to learn how to read them, it's easy enough to start. Just pick up a rock.

The East – it's wet, it's green and "real" trees grow there. But it's more. In national parks and along seashores and wild rivers east of the Mississippi, you'll find everything from northern boreal forests to grassland prairies and much in between, including sunlit beaches and dunes, verdant deciduous woods, moody cypress swamps, and even seductive subtropics.

Shore and dunes: Forest meets sea on the rockbound coast of Maine. After the Ice Age came and went, granite that was laid bare by glaciers offered new frontiers for plants. The first colonizers of the raw land were lichens, followed by mosses and sedges. Today, that same process of succession can be seen along the coast. In the tidal zone along the shore at Acadia National Park, blue-green algae, rockweed, Irish moss and sea lettuce are among the hardy pioneers that can survive the daily alternation of wet and dry conditions. The organic material these plants supply creates pockets of soil in which trees and shrubs can eventually take root.

The trees are mostly spruce and fir, their dark forms spiking through the ghostly fog that swirls around the rugged cliffs. These conifers were made for the damp, windy coast with its poor soils. In the consistent shade and moistness of this forest, mosses, mushrooms and lichens thrive. Acid-loving shrubs such as blueberry, huckleberry and bayberry, its scent spicing the air, also grow well here.

The icy Labrador Current nourishes this spruce-fir forest. "What we are looking at today," writes author Maitland Edey, "is a forest left over from an earlier postglacial past, saved from engulfment by oak, beech, maple, hemlock – a host of species that have become dominant elsewhere – by a cold climate perpetuated by frigid water flowing from the polar sea."

For a quick overview of nearly all the typical native plants of coastal Maine, stroll through the 1-acre (0.5-hectare) Wild Garden in Acadia National Park, where flowers,

shrubs, mushrooms and trees are identified.

From Cape Cod National Seashore south along the Atlantic seaboard and circling around to the Gulf of Mexico, a complex system of barrier islands exists, with beaches, dunes, bays, estuaries and salt marshes. In these dynamic coastal environments, plants encounter many challenges and provide many services. Their biggest challenge is gaining a foothold in sandy homes that are constantly on the move. Many plants have adapted to these mobile habitats, and in so doing they

eventually stabilize the dunes.

On the beaches themselves, pitch and loblolly pines, beach plum, bayberry, sassafras and sea oats are common. Beach grass, in particular, is among the vanguard of dune plants. These grasses survive rapid burial by sand through a knotty network of underground stems that holds the plants in place and literally stitches the dunes together.

At Indiana Dunes National Lakeshore on Lake Michigan, plants of the desert, oak and pine woodlands, swamps and prairies are found within a small geographic area. Dr Henry Cowles spent 20 years researching this floral "melting pot," and from this natu-

Preceding pages: autumn foliage in the southern Appalachians. **Left,** bloodroot blossoms. **Right,** sycamore leaf on haircap moss.

ral laboratory he developed a now-basic eco-logical concept called succession – the stages through which different plants establish themselves over time and space.

At Indiana Dunes, marram grass and little bluestem build dunes and hold them in place. Sand cherry, cottonwood and jack pine also grow among the dunes. The presence of these plants amounts to a self-fulfilling prophecy. As they decompose, they create new soil that in turn lets other plants become established so that succession gradually proceeds to a stable climax.

Woodlands: From the edges of the continent, we move inward to the deciduous woodlands that blanket so much of the East – ash,

and longevity command our respect and inspire our spirits.

In these mountains, hardwoods reach their greatest expression in the deep, rich, moist soils of the hollows or coves. Diversity of tree species in these cove hardwood forests is unequaled almost anywhere in the world. Beneath the towering trees grows a montage of smaller trees, shrubs and vines – dogwood, spicebush, sassafras, serviceberry, elderberry and greenbrier.

Each day in early spring brings another lovely woodland flower, bursting through the moist leaf and duff of the forest floor and blooming before the trees overhead have sprouted their leaves. People flock to woods

elm, oak, hickory, walnut, cherry, maple, beech, birch, basswood, walnut, cherry and tulip poplar trees, to name a few. Their broad leaves turn vibrant shades of yellow, gold, crimson, purple and orange in autumn before falling in winter.

Among the best places to see the deciduous forest as it once was are Shenandoah and Great Smoky Mountains national parks in the heart of the ancient Appalachian Mountains. Here the forests have begun to recover from the hectic logging days of the late 19th and early 20th centuries. Though much is second-growth, there are still pockets of virgin forest – awesome trees whose immensity

and mountains to revel in the vernal show of trilliums, violets, bluets, bloodroots, phacelias, jack-in-the-pulpits, lady's slippers, dutchman's breeches, columbines, lilies and hundreds more. In the simmering summer, when the air is hazed with moisture, the Appalachians stage an encore – this time a dazzling display of azaleas and rhododendrons. On the treeless balds high in the Smokies grow the lushest wild azalea gardens on earth.

The "balds" of the southern mountains are open, sunlit spaces. Some are grassy balds, overgrown with mountain oat grass; others are heath balds, covered with low-growing,

Lilliputian shrubs such as sand myrtle, mountain laurel and blueberry. The question of the origin of balds has long preoccupied botanists. They think the balds may be natural, but their openness has probably been maintained by cattle grazing, clearing and burning. Some botanists argue that Big Meadows, a large, treeless area high in Shenandoah National Park, may exist for many of these reasons. But unlike the balds, Big Meadows may once have been a pond. A small wetland that harbors rare plants still persists alongside the meadow.

Because Shenandoah is a transition area between the North and the South, a few plants reach their limits here. Canada yew,

gardens of the South." Finally, in September 1867, Muir set out on a 1,000-mile (1,700-km) floral pilgrimage to Florida.

He started on foot at Louisville, Kentucky, and then crossed Tennessee, Georgia and northern Florida to the Gulf of Mexico. He walked through mile after mile of the Piedmont's piney woods, marveled at the Spanish moss that draped the great live oaks, and saw the cypress, tupelo gum and perhaps the strange insect-eating sundews and pitcher plants of the swamps.

Upon arriving in Florida, the "Land of Flowers," Muir wrote: "I am now in the hot gardens of the sun, where the palm meets the pine… strange plants, strange winds blow-

balsam fir, alder-leaved buckthorn and gray birch are near the southernmost extent of their ranges. Likewise, some southern species, notably Michaux's saxifrage and Catawba rhododendron, reach their northernmost extremes here.

Marsh, bog and glade: Conservationist John Muir, known for his explorations of the Sierra Nevada in California, started his work as a botanist in the East near his father's Wisconsin farm. For many of those early years, he felt "impelled toward the Lord's tropic

Colorful contrasts: creeping phlox (left) and fragrant white water lily (above).

ing gently, whispering, cooing, in a language I never learned." Had he gotten as far south as the Everglades, Muir would truly have been in the "tropic gardens of the South." Southern Florida is the only place where the overriding temperateness of the East gives way to the subtropical.

Seminole Indians called the Everglades Pa-hay-okee, "grassy water" – and that's exactly what they are. Before humans profoundly altered the region's hydrology, the Everglades were a shallow river, 50 miles (80 km) wide and about 6 inches (15 cm) deep, creeping over flat limestone bedrock. Their flatness inspired one biologist to quip that the highest point in the Everglades National Park is at a "dizzy altitude of about 10 feet above sea level." In the winter dry season, the Everglades are a prairie. But in the spring and summer rainy season, they are transformed into a huge freshwater marsh. Covering great swaths of that marsh is a sedge called saw grass.

In places where the land surface is only a foot or two higher than the marsh, tree islands known as hammocks exist. Some hammock trees, such as red maples, hackberries, persimmons, ashes, willows and live oaks, are familiar to many. But closer to the coast, the plant life takes on a decidedly tropical air. There are mahoganies (one in the park is the

largest in the United States – more than 4 feet/1.2 meters in diameter) and trees with West Indian names like gumbo-limbo. Emerald-green ferns conceal the ground, and fat strangler figs embrace the oaks. Palm trees (there are six species in the park) sway in the warm, fragrant breezes. Shrubs like wax myrtle, buttonwood and satinleaf form the dense understory.

Lining the edges of the coast are masses of mangrove trees, impervious to the salt water and surf and invincible to all but the strongest hurricanes, by virtue of their impenetrable, entwined roots. To see exotic tropical flowers like ghost orchids, marsh pinks and crimson morning glories in bloom, you must visit the Everglades in the low season – summer. The orchids are a great draw, so much so that illegal collecting has threatened some of them. Another tropical group is the bromeliads that thrive high in the treetops. They are epiphytes, or "air plants," that depend for their existence on the dust and moisture that float on the breeze.

The prairie: "Out there back of beyond, far past the coastal ranges and the leagues of forest, the land changed and began opening to the sky." That observation was made by John Madson, writing about what early American colonists saw as they ventured beyond New England into Ohio and Indiana. Though they didn't know how or why, the land clearly was changing; the thick cloak of deciduous forest was gradually thinning.

It may come as a shock to those who think that the Midwest has always been a land of corn and soybeans, but the native plant community of much of the heartland was actually prairie. Grasses and savanna extended from northwest Indiana, took in nearly two-thirds of Illinois, and stretched into Iowa, Nebraska and beyond. It was rolling tallgrass prairie, with little bluestem and big bluestem the dominant grasses. And while grasses are the foundation of the prairies, the long-stemmed summer flowers – blazing star, bush clover, coneflower, goldenrod, milkweed, rattlesnake master and leadplant, among others – are the adornments.

Only small remnants of that prairie are left, along railroad tracks, in recovering fields or in places preserved by private groups or state agencies. As yet, a Tallgrass Prairie National Park has not been designated. For a taste of original tallgrass, try the mile-long Hoosier Prairie Trail at Indiana Dunes National Lakeshore.

We'll never again enjoy the floral scene that greeted the early colonists and explorers of the East. Cutting, burning, plowing, damming, insects, blight and building have seen to that. But in the areas of the National Park System, we can still see vestiges of that former greenery. And we can still accept the gifts of health, solace and beauty that these plants offer.

Left, orange earth tongue fungus grows in forest duff. **Right**, wild lupine bursts into bloom in a lush mountain meadow.

No foray into a national park is complete without some encounter with wildlife. It may be a moose swimming across open water at Isle Royale, a salamander beneath an old log at Shenandoah, a bald eagle soaring over the waves at Acadia, perhaps a blue heron feeding at Cumberland Island, or an alligator basking on a hammock in the Everglades, or a porcupine boldly sauntering into your campsite to munch on leaves near your tent. Whatever animals you encounter, your memories will be forever entwined with the recollection of a chance meeting with something wilder than yourself.

Sea life: In the rocky northeast outpost of Acadia National Park in Maine, you can sit at the side of a deep tidal pool and watch as crabs, fish, sea urchins, starfish, barnacles, mussels, algae and hundreds of other species go about their lives just inches away from you. Nearby, eider ducks dive for barnacles and crabs. Gulls wheel and cry overhead as lobstermen haul in their pots.

Wildlife of several different ecosystems abounds here, giving visitors the choice between watching some of the 275 sea, shore, song and migrating bird species that live in or move through the park, or catching a glimpse of large inland mammals such as deer, fox and beaver – while slapping at no-see-ums and mosquitoes raising welts on their exposed skin. You can choose between freshwater or saltwater fishing, or sit back and watch the experts – loons, herons, sea ducks, bald eagles, ospreys, seals, porpoises and whales as they seek their food from the waters of this diverse park.

Farther south, down the coast, the topography changes as you move from shorelines scoured by glaciers to those built of morainal debris, the sand and gravel dumped at the spot where the massive shields of ice ground to a halt. Cape Cod National Seashore on the Massachusetts coast is the sandy land on the seaward side of the Cape's flexed arm, and a crucial stopover for migrating birds along the Atlantic Flyway. Here are the terns, plovers, oyster catchers, and cormorants that prowl the beaches. Here is the place where your seaside picnic will be fought over by gulls, the winner to stand guard in anticipation of a meal. Striped bass, bluefish, cod and flounder haunt the salt water only a short way from where you sift the sands in search of quahog and razor clams, scallops, moon shells, horseshoe crabs and skate and whelk egg cases. You may swat a greenhead fly nipping at your calf on the shore, or catch sight of a tiger beetle.

The North Woods: Halfway across the continent and hard against the Canadian border lie the remote wildlands of Isle Royale National Park, far out in Lake Superior, and Voyageurs National Park a bit farther west in Minnesota. Both parks require boating to get around, since they include as much water as dry land. These parks define the North Woods, and the wildlife you see here is typical of deep forest. Fishing in both parks is excellent. Their waters are populated by walleye, northern pike, smallmouth bass, muskie, perch, sauger and crappie as well as lake, brook and rainbow trout. With such abundant fish, birds who like to feed on them are

Preceding pages: white-tailed buck in velvet. **Left,** Eastern screech owl. **Right,** a bobcat prepares to go on the prowl.

here as well, including nesting ospreys, eagles and great blue herons. Woodland birds are also numerous. Smaller fishing birds are also in evidence, including kingfishers, loons, mergansers and cormorants. Moose, deer, black bears, wolves, foxes, beavers and many smaller mammals live in large numbers throughout most of this region, although isolated Isle Royale Park lacks deer and bears. Isle Royale is comparatively so untouched in recent times that 99 percent of the park's land area is designated wilderness. Long-term studies of the relationship between moose and wolf populations on Isle Royale are an important window on predator-prey relationships.

vireos, catbirds, towhees and 35 types of warbler. Turkey vultures are easy to observe as they ride thermals along mountain ridges. Look down and you may find Shenandoah salamanders, mice, voles and chipmunks. Harmful and harmless snakes also live here, but both take effort to find.

Farther down the backbone of the Appalachians lies Great Smoky Mountains National Park, on the Tennessee–North Carolina border. This unique highland sanctuary, with many peaks over 6,000 feet (1,830 meters), represents such a rich and diverse ecosystem that it is one of several parks in the eastern United States to be named an International Biosphere Reserve by the United Nations.

Southern Appalachians: Shenandoah National Park, in Virginia, sits astride the crest of the Appalachian Mountains. It provides critical habitat for a number of species, several of which have been reintroduced to the park, including black bears, deer and wild turkeys. This region lacks the complexity of the North Woods and is burdened with considerable human traffic and air pollution, but black bears and deer are now abundant and often spotted by patient visitors. The park includes some 200 bird species, such as ruffed grouse, barred owls, ravens, several woodpeckers, juncos and indigo buntings. You can also see hawks, flycatchers, thrushes,

Among its most prolific inhabitants are salamanders – 27 species of them – which flourish in the warm climate and abundant moisture that provide a haven for amphibians. When not searching the undergrowth for salamanders, you may notice some of the 200 bird or 70 mammal species that populate the region. The Great Smoky Mountains contain the largest area of virgin forest east of the Mississippi. More than 600 black bears make the woods their home, along with white-tailed deer, foxes, bobcats, beavers, minks and other mammals.

Kentucky's Mammoth Cave National Park, while much smaller than some of the other parks discussed here, includes a broad array of both surface and cave-dwelling wildlife, some of them found nowhere else. Above ground, the park supports more than 40 species of mammals, 200 bird, 36 reptile and 29 amphibian species, as well as many fish (five are found nowhere else) and countless insects. This protected watershed includes 50 different species of mussels, including three on the list of endangered species. You will find most of the interesting above-ground species of other Appalachian parks here.

But the unique wild inhabitants of Mammoth Cave Park are those in the cave itself. More than 200 species spend at least some of their time in the cave, including 42 species adapted solely to cave living. While bats and crickets will come and go, eyeless fish and crayfish and the Kentucky cave shrimp can survive nowhere else. Some springfish, salamanders and spiders stay here a lifetime. Naturally there are bats – 12 species. Three of them are endangered. Mammoth Cave is also an International Biosphere Reserve.

Barrier islands: A whole family of sandy barrier islands offers opportunities to view wildlife around nearly the entire perimeter of the eastern United States. The Park Service's major eastern barrier beaches include Fire Island National Seashore in New York, Cape Hatteras and Cape Lookout national seashores in North Carolina, and Canaveral National Seashore in Florida, among others. Shore birds are always abundant on these islands, and migratory birds use them as havens and feeding stations during their annual journeys. Look for terns, ducks, sandpipers, gulls and others.

At Fire Island there are also foxes and white-tailed deer, as well as three types of ticks in the low brush. To avoid the ticks, you might surf-cast for striped bass, bluefish, mackerel or weakfish. Assateague Island in Maryland is famed for its ponies, colonial imports along with the sika deer that share grasses with native white-tailed deer. You'll hear the distinctive cry of the laughing gull here, accompanied by herons, egrets and terns, as well as the offshore play of gray seals and bottlenose dolphins. Clams and crabs are plentiful – and edible. There are

also snakes, red foxes, opossums, bats, river otters, the endangered Delmarva Peninsula fox squirrel, the meadow jumping mouse that is capable of a 10-foot (3-meter) leap, and the same ticks as on Fire Island (some of which carry Lyme disease). All of these islands down through South Carolina are home to the endangered piping plover, a tiny, attractive shore bird.

Cumberland Island National Seashore, in Georgia, is more stable than most barrier islands because of the extensive live oak and pine forest that helps hold its sands in place. It is home to white-tailed deer, wild horses, turkeys, squirrels, lots of armadillos, a few secretive bobcats, raccoons, opossums, wild

hogs and plenty of rodents. Some 250 species of birds either live here year-round or travel through, including pelicans, endangered least terns and piping plovers, ospreys, bald eagles, wood storks, white ibis, peregrine falcons, cranes and herons. Reptiles include lizards, skunks, diamondback rattlesnakes, freshwater turtles and the endangered gopher tortoise.

Not to be outdone, the Gulf Islands that stretch along the southern shore of Florida, Alabama and Mississippi also are host to an impressive number of species. More than 280 species of birds have been tallied across this area, including all kinds of pelicans,

Left, the red-spotted newt can be found from Canada to the Carolinas. **Above**, a moose grazes on water plants.

herons, plovers, gulls, terns, vultures, eagles, hawks, owls, warblers and a full range of inland birds. In the gulf surf you will find pompano, sea trout and a few jellyfish and stingrays. The protected lagoons and bayous harbor crabs, shrimp, oysters, alligators, crayfish, opossums and armadillos.

There are living coral reefs to explore at Biscayne National Park in Florida and at Virgin Islands National Park on St John in the Caribbean. Biscayne contains some of the northernmost Florida Keys, the chain of coral reefs left high and dry by changing sea levels. Biscayne was set aside as an entire bay sanctuary to preserve the range of wildlife to be seen here. St John is a volcanic

island rimmed by reefs – huge colonies of tiny animals whose slow-growing skeletons form the structures we call coral. The coral provides shelter for thousands of other species, including Christmas tree worms, the queen conch, colorful angelfish, parrotfish, the green moray, wrasses, tarpons, barracudas, rays and sharks. Birds found on St John include the plentiful nectar-sipping bananaquit, magnificent frigatebird, white-tailed tropicbird and the brown booby.

At Biscayne, five species of sea turtle are endangered or threatened. The Florida manatee, a slow-swimming plant-eating mammal, is also endangered, as is the salt-water-loving American crocodile, distinguished from the alligator by its tapered snout. Other threatened and endangered species in this park include the peregrine falcon, bald eagle, brown pelican, eastern indigo snake, Schaus swallowtail butterfly, wood stork and Antillean crested hummingbird.

River of grass: No one pretends that all is well with wildlife in the Everglades. Florida's population growth, pollution and the diversion of water seriously threaten this varied ecosystem. For thousands of years, water has flowed slowly down the Florida peninsula in a layer only inches deep but many miles wide, creating a wildlife habitat duplicated nowhere else on the planet. From Lake Okeechobee to Florida's southern tip, the ground slopes only a few feet across the "river of grass" and its slow-moving waterways. You can ease a canoe through grasses that stretch to the horizon, broken only here and there by the hump of a hardwood hammock. Where 60 years ago you would have stirred enough birds to darken the sky, today only 10 percent of the former flocks are left, represented by the endangered wood stork and Everglades kite, ibis and heron species, purple gallinule and black vulture.

In deeper waters, perhaps in a sinkhole or a small pond created by alligators in the dry season, you may see bluegill, gar, largemouth bass, snails, crayfish and the alligators themselves. Approach a hardwood hammock and spy large tree snails, barred owls, white-tailed deer and the endangered, seldom-seen Florida panther.

Move to the seashore and glide through waterways fringed with mangroves that reach down into sediments and up to shut out the sun. Here and in shallow sea-grass beds are endangered crocodiles, sea turtles and manatees, eagles, roseate spoonbills, brown pelicans and fish like the mangrove snapper.

Creatures of land, sea and air. They are alive and, for the most part, well in the cornucopia which nature offers inside America's grand preserves. Whichever parks you visit, come prepared to visit with the locals on their own wilder terms. It's what the parks are all about.

Left, diminutive tree frog. **Right**, black bears are found in wilderness areas throughout the eastern states and are especially numerous in the southern Appalachians.

It's America's most famous trail, one of the longest marked footpaths in the world, winding along for a total of 2,135 miles (3,435 km) from Maine to Georgia. And despite popular notions, it's quite a recent creation: it was only in 1921 that the Appalachian Trail was first proposed by an ardent hiker and outdoorsman from Massachusetts named Benton MacKaye.

MacKaye died in 1975 just short of his 97th birthday, so he had ample time to see his dream become real. He once wrote about his great project: "The ultimate purpose? There are three things: 1) to walk; 2) to see; 3) to *see* what you see... Some people like to record how speedily they can traverse the length of the Trail, but I would give a prize for the ones who took the longest time."

Wild trail: MacKaye first imagined the establishment of a wild trail during long rambles in the New England mountains. He believed that wilderness outings conferred beneficial effects on the physical and mental health of an increasingly urban population, and his idea was for a super-trail that would run the length of the industrialized East Coast. This would be a trail that was wild and yet within reach of major urban centers and their throngs of workers alienated from outdoor life. He felt that the trail would grace all who spent time on it with the healing tonic of wilderness, and he wanted it to be accessible to just about everybody.

He laid out his scheme in a landmark article in the October 1921 issue of the *Journal of the American Institute of Architects*. The article was entitled "An Appalachian Trail: A Project in Regional Planning," and the response was positive indeed.

Hiking clubs along the proposed route quickly picked up the idea, and in 1922 the first miles of the trail were constructed by volunteers in the Bear Mountain region of New York and New Jersey. Soon, hiking clubs were busy building sections in New England and Pennsylvania, and within a few years volunteers up and down the Appala-

chians from Maine to Georgia were hard at work. The volunteers' energy and enthusiasm for turning his vision of a wilderness super-trail into reality surprised even Benton MacKaye.

Under the leadership first of MacKaye, then later of Judge Arthur Perkins of Connecticut and especially Myron Avery, a rather bullheaded lawyer from Lubec, Maine, who became the first person to walk its entire length, the Appalachian Trail was pushed through to completion in 1937.

"To say that the trail is completed," Avery said, "would be a complete misnomer. Those of us who have physically worked on the trail, know that the trail, as such, will never be completed." He foresaw what thousands have since learned: the Appalachian Trail is not merely a line drawn upon a map but a deeply fulfilling experience.

A thin green line: The trail, essentially a linear national park, extends from Springer Mountain in northern Georgia to Katahdin, a giant windswept monolith rising above the vast boreal forests of northern Maine.

Along the way, it follows the skyline, touching the tops of most of the states it

Preceding pages: enjoying the view in Virginia's Blue Ridge Mountains. Left, hitting the trail in New York State. Right, backcountry banquet.

enters. Winding from north to south, it traverses the many distinct ranges that make up the Appalachian chain, including the White and Green mountains, Berkshire Hills, Kittatinny Ridge, Blue Ridge Mountains, and the Alleghenies and Great Smokies. Though a part of the whole, each range has its own personality. The trail also passes through several national parks, including Great Smoky Mountains, Shenandoah, Harpers Ferry and Delaware Water Gap.

And yet, though seeking the high, wild country above the settled valleys, the trail maintains contact with the peopled landscapes below. This relationship is deliberate and was an essential part of the original

chian Trail remains at the head of the class, enjoying celebrity status among the many great trails of the world.

It's hard to say exactly why this is so. The Appalachian Trail is wild, but there are trails that are wilder. It is tough, but others are even more challenging. It crosses high summits, but there are others that traverse higher ground. Still, the feeling hikers get when they set foot on the "AT" is unique.

For most, it is not just another hiking trail, it's a part of history. This is why many who have traveled it consider the experience so memorable. It explains why hundreds of volunteers spend their free time repairing and maintaining the trail. There is a special

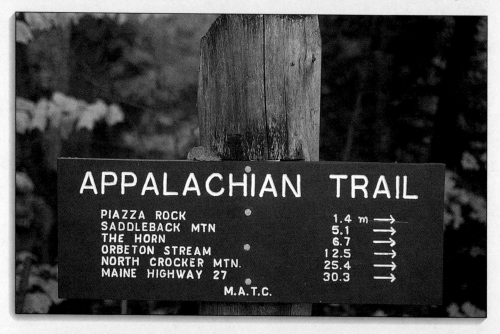

concept. MacKaye wanted the trail to be within reach of city folk, and he hoped that they would take up the invitation to walk into the wilderness as far as their legs were able to carry them.

Though not the first long-distance footpath in America, the Appalachian has become our flagship trail. Vermont's Long Trail, a 262-mile (422-km) stretch that traverses the length of Vermont from Quebec to Massachusetts, was begun earlier, in 1910. And the Pacific Crest and Continental Divide trails cover comparable distances through what their many supporters claim is superior scenery. Nevertheless, the Appala-

feeling, a certain pride, in belonging to the Appalachian Trail community, of being a part of a great tradition.

The long walk: Thousands hike sections of the trail every year, taking a day or a week away from day-to-day cares. For these legions, most of whom are not necessarily very experienced in the outdoors – and most of whom will never see either end of the trail – the mere fact that it keeps going and going is an inspiration. For them, the AT offers an outlet, an escape valve. They know the trail is there when they need it, for as long as they need it, just as MacKaye had envisioned.

Every summer there is another group on

the path, an odd collection of individuals – usually fewer than a couple of hundred in all – whose goal is to hike the entire trail from end to end. These dedicated long-distance travelers call themselves the thru-hikers, and each year they start at one end – usually Springer Mountain in Georgia to take advantage of the southern spring – and continue until they reach the summit cairn atop Katahdin in faraway Maine.

So, gathering atop Springer Mountain in March or April (still deep winter in Maine), they move north with the seasons. By May, the thru-hikers have advanced through the Carolinas and are crossing the Virginia line. By July they are passing Harpers Ferry and

ranges are shocked when, after a few days, the AT has them begging for mercy. This is indeed one very tough trail, and the challenges are many. Looked at from any angle, more than 2,000 miles is a long way to walk anywhere, much less along the length of a mountain range. To cover the distance, AT hikers must spend five months sleeping on the ground, living out of a backpack, and eating a diet of camp food; not to mention dealing with sore muscles, tired feet, blisters and bruises, and highly aromatic socks.

Then there is the trail itself. Unlike western trails, the AT surprises hikers with sharp gains in elevation and almost no switchbacks to level out the grade. Indeed, the AT seeks

striking into Pennsylvania. The next few weeks find them progressing through New Jersey and New York, poised to spend August in the high mountains of Vermont and New Hampshire. By September, most of the thru-hikers have crossed into Maine and are drawing a bead on Katahdin itself.

Many people underestimate the challenges posed by the Appalachian Trail. Western chauvinists who denigrate the Appalachians while loudly touting the virtues of their home

Left, the Appalachian Trail is 2,135 miles (3,435 km) long and runs through 14 states. **Above**, a hiker atop Katahdin, the AT's northern terminus.

altitude in the most direct way: straight up. Compound the contrary nature of the path itself with the heat, humidity and rain of the East, and you are faced with one tough physical challenge.

The mental challenges are equally daunting. Hikers must somehow cover a certain mileage each day, because finishing the trail becomes logistically impossible in a race against winter. Food drops must be arranged at post offices along the route a certain number of days apart. Caloric intake must be calibrated well in advance, long before hikers have any idea just how ravenous they will be halfway through their hike. These physical and mental challenges require advance preparation and careful planning. Few, if any, start hiking from end to end without having done their homework prior to lacing their hiking boots for the start of the journey.

Radical repeaters: Why do the thru-hikers do it? Some may be taking time away from troubled lives back home, and relish the chance to spend five months alone in the outdoors doing something they consider absolutely worthwhile. Others are between jobs, or at some critical juncture in their lives.

For many, the sheer physical challenge is invitation enough. For others, the trail is an opportunity to discover more about themselves in a setting well removed from the

hustle and bustle of the modern world.

Regardless of why they do it, most thru-hikers find the experience deeply satisfying. For them, every day marks a major accomplishment. Tasks are straightforward, goals are achievable, rewards are simple and immediate. Each day a new section of trail is conquered. At night, sleep is deep and well deserved, and the sky is crowded with stars. Needs are reduced to the basics: a snug shelter in foul weather; a hot, filling meal when one is famished from a long day of hiking; a refreshing swim in a mountain pool on a blazing summer day; a shady spot to rest aching feet. The trail makes only two de-

mands: that hikers pay attention to it and to the immediate surroundings, and that they grant themselves a five-month reprieve.

Some of the thru-hikers are so taken with the trail that they turn around at Katahdin and start hiking back to Georgia! One thru-hiker said that he was hiking back "as a gift to myself." Others hike the trail again the next year or perhaps several years later. Some of these "radical repeaters," as they are known in AT circles, have hiked the trail eight or nine times. Again, this phenomenon of repeat hiking appears to be unique to the AT. Apparently neither the Pacific Crest nor Continental Divide trails inspire such steadfast loyalty and devotion.

But then the AT does cast a kind of spell on those who hike it. After even a few days, it starts to work its magic. And after weeks and months, one day blends seamlessly into the next, temporal cares slip away, and the outside world seems at first distant, then irrelevant, and ultimately is forgotten altogether. Hiking the AT becomes a way of life, the woods and mountains become home, and fellow hikers and other creatures form a close circle of family and friends.

Of course, most hikers spend only a few hours on the trail. But even these brief jaunts are enough to get a feeling for the AT's charms – the sun-dappled forests, breathtaking vistas, secluded glades, and its fascinating variety of plant and animal life. Although much of the trail is devoted to remote, backcountry areas, many spots are easy to reach by car or on a short walk. And it doesn't take long to feel removed from the hustle and bustle of daily life. After only 10 or 15 minutes, you'll feel as if you have entered another world.

Perhaps more than any other trail, the Appalachian is a community, a refuge and a necessary counterbalance to the pressures of modern, urban life. It provides hikers with a broad view of the ecology of the Appalachian chain, tests their endurance and determination, offers the scenic beauty of the East's highest peaks and, to borrow a phrase from the trail's founder, Benton MacKaye, allows them to really *see* what they see in the land and in themselves. MacKaye would certainly approve.

Left, a frosty look. **Right**, a winter hike through Nantahala National Forest in North Carolina.

Steve Shepard is a high-powered tax attorney whose job keeps him operating at a high level of stress from early Monday to late Friday. So what does he do to wind down? He climbs up. You'll find him on many summer weekends clinging to sheer cliffs by his fingertips. Pushing himself to the limit is the way he keeps himself together. The sport of rock climbing gives him a lift.

"I become so focused a thousand feet above the valley floor," he says. "A tough climb takes my mind off work completely."

Rock climbing started to take off in popularity in the 1970s. Today it's one of the older of the new high-risk sports that are being undertaken throughout the East. Changes in life-style and technology are making profound inroads in the way we experience the outdoors. New forms of recreation are taking their place alongside the traditional arts of canoeing, horse-packing and mountain climbing.

Wilderness fix: Testing oneself in the wilderness has long been an American tradition, almost a rite of passage. But in today's fast-paced world of longer workdays and shorter vacations, most people don't have the time for extended forays into the wilderness. And that's partially why so many modern-day adventurers go for the quick hit – a day or two of high-action sport that puts them in direct contact with the elements.

"On the rock I become totally immersed in my surroundings," Shepard says. "Where a simple mistake can have big consequences, there's no room for less than complete concentration. These moments of intensity keep me going. My job in the city is so time-consuming, I can't just take off for a week or ten days at a time. So I opt for these adrenalin shots instead. By late Sunday afternoon I'm physically spent and ready to go back to work."

Paradoxically or not, the thirst for outdoor adventure seems to be growing stronger even as American wilderness constricts. Increasing

numbers of thrill-seekers flock to the parks seeking exotic recreation, eager to confront physical and mental challenges not found on home turf.

"To most of mankind," conservationist Robert Marshall observed in 1930, "a very powerful desire is the appetite for adventure. But in an age of machinery only the extremely fortunate have any occasion to satiate this hankering, except vicariously. As a result people become so choked by the monotony of their lives that they are readily amenable

to the suggestion of any lurid diversion."

Freewheeling: Also big nowadays is the sport of mountain biking. Although the national parks generally permit biking only on paved or gravel roads and some designated trails, it is a great way to get out from behind a windshield and see the scenery. In Acadia National Park, for example, there are more than 50 miles (80 km) of unpaved paths used by bikers to crisscross the terrain. At several other parks, including Big South Fork and New River Gorge, a network of old mining and logging roads have been converted into bike trails.

"Mountain biking is a totally different way

Preceding pages: white-water adventure at the Ocoee River Hell Hole. **Left,** a rock climber traverses the Endless Wall area of the New River Gorge. **Right,** freewheeling in West Virginia.

to cover ground," says Marty Davis, a self-described "weekend warrior" from Boston. "It's much faster than hiking, you get a terrific aerobic workout, and the feeling you get when you've reached the top of a long, steep climb is nearly indescribable."

Davis says the thrills begin on the way down. "Mountain biking calls for steel nerves, great leg and arm strength, aerobic capacity, and quick reflexes. For me, it's a total workout and a total thrill. Picking your way down a steep boulder-strewn trail, staying back on your seat to keep from going over the handlebars, riding by the seat of your pants while the wind blows past your face – it's so cool. That's why I mountain bike."

numerous rivers and streams cutting through the Appalachian Mountains. "There's no avoiding the tossing and turning, the bucking and slam-dunking of a big brawling river. I think fear is a big part of white-water paddling – it's always there. But overcoming that fear – taking a breath and going for it – making it through with your wits and skills, that's what it's all about for me. The feeling is pretty incredible. It's a tangible feeling of achievement. The results are so immediate – you either make it or you get "Maytagged" and go for a long swim. You just don't get that anywhere else. At least I don't."

If the churning froth of a white-water stream isn't for you, then consider sea

Water works: Still another sport gaining in popularity is white-water canoeing and kayaking. As with climbing and biking, paddlers have taken the most demanding aspect of boating – running the rapids – and created a whole new sport that consists solely of negotiating the most difficult stretches of white water they can find. In the old days, canoeists carried (or portaged) their boats and gear around dangerous stretches of white water, but today's paddlers deliberately seek out the challenge – and the fun.

"It's a lot like rodeo, I imagine" says Cathy Campbell, an avid paddler who spends her free time testing her skills against the

kayaking. One of the fastest-growing outdoor sports on both coasts and in the Great Lakes region, sea kayaking is a sport that appeals to people of all ages and varying levels of physical ability.

The modern sea kayak is a fiberglass or plastic version of the sealskin craft used by Eskimo hunters for millennia. Today's adventurers have taken the vessels out of the Arctic, and they can be found island-hopping off the coast of Maine, poking into estuaries along the Atlantic Coast, cruising the Everglades, and circumnavigating the sandy beaches of Cumberland Island off the coast of Georgia.

"Paddling a sea kayak is total immersion in the scenery," says Mary O'Donnell, a school administrator in Massachusetts. "You get a loon's-eye view of the water and the surrounding seascape. It's as if you and your boat are one, and you feel every swell, every breath of wind, every nuance in the environment. You can poke into little coves that motorboats and sailboats can't get into. As far as I know, there is no better way to explore the coast."

Of course, sea kayaking has its own challenges, and more experienced paddlers are undertaking long crossings and sometimes dangerous circumnavigations in remote locations where intricate knowledge of wind,

a sea kayaker is a generalist, not a specialist. You have to be able to paddle the roughest water and have the stamina to make miles on calm days. And unlike the white-water paddler, who has a vehicle at either end of the run, you also have to be completely in tune with your environment. I'm constantly watching the sky, watching the surface, and keeping an eye on the wind. Although I never feel more relaxed than when I'm out in my boat, I'm constantly monitoring the scene. I don't think I miss very much. It's amazing how aware you become."

Sky high: If you are looking for a more uplifting experience, consider strapping on a pair of wings and flying off into the sunset.

water and tide are critical. In addition, expedition kayakers must be expert in the arts of navigation and wilderness camping. But perhaps most importantly, they must also have the judgment to know when to proceed and when to stay in camp and wait out a storm.

"The ocean is beautiful and serene," O'Donnell says. "But it is also powerful and can be dangerous. Winds can come out of nowhere, and crosscurrents can sweep you off course. Unlike the white-water kayaker,

Left, testing the waters. **Above**, soaring over the dunes on North Carolina's Outer Banks.

"For some time now," Wilbur Wright wrote in 1900, "I've been afflicted with the belief that flight is possible to man." But not even the visionary Wright Brothers could have foreseen the freedom with which hang gliders now take to the air.

"It's like cheating nature," says Bruce Weaver, manager of the flight school at Kitty Hawk Kites in Nags Head, North Carolina. "Every time your feet leave the ground, you're doing something that you're not supposed to be able to do."

Thanks to improvements in technology and design, learning to hang glide has become easier than ever. Weaver's students get airborne on the first lesson, which usually includes several short flights (lasting around 10 or 15 seconds each) over the forgiving sand dunes of the Outer Banks, the same location that was used by Orville and Wilbur Wright to try out their newfangled flying machine in 1903.

"People are under the misconception that it takes a lot of work to hang glide, but it's really pretty effortless," Weaver says. "The most common mistake beginners make is trying to do too much. It doesn't take a whole lot of effort to fly. You can just lay there and the kite will fly itself."

And what about the risks? "Hang gliding is as dangerous as any other form of aviation.

But it's certainly less dangerous than other extreme sports like rock climbing or white-water kayaking."

And the sensation is almost indescribable. "It's exhilarating and soothing at the same time," says Weaver. He should know: he has stayed airborne for as long as eight hours during a single flight and has soared as high as 12,000 feet (3,658 meters).

"A lot of people say that it gives them the same feeling that they have in their dreams – weightlessness, silence, total freedom. It feels like what a bird looks like."

Hit the trail: Need a few more ideas for outdoor adventure? How about exploring

the sea? Just slip on a diving mask, snorkel and a pair of fins and get a firsthand look at the stunning coral gardens that grow at several national parks, including Biscayne, Virgin Islands, Dry Tortugas and Buck Island Reef. Licensed scuba divers can swim even deeper and explore the many sunken ships that lie on the ocean floor and beneath the frigid waters of the Great Lakes.

There are any number of other ways to experience nature in the eastern national parks. How about windsurfing off the coast of Cape Cod, for example? Exploring sub-terranean passages at Mammoth Cave? Cross-country skiing at Voyageurs? Snowshoeing at Acadia? Horseback riding at Big South Fork? Birdwatching in the Everglades? Fishing at Isle Royale?

But perhaps the best way to experience the outdoors, the way that costs nothing in monetary terms, that requires no skills and that puts you in closest contact with the environment, is the simple practice of walking. Just lace up a pair of sneakers or lightweight boots and set out across the parks.

As with the other, more "radical" outdoor activities, walking is a great way to clear your mind, rejuvenate your spirit and refresh your soul. All of the great advocates of wilderness were great walkers, too. Robert Marshall was known to scale numerous Adirondack peaks in a given day, often putting in 30 miles (48 km) between sunup and sundown. John Muir, too, reveled in hopping the back fence and taking off for the wilderness with little more than a few bread crumbs and a blanket. And when he wasn't exploring the Maine woods by canoe, Henry David Thoreau made his rounds of the forests and fields of Concord on foot.

"I think that I cannot preserve my health and spirits," Thoreau wrote, "unless I spend four hours a day at least – and it is commonly more than that – sauntering through the woods and over the hills and fields, absolutely free from all worldly engagements."

Since those words were written about 150 years ago, millions of Americans as well as people from all over the world have come to the national parks and, as Thoreau suggested, renewed themselves with "the tonic of wilderness."

Left, riding the wind at Cape Cod National Seashore. **Right**, undersea exploration.

Bill Terry is a ranger with the National Park Service. On a busy Saturday morning in July, he is maneuvering his patrol boat upstream to check out a report that some disorderly canoeists are swimming and mucking around in one of the fragile springholes that issue into the Current River – a violation of the rules within southeast Missouri's Ozark National Scenic Riverways.

After cruising along for a few hundred yards, Terry is forced to a dead stop below a rocky shoal. It's not the shallow water that poses a problem. It's a flotilla of canoes heading downriver, and clogging up the narrow chute.

Unperturbed, Terry waits for a break in the traffic before moving on. "If this was a real emergency, I'd force my way through there," says the 40-year-old park ranger. "But if I did, the wake from my boat would definitely swamp a bunch of canoes, and I'd probably be cussed out pretty good."

Finally, there is a lull in the procession, and Terry guns the motor, sending the long, flat-bottomed johnboat barreling against the current. Upstream of the shoal, a montage of paddlers smile, stare, wave and exchange greetings with the park ranger. Two questions are repeatedly asked of him: "How much farther is it to the take-out?" and "How come you get to use a motor and we don't?"

Bill Terry has heard it all before, yet he's just as enthusiastic now about being a ranger as when he started with the Park Service in the mid-1970s. He answers each inquiry with words of encouragement or witty one-liners. "You have to like people and enjoy communicating with them to succeed in this line of work," he says. "Those who don't, or can't, are weeded out of the Park Service pretty quick."

At 6' 3" (190 cm) and a solid 200 pounds (91 kg), Terry strikes an imposing figure in his forest-green and gray uniform, with a holstered .357 magnum revolver strapped to

Preceding pages: a gathering of rangers at Mammoth Cave National Park. **Left**, conducting research at Buffalo National River, Arkansas. **Right**, releasing turtles at Cape Lookout National Seashore, North Carolina.

his hip. As a commissioned park police officer, he is authorized to make arrests. "At one time there was extremely little crime or violence in our national parks; not so any more," he says. "We deal with anything a big-city cop would do. The only difference is we do it in a more scenic location."

Most of the arrests in the Riverways deal with alcohol or drug use, but there are also traffic infractions, littering, illegal tree cutting, and violations dealing with campground quiet hours, fish-and-game laws, and boat-

ing regulations. "Some weeks I issue quite a few citations, some weeks none at all," Terry says, as he weaves his boat skilfully through the throng of canoes. "I try and treat everyone like they're doing good until they're doing bad. Usually it takes only a gentle warning for people to do the right thing."

In addition to his role as a park cop, Terry's other responsibilities include search and rescue, resource management, lifesaving, and structural and wildland fires. During an average summer, he will be involved in everything from attending to injured visitors requiring emergency medical attention and evacuation, to searching for missing canoeists and dealing with flash floods. He will also assist biologists reintroducing river otters and be called upon to fight prairie burns.

"Being a national park ranger is not what most people think it is," he says. "We wear many different hats that the public rarely sees. But that's the aspect of the job that I enjoy the most. No two days at work are alike."

A way of life: Of course, all is not perfect in the ranger profession. Over the past few decades, the Park Service has seen its budget eroded and operating costs inflated. The number of ranger personnel available to assist the public has dwindled as their responsibilities have increased. Says Terry: "It's a

classic case of doing more with less. But I'm not complaining. When nine out of ten people I meet tell me how lucky I am to work as a park ranger, I know I've got a good thing."

Because of the budget crunch, it's harder than ever to get a ranger job, according to Amy Vanderbilt, a public affairs officer for the National Park Service. "Ninety-nine percent of all rangers who end up permanent get their start as seasonal park rangers," she points out. "Seasonals (their positions generally last three to four months during the peak visitation seasons) are the backbone of the Park Service."

Vanderbilt cautions, however, that it takes

persistence to get hired. "The number of applicants far outnumber the positions available every year, particularly at larger, well-known parks."

Once in the system, most rangers never leave. But as in any profession, they have their gripes. When rangers get together to talk shop, their chief complaint is their low pay scale relative to other federal agencies.

Terry, now approaching the springhole with its miscreants, says that "rangers are the most highly trained employees in the federal government, and the most underpaid. Still, I would rather give up the bigger paycheck for the scenery. Look where I work, look what I'm able to do. Rangering is more than a job, it's a way of life. I can't imagine doing anything else."

Another view of rangering comes from Interpretive Ranger Edge Wade. Today, she will be patrolling by canoe a 16-mile (26-km) section of the Upper Current, a trip that generally takes 6 to 7 hours. She calls it "a beautiful stretch of river, one of the best in the park."

Wade is a 46-year-old former technical writer with a master's degree in environmental studies, and this is her first stint as a seasonal park ranger. "You might say I was going through a life change when I applied to the Park Service," Wade says. "I never thought I'd get the job, but here I am." Today, about one-third of the Park Service's 21,000-member work force are women, a far cry from the old days when rangering was almost exclusively a male preserve.

Along with several other seasonal rangers, Wade reported to work in mid-May and will stay on until after Labor Day. Her first two weeks on the job were on-site training, covering everything from the area's history, the roles of different Park Service divisions, wearing the uniform, canoeing skills, and water rescue. "In a way, it was like going to college all over again," she laughs.

Paid in sunsets: Like most rangers, Edge Wade is not in it to get rich. Her GS-4 federal rating translates to $7.27 per hour, considerably less than what she was earning before. "The standard line among rangers," she says, "is that we get paid in pretty sunsets."

As Wade finishes some paperwork, the first fleet of concessionaire buses rolls in. Each of the old school buses is loaded with soon-to-be floaters. Most appear to be of high school or college age, with a sprinkling of others older and younger. One of Wade's duties is to accompany a bus hauling paddlers and canoes upriver to a popular put-in. En route, she explains the rules of the park to the canoeists, offers canoeing safety tips and answers questions, no matter how inane.

"No, those aren't owls soaring overhead," she points out to a young man who obviously isn't a biology major. "They're turkey vultures." To another, she replies, "No, I'm not a game warden or a forest ranger; I work for the National Park Service."

At 10.30am the buses arrive at the put-in and disgorge their loads. The scene is chaotic. Hundreds of people are busily launch-

instructs the cliff-jumpers that what they are doing is against park regulations and that to avoid injury they need to climb back down immediately. The boys comply sheepishly.

Moving on, Wade guides the canoe into an eddy in the cool shade of a limestone cliff. "An interpretive ranger has no law-enforcement authority," she explains, "so my main patrol objective is to try and make positive contact with everyone I meet on the river. I want them to know that a park ranger is on duty and is here to help them have a safe and enjoyable visit. I also want to get across the message that, as park users, they should care about this place. We have a beautiful river here and we'd sure like to keep it that way."

ing canoes, while bank-to-bank canoes are already easing down the river. Wade is the only park ranger around. Throwing her work kit into her government-issue canoe, she points the bow downstream and joins the busy weekend throng.

Paddling at a leisurely rate, Wade soon arrives at a gravel bar teeming with happy boaters. A half-dozen teenagers have scrambled up a rock wall and are about to jump into a deep pool. In a firm but friendly voice, she

During the next few hours, she assists a few floundering canoes, offers paddling pointers to inexperienced boaters, and tries to maintain some semblance of order before meeting up with Bill Terry. They compare notes, and then Wade pushes off from the johnboat and bids goodbye. "Don't mean to rush off, Bill, but I've got to get back," she says. "Tonight's my turn to lead a cave tour."

Bill Terry's shift is almost over, too, but not quite. He still has to put the boat away and meet with the district ranger to fill out some reports. Then, tomorrow morning he'll be back on patrol, not knowing for sure which of his many hats he'll have to wear.

Left, a ranger leads a nature walk. **Above**, keeping an eye on the tourists at Ozark National Scenic Riverways, Missouri.

HISTORIC TREASURES

A great deal of history is celebrated at the national parks. As well as flora and fauna, many illustrious people and famous events are celebrated here. Indeed, more than half of the areas of the National Park System are historic sites, sprinkled like small treasures among the large scenic preserves.

These national treasures weren't always under the aegis of the National Park Service. Originally, military and other historic areas were controlled by several government agencies, including the War Department. Then in 1930, Horace Albright, the second director of the Park Service, argued that his agency was better equipped to manage such sites than the War Department. Congress agreed.

The legislators created George Washington Birthplace National Monument and placed it under the Park Service's supervision. Later it transferred all historic sites managed by the federal government to the Park Service. Since then, well over 100 monuments and memorials have been added to the system, which cover everything from ancient Indian civilizations right up to contemporary politics.

A 13-acre (5-hectare) site in Ohio, for example, contains 23 burial mounds constructed by the Hopewell Indians more than 1,000 years ago. Filled with obsidian tools, jewelry and trade goods, the site offers an enticing glimpse of a complex Indian civilization that once occupied much of the Midwest.

A score of sites are associated with America's chief executives, from George Washington to those of present times, including the Jimmy Carter National Historic Site in Georgia and the Boston suburb in which John F. Kennedy spent his boyhood years.

Long before the Pilgrims landed at Plymouth Rock, there were French and Spanish explorers and settlers, and they left behind impressive structures. In Florida, for example, there is De Soto National Memorial, marking the site where Hernando de Soto is thought to have landed, and Castillo de San Marcos National Monument in the nation's oldest city, St Augustine.

Holding a specially revered status in the American historical consciousness is the place in Philadelphia where the momentous events that led to the founding of the Republic and the setting up of its unique form of government took place. This is, of course, Independence National Historical Park. The Liberty Bell is here, outside the hall where the Declaration of Independence and the Constitution were forged, and it is a must-see for countless numbers of visitors from around the world.

Also sacred in American heritage are the places where kinsman fought kinsman with such awful ferocity during the American Civil War of 1861–65. From the opening shots at Fort Sumter in South Carolina to the bitter denouement at Ford's Theatre in the District of Columbia, the Park Service tracks the great struggle in memorials and monuments throughout the eastern states.

Preceding pages: sunrise at Gettysburg; fireworks over Independence Hall. **Left**, a Park Service worker scrubs the Lincoln Memorial.

HISTORIC SITES

The National Park Service is best known for its great scenic preserves, but it also protects some of the nation's most important historic sites. From early Indian cultures right up to modern issues, the national parks chronicle the great people, events and institutions that have shaped American history.

The Park Service began acquiring historic sites in the East in the 1930s. Back then, more than a few people were skeptical. But today, most Park Service personnel consider the task of interpreting American history as a vital extension of their original mission.

"Being a park ranger at a historic site is very similar to being a ranger at a natural area," says Vicki Tise, a ranger at Adams National Historic Site in Massachusetts. "But in addition to making sure people have a good time, we try to get visitors to appreciate the past and learn from it."

Executive homes: Among the most popular and interesting sites are the presidential homes. These include everything from the birthplaces to the retirement homes of more than 20 chief executives. At each, you will find a wealth of revealing details about the private lives of America's most powerful men.

Appropriately, the first presidential home to be managed by the Park Service was **George Washington Birthplace National Monument**. The "father of our country" was born in northern Virginia in 1732. On the site is a 1930 reconstruction of a typical plantation house of the period (the actual house in which Washington was born burned down in 1779). Approximately 30 of Washington's ancestors are interred at a family burial ground in the park.

If one small site can bring to life a presidential family, it is **Adams National Historic Site** in Quincy, Massachusetts. It is the only national park site to tell the story of two presidents. Unlike most presidential homes, "The Old House," as the Adamses called it, never passed out of family hands, and its fur-

nishings never had to be sought out or replaced. John and Abigail Adams bought the house in 1787, a decade before he became the second president of the United States. There they raised their son John Quincy, who became the sixth president. Park rangers take visitors through 15 of the rooms, including the study where John Adams conducted the nation's business and where he died, at the age of 90, on July 4, 1826. On the west side of the Old House is the elegant and inspiring library, housing nearly 12,000 volumes. The site's grounds include one of the best-kept 18th-century formal gardens in New England.

On an island sprawling across the Canada–US border in Maine is a unique presidential park jointly operated by the two countries. The **Roosevelt Campobello International Park** preserves the summer home and grounds on Campobello Island where President Franklin Roosevelt vacationed from 1883, when he was an infant, until he was stricken with polio in 1921. The family's Dutch colonial "cottage" of 34 rooms, given to

Franklin and Eleanor as a wedding gift, is maintained with most of its original furnishings.

Roosevelt's liking for Campobello was rivaled only by his love for Hyde Park, New York. The **Eleanor Roosevelt National Historic Site** preserves her personal retreat, Val-Kill Cottage, among the fields, trees and ponds of Hyde Park.

Among the many other presidential sites managed by the Park Service in the East are two dedicated to more recent presidents: the **Jimmy Carter National Historic Site** in Georgia and the **John Fitzgerald Kennedy National Historic Site** in the Boston suburb of Brookline, where Kennedy was born.

First Americans: The history of the United States is, of course, much more than the men who have led the government. In the East, you can trace the rise of this country to modern times by starting at the very beginning.

Mound City Group National Monument is an ancient necropolis on the banks of the **Scioto River** in Ohio. The 13-acre (5-hectare) park, about three miles (5 km) north of **Chillicothe**, contains 23 Hopewell burial mounds, one of the largest concentrations of this type. Rather than simply burying their dead, the Hopewell of this area cremated the body and buried it with a variety of objects, such as copper breastplates, stone pipes and ornaments made from the teeth of grizzly bears. When the burial basin was filled, it was mounded over with dirt. The visitor center explains the burial rituals and what they have to tell us about the people who lived here from 200 BC to AD 500.

The **Ocmulgee National Monument** east of **Macon**, Georgia, contains traces of more than 10,000 years of continuous human occupation, including the massive temple mounds of the Mississippians, a farming people who thrived between AD 900 and 1100.

European exploration: The first contact between Native Americans in the East and white Europeans was not made when the Pilgrims set foot on Plymouth Rock. A century earlier, the French and Span-

The "Big House" at Hopewell Furnace National Historic Site, Pennsylvania

ish established themselves in the Southeast. Throughout the region are examples of Spanish and French forts. These impressive structures remind us that America began as an outpost of the Caribbean trade system.

Hernando de Soto sailed into Tampa Bay in 1539 to conquer and colonize *La Florida*. **De Soto National Memorial** in Bradenton marks the spot where he is thought to have landed and commemorates the four-year journey that opened the Southeast to colonization.

The stone fort at **Castillo de San Marcos National Monument**, begun in 1672, is the oldest in the country and guards the nation's oldest city, St Augustine in Florida. The fort represents 300 years of history, reaching back to the years just after Christopher Columbus landed in the New World.

The **San Juan National Historic Site** in Puerto Rico includes the Spanish-built forts of El Morro, San Cristóbal and El Cañuelo and the city walls of old San Juan, founded in 1521.

English colonists arrived in the Northeast relatively late during this initial period of exploration. They established their first permanent settlement in 1607 at Jamestown, now part of **Colonial National Historical Park** in Virginia.

Road to independence: You can retrace the rocky road to independence by following the **Freedom Trail** to the sites of **Boston National Historical Park.** Highlights of the tour include the **Old State House**, seat of the colonial government; **Faneuil Hall**, known as "the Cradle of Liberty" because protests against the British were held here; the **Old South Meeting House**, where Bostonians met in 1773 to consider the new tax on tea that precipitated the Boston Tea Party; the **Paul Revere House**, the oldest in Boston; and the **Bunker Hill Monument**, which marks the first major battle of the Revolution, on June 17, 1775.

Although no battles were fought here, **Valley Forge National Historical Park** in southeastern Pennsylvania honors the place where some 2,000 soldiers died of disease and exposure during the winter of 1777–78. A visitor center, exhibits and tour guides in uniform tell the story of George Washington's troops as they trained for combat.

Hostilities had commenced on April 19, 1775, when British troops marched from Boston to Concord and exchanged fire with the Massachusetts militia at North Bridge. **Minute Man National Historical Park** follows much of the road from Lexington to Concord, including **Bloody Angles**, where colonial militia ambushed British troops.

The first land battle fought in the South is at **Ninety-Six National Historic Site** in South Carolina. To the north, **Saratoga National Historical Park** in New York's Hudson Valley marks what may have been the turning point of the war. Most of the fighting ended when British troops surrendered to Revolutionary forces at Yorktown in 1781. The battlefield is part of Colonial National Historical Park in Virginia.

Nation-building: Once the American Revolution was over and the United States had won independence, the fledgling government needed a permanent

The Gateway Arch at Jefferson National Expansion Memorial in St Louis, Missouri.

place to do business. The site chosen in 1790 for the nation's capital city was the marshy confluence of the Potomac and Anacostia rivers. Since 1800, the **US Capitol** has been the seat of Congress and the **White House** has been the official residence of the president, but the District of Columbia grew slowly and was almost abandoned at one point. Finally, after years of neglect and political infighting, the **Washington Monument** was finished in 1884, the **Old Executive Office Building** in 1888 and the **Library of Congress** in 1897, marking the government's irrevocable commitment to the city.

At the turn of the century, the government turned its attention to the "Grand Avenue," the mile-long (1½-km) mall of muddy land stretching from the Capitol. Today, **the Mall** is a magnificent avenue of world-famous museums and memorials, and has been home to the Smithsonian Institution's first building, known as the **Castle**, since the 1850s. Since then the original Smithsonian has been joined by many museums dedi-

cated to history, the arts, natural history and technology. And the Mall continues to grow. The **Vietnam Veterans' Memorial**, dedicated in 1982, and the newer **Holocaust Memorial Museum** are two of its most moving sites.

One of the best kept secrets of the National Park System is found in Fayette County, Pennsylvania. It is **Friendship Hill National Historic Site**, home of Albert Gallatin from 1789 to 1825. He was Secretary of the Treasury under Presidents Thomas Jefferson and James Madison and played an important role in the early years of the Republic. The park preserves Gallatin's plain brick house and samples of his work.

The Big Apple: While the new government was struggling to build its capital, New York was surpassing Philadelphia and Boston as the nation's largest metropolis. The city has held that title since the early 1800s, even before its population was swelled by the great wave of immigration later in the 19th century. Park sites throughout New York preserve the city's illustrious past.

St Paul's Church, established in the 17th century, is home to the twin of the famous Liberty Bell. The first meeting of Congress took place at the original **Federal Hall**, now marked by an 1842 Greek Revival building. Also in the city are Alexander Hamilton's 1802 home **The Grange**, and **Theodore Roosevelt's Birthplace**.

Originally built in 1808–11 as a fortress and later used as an immigration center, **Castle Clinton National Monument** is the main visitor center for the national parks in New York City and the ticket office for ferries to the **Statue of Liberty** and **Ellis Island**. The turreted brick-and-limestone immigration center at Ellis Island, through which millions of new Americans passed from 1892 to 1945, was recently renovated and converted into a museum of immigration, including a collection of family heirlooms brought by immigrants, oral histories and educational facilities.

Industry, arts and science: The flood of immigrants pouring through Ellis Island helped fuel America's Industrial Revolution. The site that best focuses

Thomas Edison's office at Edison National Historic Site, New Jersey.

on this subject is **Lowell National Historical Park** in Massachusetts. Lowell was America's leading textile manufacturing center in the 1820s and its first great industrial city. Exhibits and tours offer a glimpse of everyday life and work during the Industrial Revolution. Among the important sites are the boardinghouse where the mill girls lived, and a working power loom.

Other industrial sites include **Hopewell Furnace National Historic Site** in Pennsylvania, a fine example of a 19th-century, rural iron-making community, and **Salem Maritime National Historic Site** in Massachusetts, a remnant of the prosperous commercial shipping industry of the 18th century.

Several parks, such as the **Edison National Historic Site** in West Orange, New Jersey, commemorate scientific and artistic achievements. Thomas Alva Edison set up his "invention factory" here in 1887. By the time he retired, he had developed the phonograph, motion-picture camera, fluoroscope and electric storage battery. His home, **Glen-**

mont, is located about a half-mile (1 km) from his laboratory.

The **Wright Brothers National Memorial** in Kill Devil Hills, North Carolina, is the site of the first powered flight, on December 17, 1903. The visitor center has a full-scale reproduction of the original plane, *The Flyer*.

The **Frederick Law Olmsted National Historic Site** in Brookline, Massachusetts, is the home and office of the country's most influential landscape architect. His legacy of wilderness areas, green spaces and urban parks, including New York's Central Park, helped define how America looks today.

The home, studio and gardens of one of America's most noted sculptors are preserved at the **Augustus Saint-Gaudens National Historic Site** in Cornish, New Hampshire. In Flat Rock, North Carolina, is the **Carl Sandburg Home National Historic Site**, last home of the Pulitzer Prize-winning poet.

A broader legacy: The Park Service has been criticized for placing too much emphasis on the deeds of white males

"The Wall,"
Vietnam
Veterans
Memorial,
Washington,
DC.

and the march of progress. But a more fitting representation of the achievements of women and African-Americans is gradually being achieved.

The **Women's Rights National Historical Park** in Seneca Falls, New York, includes the **Wesleyan Methodist Chapel**, a landmark in women's struggle for equal rights since 1848. The **Sewall-Belmont House National Historic Site** on Capitol Hill in Washington has been the National Women's Party headquarters since 1929. Also on Capitol Hill is the **Mary McLeod Bethune Council House National Historic Site**, headquarters of the National Council of Negro Women, established by the famous black educator in 1935.

The **Frederick Douglass National Historic Site** is in Washington's Anacostia neighborhood. The 21-room mansion, called **Cedar Hill**, was the home of this black abolitionist from 1877 to 1895. Born a slave, Douglass was a self-taught speaker, author and journalist who was named minister to Haiti in 1889. By purchasing this house

in a whites-only neighborhood, he was one of the city's first "block breakers."

Booker T. Washington founded a college for black Americans in 1881 in Alabama, now preserved as the **Tuskegee Institute National Historic Site** and still an active institution. A short drive east of the Blue Ridge Parkway in Virginia is the **Booker T. Washington National Monument**, a reconstructed slave farm and cabin where Washington was born in 1856.

The **Martin Luther King, Jr, National Historic Site** in Atlanta includes the boyhood home, church and grave of the civil rights leader, as well as significant sites in the neighborhood. In the summer of 1990 a historic building collapsed there because the park had insufficient funds to maintain the decaying house. This was a dramatic illustration of one of the main problems facing the Park Service: historic buildings are in a constant state of decline, as are funds for upkeep and improvements.

The **Boston African-American National Historic Site** focuses on the political, social and educational aspects of black life during the struggle for independence and citizenship. The park includes 15 pre-Civil War black history structures, including the African-American Meeting House, the oldest existing black-founded church in the US.

At the old **St Louis Courthouse** in Missouri, Dred Scott, a slave, lost his bid for freedom on a legal technicality. More importantly, the trial led to the infamous ruling in 1857 that blacks were not "persons" and had no legal rights. Today the courthouse is part of the **Jefferson National Expansion Memorial**. The memorial is better known for the **Gateway Arch**, a 630-foot (192-meter) structure, below which is the **Museum of Westward Expansion**. The memorial pays tribute to Thomas Jefferson, who negotiated the Louisiana Purchase, thereby doubling the size of the nation, and to the explorers, traders and settlers from the East who used St Louis as a gateway to the West.

● *For an extended list of historic sites, see Travel Tips at the end of this book.*

Left, Thomas Edison's chemistry laboratory. Right, interior of the Capitol dome, Washington, DC.

INDEPENDENCE

It's been called America's "most historic square mile" – Philadelphia's **Independence National Historical Park** – home to the nation's most sacred shrines and symbols. This is where a young journeyman printer named Benjamin Franklin set up shop, where Thomas Jefferson composed the Declaration of Independence, and where the Constitution was drafted and a new kind of nation created.

This storied district is more than just a journey into the past. It is also a study in urban renewal. In the early 1950s, the National Park Service took over much of the district, cleared away the dreck and restored the area's historic sites. Rehabilitation spawned a clutch of shops, galleries, restaurants and hotels. History remains the big attraction, however, and no matter where you go, you will bump into a reminder of Philadelphia's illustrious past.

Colonial core: Start your tour at the visitor center at 3rd and Chestnut streets, where park rangers dispense free maps and information. Exhibits focus on various aspects of American history, and a short film, *Independence*, that was directed by John Huston, is shown every 30–45 minutes.

The visitor center is surrounded by some of the city's most distinguished and dramatic buildings. Directly across 3rd Street, the **First Bank of the United States** stands in "lonely grandeur." Completed in 1797, this regal neoclassical structure is a monument to the political vision of Alexander Hamilton who, as the nation's first Secretary of the Treasury, insisted that government finances be handled by a central institution.

To the south of the visitor center is the **Philadelphia Exchange**, a magnificent Greek Revival structure designed by William Strickland and opened in 1834 as the nation's first stock exchange. Be sure to walk to the rear of the building for a look at the graceful curved portico. The wide cobbled way that wraps around the Exchange is **Dock Street**, formerly

Dock Creek, where ships tied up to unload their cargo in the late 1700s.

A short walk along Walnut Street to the corner of 2nd Street brings you to the **City Tavern**, a fully functioning reconstruction of the 18th-century inn where Benjamin Franklin, George Washington, John Adams and others wrangled over weighty issues.

Around the corner on 2nd Street, **Welcome Park** is a tribute to William Penn, who occupied a slate-roof house on the site during his second and final visit to the colony. Designed by the prize-winning Philadelphia architect Robert Venturi, the park is a model of Penn's original city plan. Next door, the **Thomas Bond House** is an 18th-century restoration operated by the Park Service as a bed-and-breakfast inn.

Return to Walnut Street and turn right toward the lovely row houses and gardens between 3rd and 4th street. The first is the **Bishop White House**, built in 1786 and occupied until 1836 by Episcopal Bishop William White, rector of **Christ Church**. Fully re-

stored, the house evokes 18th-century affluence, with a beautifully appointed dining room in which Washington, Jefferson, Franklin and others dined, the bishop's well-stocked library, and – a sign of real wealth – an indoor privy.

At the other end of the block is the **Todd House**, built about 10 years earlier than Bishop White's house and, judging by the tiny rooms and outdoor privy, meant for a family that was less privileged. John and Dolley Todd lived here for two years before John, an attorney, died in the yellow fever epidemic of 1793. Dolley later married "the mighty little Madison" – James Madison, the "master builder of the Constitution" and the nation's fourth president. Tickets to the Todd and Bishop White houses are free at the visitor center. Tours are limited to 10 people and begin about every 30 minutes.

From the Todd House, it's a short walk through the Park Service's **18th-century Garden** into a lovely mall shaded by enormous willow and dogwood trees. Straight ahead is **Carpen-**ters **Hall**, a beautifully proportioned Georgian structure built in 1770–74. This is where the First Continental Congress met in September 1774 to air colonists' grievances against George III.

At the front of **Carpenters Court**, two smaller buildings face Chestnut Street. The **Marine Corps Memorial Museum**, a reconstruction of New Hall built in 1791, houses a modest collection of revolution-era weapons. The **Army–Navy Museum**, quartered in a reconstruction of a colonial house, details the development of the military in the late 1700s.

A very good house: Just across the street, an alleyway leads to **Franklin Court**, site of Benjamin Franklin's last home. Franklin started work on the house in 1763 but didn't move in until 1785, when he retired from his diplomatic posts in Britain and France. "'Tis a very good house that I built so long ago to retire into," Franklin wrote. Even in retirement, however, Franklin had little rest. He served as president of Pennsylvania for three years and, at the age of

A "redcoat" plays the fife

80, as a delegate at the Constitutional Convention. The house was torn down in 1812 by Franklin's grandchildren. Lacking plans for the structure, the Park Service erected "ghost structures" that represent the outline of Franklin's house and his grandson's printing office.

At the opposite end of Franklin Court, facing Market Street, a row of homes built by Franklin in the late 1780s now accommodate a park bookshop, a post office and an 18th-century printing shop where his firebrand grandson, Benjamin Franklin Bache, once published the *Aurora*.

The exhibits continue in Franklin Court's underground museum, which features a portrait gallery, replicas of Franklin's inventions, a display detailing his work as a scientist, statesman, philosopher and printer, and an audio-drama explaining Franklin's imposing presence in the revolution and the Constitutional Convention. Best of all, you can pick up a telephone at the "Franklin Exchange" and hear what Washington, Mark Twain, D.H. Lawrence and others

had to say about "the wisest American" – not all of it kindly.

Walk back to Chestnut Street and turn right for the glorious, if somewhat faded, facade of the **Second Bank of the United States**, yet another of the park's Greek Revival jewels built in 1824. Today, the bank serves as Independence Park's portrait gallery. Many of the works are by Charles Willson Peale, one of the premier American painters of his day. Works by James Sharples, Gilbert Stuart, Thomas Sully and Peale's son, Rembrandt, are also part of the collection. During the summer, cool drinks are offered in a colonial-style tea garden at the side of the building.

Library Hall stands next to the Second Bank. The original building was completed in 1789 for the Library Company of Philadelphia, destroyed in 1884 and then reconstructed in the 1950s as the library of the American Philosophical Society. The structure now houses all sorts of historical goodies, including letters and other documents written by Franklin, Jefferson and other eminent

Americans. Most of the holdings are reserved for serious scholars, but visitors can sneak a peek at a few choice samples in the lobby.

Let freedom ring: Crossing 5th Street from Library Hall puts you smack in the middle of **Independence Square**. The two buildings hugging the corner are **Old City Hall** – home of the Supreme Court from 1791 to 1800 and to city government between 1800 and 1870 – and **Philosophical Hall**, headquarters of Ben Franklin's American Philosophical Society, which has occupied the building since 1789. Today, Old City Hall houses exhibits dealing with the early years of the Supreme Court. Philosophical Hall is closed to the public.

Not to be missed, of course, is **Independence Hall**, locus of the American historical experience. It was built between 1732 and 1756 as the Pennsylvania State House but was destined to play a key role in the birth of the nation. This is where the Second Continental Congress convened in 1775 to make its case against the British and, ultimately, to draft a revolutionary Declaration of Independence. Eleven years later, the Constitutional Congress met to amend the irresolute Articles of Confederation – and ended up forging an entirely new government. Tours of Independence Hall start in the east wing and guide visitors into the **Assembly Room**, where John Hancock presided over his rebellious countrymen in 1776 and George Washington, the preeminent revolutionary icon, served as guiding light during the secretive proceedings of the Constitutional Convention in 1787.

Although most of the original furnishings were destroyed by the British during the war, a few original touches remain, including the silver inkstand used for the signing of the Declaration of Independence, the "rising sun chair" used by Washington, and Thomas Jefferson's walking stick. The rest of the furniture dates to the late 1700s. Independence Hall also houses period restorations of the **Pennsylvania Supreme Court** and, on the second floor, the **Governor's Chamber** and the **Long Room**, used as a prison hospital for American soldiers during the war, a reception hall for foreign dignitaries in the 1790s and, later, as Charles Willson Peale's museum of art and science.

Now closed to the public, the bell tower was erected in 1828, about 37 years after the unsteady original was torn down. The bell hanging in the steeple is not the famous Liberty Bell but a substitute – the **John Wilbanks Bell** – installed in 1828 and still rung on national holidays. Finally, standing off Independence Hall's west shoulder, **Congress Hall** housed the United States legislature between 1790 and 1800. Inside, the Senate and House chambers are replete with fine studded leather, mahogany furnishings and other 18th-century fineries.

The real **Liberty Bell** has, since 1976, occupied a glass-and-steel pavilion in the plaza directly across Chestnut Street. This is probably the most famous bell in the world, which is somewhat ironic given its checkered history. First of all, there is that giant crack marring its face. Consider, too, that the colonial Phila-

The inkstand used to sign the Declaration of Independence

delphians who lived nearby were wont to grumble about its insistent clanging at inopportune moments. And later, in the 19th century, plans to scrap it as an antiquated heap of metal were considered on more than one occasion. Indeed, the circumstances surrounding the very making of the bell represent a kind of comedy of errors.

Intended for the State House tower, the bell was cast in London by the venerable Whitechapel Bell Foundry and sent to Philadelphia in 1752. Before it could be installed, someone decided to put it to the test and, perhaps ineptly, gave it a ring that promptly produced a crack. The bell was recast by two Philadelphia craftsmen, John Stow and John Pass. To their chagrin, this second version sounded a rather unmelodious bong, and Pass and Stow recast it once again – in the process immortalizing themselves with the inscription "Pass and Stow" on the bell's waist.

The bell tolled a number of times during and after the American Revolution, but it cracked again in 1835 while being rung for the death of Chief Justice John Marshall. It tolled one more time on Washington's birthday in 1846, and since then it has remained mostly mute.

Beyond the bell: If time allows, consider a few side trips to some of the other sites administered by the Park Service. The **Graff House**, a reconstruction of the house in which Thomas Jefferson composed the Declaration of Independence, is only a few blocks from Independence Hall. The **Thaddeus Kosciuszko National Memorial** is situated in a lovely 18th-century house just a short walk to the south in Society Hill. And **Old Swedes Church** – Pennsylvania's oldest – is on the corner of Christopher Columbus Boulevard and Christian Street near the waterfront.

Farther afield, the **Deshler-Morris House** and **Cliveden** preserve a portion of the 18th-century village of Germantown, and the **Edgar Allan Poe National Historic Site** in North Philadelphia is the house where the melancholy poet penned some of his best work while living in the city.

The Independence Hall bell tower, former home of the Liberty Bell.

CIVIL WAR SITES

In his famous address at Gettysburg, Abraham Lincoln spoke movingly of hallowed ground. Many of the battlefields of the Civil War are included in the National Park System, and for Americans none of the land which the nation has set aside for preservation bears the peculiar emotional force of these consecrated places. Brutal battles were fought here, pitting kinsmen against kinsmen in an awful conflict that scarred the national psyche. Fighting raged across most of the eastern states for four years, killing more than 600,000 men and nearly destroying the young republic.

The sites administered by the Park Service include battlefields, cemeteries, memorials and other historic places. Some parks are clustered together and can easily be visited in a day or two. Others require long-distance driving and a serious investment of time.

The opening volley: It was the fanatical John Brown who touched off the powder keg and turned angry rhetoric into explosive violence. The year was 1859, and the place where he did it is commemorated at **Harpers Ferry National Historical Park**. The park is in West Virginia, where the Shenandoah and Potomac Rivers meet, upriver from Washington, DC; George Washington himself had picked it as a strategic site for a national armory.

For John Brown, it was the perfect spot to launch the final offensive in his great crusade to end the "peculiar institution" of slavery. On October 16, his 21-man "army of liberation" overran the armory and several outlying buildings. Two days later, his contingent was attacked by US Marines under the command of Colonel Robert E. Lee.

The end of Brown's quixotic mission came six weeks later when he was hanged for insurrection. Hours before his execution, the fiery abolitionist wrote: "I, John Brown, am now quite certain that the crimes of this guilty land will never be purged away but with blood." Total war erupted 16 months

later, and during the long hostilities Harpers Ferry would be taken and retaken several times.

A year after the incident at Harpers Ferry, Lincoln was elected president, and momentous events now came in a rush. On December 20, 1860, an angry South Carolina convention voted to secede from the Union, followed quickly by Alabama, Florida, Georgia, Louisiana and Mississippi. The Confederate States of America formed in February 1861, electing Jefferson Davis as president. Texas joined the coalition, and nearly all Federal forts in the South were seized by Confederate forces.

In South Carolina, Major Robert Anderson realized that Fort Sumter was the only defensible fort of the four Federal installations in Charleston, and he consolidated troops there. When Lincoln took office on March 4, 1861, he made clear that he would hold the fort. At 4.30 on the morning of April 12, Confederate batteries opened fire on Fort Sumter. The Civil War had begun.

Anderson surrendered late the next

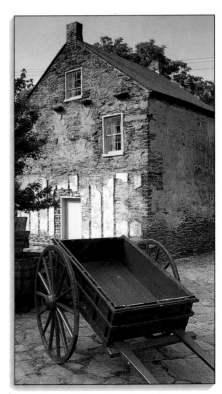

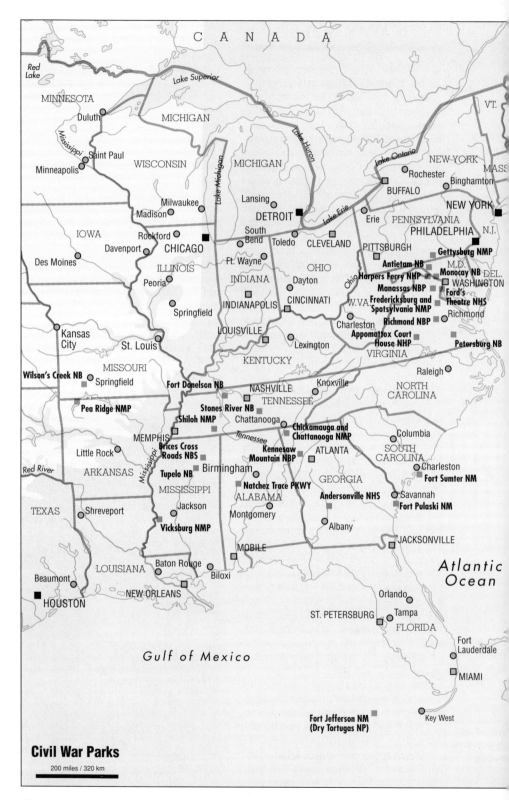

Civil War Parks

200 miles / 320 km

day. The Union Army laid siege to the fort for 22 months, but never retook it; Confederate troops remained until 1865. Today, National Park Service boats carry visitors to **Fort Sumter National Monument** from April 1 to Labor Day.

Just west of Washington, DC, **Manassas National Battlefield Park** in Virginia was the site of two major clashes. General Irvin McDowell led 35,000 Union troops toward a key railroad junction at Manassas on July 18, 1861, expecting to take Richmond, the Confederate capital, easily and end the war quickly. But waiting there, near the Stone Bridge on Bull Run Creek, was General Pierre G.T. Beauregard and 22,000 Confederate troops. Another 10,000 Confederates arrived later in the day.

Confederate soldiers rallied behind General Thomas J. Jackson's fresh Virginia brigade. Jackson "stood there like a stone wall" – hence his nickname, "Stonewall" Jackson. Union forces fled in disarray, hindered by the carriages of sightseers who came to watch the fighting. Some 900 soldiers died on the first day alone.

A mile-long (1½ km) self-guided walking tour follows the course of the battle. A second walk covers the area of the Stone Bridge. Union troops who were wounded here received aid and medicine in an effort organized by Clara Barton. At the age of 40 she had quit her US Patent Office job, and would later found the American Red Cross.

The second Battle of Manassas (Bull Run) came more than a year later, this time involving not raw recruits but veteran soldiers. Robert E. Lee, the new commander of the Confederate Army of Northern Virginia, dispatched Stonewall Jackson's force to engage General John Pope's Union troops. After several battles and tactical mistakes by Pope during the engagement, Jackson sent Union forces fleeing once again. The confrontation killed 3,300 men. A 12-mile (19-km) driving tour covers much of the large area of the second battle of Bull Run.

General George B. McClellan rebuilt the fleeing Federals into the 100,000-man Army of the Potomac and in May 1862 marched on the heavily fortified Confederate capital at Richmond, Virginia. On May 15, Confederate fire drove off five Union ironclad ships that had been moving up the James River toward Richmond. June 26 was the start of seven days of fierce battles on Richmond's eastern outskirts. Lee's forces repulsed McClellan's Union troops, with casualties on both sides numbering 35,000.

Richmond was not safe for the Confederates, however. Battles in regions north of the city continued throughout the coming months. In March 1864, Ulysses S. Grant became commander of the Union field forces, and immediately proclaimed as his chief objective the capture of Richmond.

The battlefield at **Cold Harbor** sits midway between two roadside taverns. When Grant's soldiers attacked there on June 3, they suffered 7,000 casualties in 30 minutes, forcing him to change to a siege strategy. Union soldiers, including several regiments of African-American troops, took Fort Harrison on Sep-

Many historic sites are threatened by encroaching development.

tember 29. Richmond held on until April 1865, falling only after Lee's forces withdrew. You can trace the progress of the encounter at the 10 units of **Richmond National Battlefield Park**. A complete tour requires an 80-mile (129-km) drive.

War for the West: Far to the west, both sides coveted the state of Missouri, with its position on both the Missouri and Mississippi rivers. Control of the region was contested throughout the war, but Union forces gained the upper hand after the Battle of Wilson's Creek, 10 miles (16 km) southwest of Springfield. Brigadier General Nathaniel Lyon, commander of the US Arsenal at St Louis, learned of the governor's plans to take the arsenal for the Confederacy and attacked first on May 10, 1861. Brigadier-General Lyon drove Missouri Governor Claiborne F. Jackson to the southwest corner of the state.

Joined by other Confederate groups, Jackson's forces swelled to 12,000 as he prepared to retake Missouri. Again, Lyon moved first, attacking the Confederates at **Wilson's Creek** with his force of 5,400 early on August 10, 1861. A five-hour battle on **Bloody Hill** cost more than 2,500 casualties on both sides. Lyon was killed at Bloody Hill, and Union forces retreated. A 5-mile (8-km) auto tour covers all the key points of **Wilson's Creek National Battlefield**.

The battle for Missouri moved to a climax at the beginning of 1862, when Union Brigadier General Samuel R. Curtis launched a drive to push Confederate forces from the state. Confederate troops regrouped south of Fayetteville in Arkansas under Major General Earl Van Dorn. Van Dorn's forces marched toward Missouri but met Curtis's troops at Pea Ridge in Arkansas. The battle raged March 7 and 8, until Van Dorn's Confederate troops withdrew after running low on ammunition. **Pea Ridge National Military Park** is 10 miles (16 km) northeast of Rogers, Arkansas.

Until 1862, the Union military seemed unable to win an important victory. Confederate defensive lines had few weak points, but Union commanders decided to test the line in western Tennessee, where Fort Henry on the Tennessee River and Fort Donelson on the Cumberland River sat just 12 miles (19 km) apart. Union ironclad gunboats opened fire on Fort Henry on February 6, 1862, while the virtually unknown Brigadier General Ulysses S. Grant led a ground assault. Grant was slow in reaching the fort, and by the time he arrived, the ironclads had destroyed it and almost the entire garrison had fled to Fort Donelson.

When Union forces attacked on February 14, gunboats could not duplicate their feat against Donelson's heavier guns. Changing tactics, Grant encircled the fort and laid siege. The Confederates surrendered on February 16. These were the Union's first big victories; Grant had made a name for himself. Driving and walking tours are available at **Fort Donelson National Battlefield**, a mile west of Dover in Tennessee.

After the losses at Fort Henry and Fort Donelson, Confederate forces withdrew. In Mississippi, General A.S. Johnston consolidated a force of 44,000

President Abraham Lincoln reviews the military situation at Antietam, 1863.

troops at Corinth, planning to overwhelm Grant. Grant, in turn, moved his own 40,000-man Army of the Tennessee to an encampment around **Shiloh Church**, 22 miles (35 km) northeast of Corinth. Grant drilled his new recruits but set up almost no defenses. Johnston's attack on April 6, 1862, caught Union forces by surprise. Grant's troops spent the entire day in fierce, retreating battles at locations such as **Hornet's Nest**. Confederates used a barrage of 62 cannons – the largest artillery assault of its day – to inflict huge losses on a Union division. Johnston was killed in action and P.G.T Beauregard assumed command. By the end of the day, Grant's remaining forces reached **Pittsburgh Landing** and set up a position fortified by gunboats and thousands of men.

By the morning of April 7, Grant's forces numbered 55,000, but, unaware of the reinforcements, Beauregard attacked. By the time Beauregard retreated, his troops were low on ammunition, and Confederate casualties swelled to 15,000. **Shiloh National Military Park** includes a visitor center and a self-guided driving tour.

Even before the battle at Shiloh, Union forces were preparing to attack Fort Pulaski, a newly completed fort, now in Confederate hands, which guarded the river approaches to Savannah in Georgia. After taking Hilton Head Island, Union forces moved 10 experimental rifled cannons into position on Tybee Island, a mile (1½ km) away from the fort. On April 10, 1862, the Union's new cannons opened up on Pulaski's brick walls, which ranged in thickness from 7½ to 15 feet (2–5 meters). Confederate Colonel Charles H. Olmstead and his troops held on through 30 hours of devastating high-technology barrage.

By noon on April 11, explosive shells opened an outer wall and exposed the fort's main powder magazine. Fearing that an explosion might destroy not only the fort but also the men inside, Olmstead surrendered. **Fort Pulaski National Monument** is reached via Highway 80 from Savannah.

As 1862 drew to a close, Major Gen-

Train trestle guarded by troops at Manassas (Bull Run), 1863.

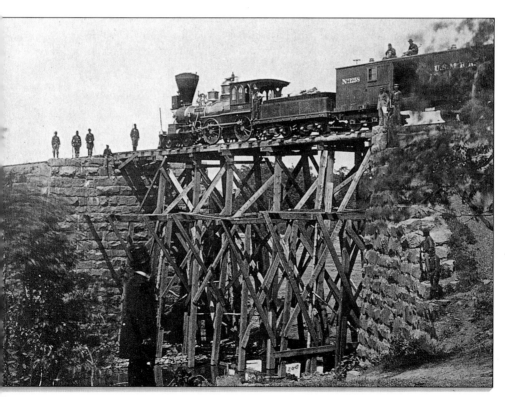

eral William Rosecrans took command of the Union Army of the Cumberland, charged with driving Confederate forces under General Braxton Bragg out of Tennessee. Rosecrans found Bragg waiting for him in a grove of cedars near the **Stones River** in **Murfreesboro,** Tennessee, 27 miles (46 km) southeast of Nashville.

Troops on both sides acted out one of the heartbreaking ironies of warfare as they camped within sight of one another on December 30, 1863, singing rousing songs well into the evening. Then, at dawn on December 31, in a day that went badly for Union forces, they were driven back nearly a mile (1½ km) before establishing a new line. There was neither music nor fighting on New Year's Day. On January 2, Bragg's forces drove Union soldiers back to Stones River, where Rosecrans's superior artillery was waiting. Bragg lost 1,800 soldiers at the river, and the battle ended as his forces retreated. The Confederates had lost Tennessee. The casualties after two days of fighting were

13,000 Union and 10,000 Confederate. **Stones River National Battlefield** lies in the northwest corner of Murfreesboro and includes a driving tour.

Only 30 miles (48 km) west of Jackson, the Mississippi state capital, lies **Vicksburg National Military Park**, the site of the last Confederate stronghold on the Mississippi River. When the war began, Confederate forces set up posts along the river, knowing that the Union would fight hard for access to the Mississippi. If the Federal Army could keep the river free of rebel forces, it could use it to maintain a steady flow of troops and supplies moving into the Confederate territory.

By the summer of 1862, Union troops had captured all of the river's Confederate fortifications – except for Vicksburg and Port Hudson. In October, Ulysses S. Grant was appointed commander of the Department of Tennessee and charged with clearing the river of the last of the Confederate forts. After capturing Jackson on May 14, 1863, he moved west to Vicksburg, where Confederate forces rallied. Realizing that direct attack would fail, Grant surrounded the Confederate Army. On July 4, 1863, Confederate Lieutenant General John C. Pemberton surrendered to Grant. When Port Hudson fell on July 9, the Mississippi belonged to the Union.

When Grant first attempted to take the river, he did so by boat, but his "Bayou Expeditions" failed. He did, however, make naval history: the ironclad Union ship *Cairo* became the first vessel in history to be sunk by an electronically detonated mine. You can see all sorts of items recovered from the ship at the **Cairo Museum**, built in 1980 after the sunken boat was discovered. More than 1,400 monuments erected at Vicksburg National Military Park mark army positions. Visitors can also walk through the serene **Vicksburg National Cemetery**, the final resting place of 17,000 Union soldiers.

The bloodiest day: As tragic as Vicksburg was, it was only a hint of what was to come. Autumn of 1862 brought the costliest battle of the Civil War – the Battle of Antietam, fought on

A medical team reenacts the war.

both sides of **Antietam Creek** near **Sharpsburg** in Maryland.

Buoyed by his August victory at Manassas, General Robert E. Lee moved into Maryland to set the stage for his first foray into the North. Lee, who had lent troops to Stonewall Jackson to capture Harpers Ferry, had only 40,000 troops left to lead against the Federal Army's 87,000. Although outmanned, the Confederates didn't lose; there was no decisive victory at Antietam, where, on September 17, 1862 – the bloodiest single day of the entire four-year conflict – more than 23,000 men fell.

At 12-sq.-mile (31-sq.-km) **Antietam National Battlefield**, you can follow the battle, perhaps lingering at the **Miller Corn Field**. Union General Joseph Hooker, who earned his nickname "Fighting Joe" at Antietam, wrote of the cornfield, "Every stalk of corn in the northern and greater part of the field was cut as closely as could have been done with a knife, and the slain lay in rows precisely as they had stood in their ranks a few moments before." Pause at

the beautiful **Burnside Bridge**, named after Union General Ambrose E. Burnside, whose troops were pinned down at the bridge for hours.

Although the battle was not lost, the Confederate Army had taken a step toward losing the war. On September 22, President Lincoln issued the Emancipation Proclamation, which on January 1, 1863, freed slaves in states "in rebellion against the United States." Only then did emancipation become a formal objective of the war.

After visiting Antietam, you may want to travel toward **Rockville** to tour **Monocacy National Battlefield**, a new national park honoring another Maryland site where, much later, the Confederate Army made yet another failed attempt to cross Northern lines. In July 1864, General Jubal Early led rebel troops down the Georgetown Pike, only to encounter Federal troops in a battle on the Monocacy River.

General Early, slowed down but not stopped, battled on – until veteran Federal forces, who had traveled by steam-

boat from southern Virginia, arrived at Monocacy and drove his troops back.

One could "take the pulse" of the war farther south, at **Fredericksburg** in Virginia. The city's proximity to Washington, DC, and Richmond – it lies halfway between – had been a blessing before the war, but after secession its strategic location became a curse. One hundred thousand men died near Fredericksburg in four major battles. **Fredericksburg and Spotsylvania National Military Park** encompasses 7,775 acres (3,146 hectares) of land that includes four battlefields and three historic buildings.

Begin at **Fredericksburg Battlefield**, where Burnside's Union troops crossed the Rappahannock River in December 1862 to attack Lee's forces, commanded by Stonewall Jackson. Heavily defended on hills west of Fredericksburg, Jackson handily won the battle, inflicting big losses on the Federal troops. More than 15,000 Union soldiers are buried at **Fredericksburg National Cemetery**. Visit **Chatham**, a Georgian mansion used as a field hospital, where volunteer Clara Barton and poet Walt Whitman tended to injured soldiers.

Stonewall falls: Next, drive west to the **Chancellorsville Battlefield**, where in May 1863 Jackson's forces again won a victory against Federal troops. Here Jackson was shot by "friendly fire." Following the amputation of Jackson's left arm on May 4, General Lee wrote to him, "You are better off than I am, for while you have lost your left, I have lost my right arm." Jackson died of pneumonia on May 10 at **Guinea Station**, 15 miles (24 km) south of Fredericksburg, where the **Stonewall Jackson Shrine** now stands.

To the west is **Wilderness Battlefield**, where Lee and Grant first faced each other in an indecisive battle on May 5–6, 1864. Grant broke away from that battle to march toward the **Spotsylvania Court House**. Lee's army actually reached Spotsylvania first, and he fended off several small Union attacks. When more Union troops arrived, along with a thick fog, the fighting grew

Monuments and cannons at Chickamauga and Chattanooga National Military Park in Georgia.

104

more savage. After 20 hours of hand-to-hand combat and several days of a staunch Confederate defense, Grant pulled his troops out and called the fight at "Bloody Angle" a Union victory, a key to winning the war.

Lee lost his right-hand man in Stonewall Jackson, but not his fighting spirit. On June 3, Lee began a march west into Pennsylvania. He was to lead troops into the fateful Battle of Gettysburg, where his 70,000 soldiers would clash with General George G. Meade's 93,000 Union troops. In three days, the two armies suffered 51,000 casualties – the greatest losses of any battle ever fought in North America. **Gettysburg National Military Park** features an 18-mile (29-km) auto tour through the battlefields.

The most famous spot of all is the **High Water Mark**, the site of the heroic but doomed Pickett's Charge. General George E. Pickett, only 38 years old, marched more than 12,000 Confederate troops across an open plain surrounded on three sides by Union forces, toward **Cemetery Hill**. Union soldiers

cut down more than 6,000 Confederates, and the Battle of Gettysburg was over. The war had taken its most significant turning point toward Union victory.

At the dedication of the **Gettysburg National Cemetery** on November 19, 1863, President Lincoln delivered a "few appropriate remarks" that would transform Gettysburg into an inspiration and change the way we view the nation. It took only two minutes for Lincoln to give his 272-word Gettysburg Address, which is displayed in the park in summer.

Struggle for the South: A visit to **Chickamauga and Chattanooga National Military Park** in Georgia, just miles outside Chattanooga in Tennessee, stirs the imagination and provides insight into the struggle for the South. As you hike over its fields, hills and hardwood forests, picture two battles – one an empty Confederate victory on September 18–19, 1863, at **Chickamauga Battlefield**; the next, a Union triumph in the Battle of Chattanooga on November 23–25. You can best imagine this battle by hiking up to **Point**

Elkhorn Tavern at Pea Ridge Military Park in Arkansas.

Park on **Lookout Mountain**. From here you can see all of Chattanooga.

After Ulysses S. Grant was named supreme commander on March 9, 1864, the Union Army traveled south from Chattanooga toward Atlanta: "too important a place in the hands of the enemy to be left undisturbed," said General Sherman. The Federal Army wanted to get its hands on the weaponry, the foundries "and especially its railroads, which converged there from the four great cardinal points," Sherman said.

Kennesaw Mountain National Battlefield Park memorializes the 1864 Atlanta campaign, which began when Sherman led 100,000 troops out of Chattanooga in early May, only to confront 65,000 Confederate troops in the mountains of northwest Georgia. For months the two armies battled for key points along the Western and Atlantic Railroad, which ran from Chattanooga to Atlanta. A climax was reached on June 22 at **Kennesaw Mountain**, just northwest of Atlanta. Hand-to-hand combat killed more than 2,000

of Sherman's men at Kennesaw, while the Confederates lost several hundred men in their winning battle.

Still, Sherman pushed General Johnston's Confederate troops south into Atlanta by July 9. After several attacks, Sherman placed the city under siege, concentrating on the railroads. He won the last one, the Macon & Western, on August 31, and telegraphed the fall of Atlanta to Washington on September 2. Riding the victory, Lincoln was reelected on November 8. A week later, Sherman began his horrific March to the Sea.

Hiking trails from 2 to 10 miles (3–16 km) take you to the important sites. These are **Kennesaw Mountain**, where the armies clashed and where you will see a vista of northern Georgia; **Pigeon Hill**, where a foot trail leads to Confederate entrenchments; **Cheatham Hill**, site of the most savage fighting; and **Kolb's Farm** (not open to the public), headquarters of General Joseph Hooker.

Last days: Two small parks in Mississippi mark strategic points in the struggle for the South. Sherman's army needed to defend the Nashville–Chattanooga Railroad, a critical Union supply line. In June 1864, the Confederates, under General Nathan Bedford Forrest, an unschooled farm boy who had become a millionaire, routed Union soldiers at **Brices Cross Roads**, displaying brilliant military tactics and taking advantage of torrential downpours that mired Union troops in mud. Victory in battle, however, didn't help the Confederate position, as Sherman was still able to defend the railroad. You can see the battlefield and markers from the 1-acre (half-hectare) **Brices Cross Roads National Battlefield Site**.

Only a month later, arid, hot weather created as many difficulties as did the earlier rain, tiring soldiers on both sides. Again Federal troops battled Confederate men to protect their southern supply line. On July 14, the two sides met at **Tupelo**, Mississippi, with exhausted, ill-fed Union troops winning a close victory. For two months, the two sides skirmished. Finally, in September, Confederate troops pushed north past Federal soldiers into Tennessee. But Sher-

Black soldiers played a significant role in the Civil War.

man's forces no longer needed to protect the railroad; they had already won Atlanta and were on their way to the sea. **Tupelo National Battlefield** is located within Tupelo city limits, about a mile east of the **Natchez Trace Parkway**.

Grant's army was everywhere during the spring of 1864. Even while Sherman waged the Atlanta campaign and smaller forces defended the Nashville–Chattanooga Railroad, Federal troops were focused on Richmond. The Union Army reached Petersburg, which Grant called "The key to taking Richmond," in mid-June 1864. For 10 months, Grant kept Petersburg under siege. He cut Lee's supply lines from the south, diminishing troop strength through direct attack, hunger and demoralization. Petersburg finally surrendered on April 2, 1865. On the same day, Richmond fell.

One of the most interesting sites at **Petersburg National Battlefield** is the **Crater**. Here, the 48th Pennsylvania Infantry, which included many former coal miners, dug a tunnel toward a Confederate fort at Pegram's Salient. In this tunnel they blew up four tons of gunpowder, planning to send Union troops through the gap it would create, with the intention of shortening the siege. The explosion, which blew up Confederate artillery, created a crater 170 feet (52 meters) long, 60 feet (18 meters) wide and 30 feet (9 meters) deep. The Union Army went directly into the crater but were unable to go any farther. They sustained 4,000 deaths when Confederate troops attacked. The battlefield is within Petersburg city limits.

From here, visit the 27 historic structures within the restored village of **Appomattox Court House** (20 miles/32 km east of Lynchburg), where Lee surrendered to Grant only one week after Richmond fell. Imagine the meaning of the victory, which overwhelmed the descriptive capabilities of *The New York Times*: "No brilliant rhetoric, no vivid word-painting, no oratorical eloquence can portray the sublimity and immensity of the great victory," its correspondent reported on April 10.

The aftermath: Lincoln's presidency

Memorial at Gettysburg National Military Park.

was bounded by the war, which began before he took office and ended only one week before John Wilkes Booth, a 27-year-old actor, shot Lincoln at **Ford's Theatre** in Washington, DC, on April 14, 1865. Booth escaped but was found on April 26 and was killed either by his captors or by committing suicide. You can visit the **Lincoln Museum**, in the basement of **Ford's Theatre National Historic Site**, and the restored **House Where Lincoln Died** across the street. The theatre itself has been restored to its Civil War appearance and is home to plays from September through May.

To take a look at one of the saddest sites of the Civil War, visit **Andersonville National Historic Site** in Georgia. At Andersonville, the largest encampment housing Federal prisoners, almost 13,000 Union soldiers died – a third of those confined here. When it was built in 1864, most people thought the war would soon be over. The Confederate government built the prison to hold 10,000 prisoners, but soon 32,000 men were suffering the filthy conditions of the prison camp. Prisoners died of disease, poor sanitation, malnutrition, overcrowding or exposure to the elements.

Following the war, the prison commander, Captain Henry Wirz, was hanged as a war criminal, although his crimes were simply those of the ailing Confederate government, which had no money or resources with which to feed and house its own troops, much less its prisoners. Andersonville's life as a prison ended in early 1865. In July and August, Clara Barton, working with Dorence Atwater, a former prisoner who had chronicled the prisoners' deaths, identified thousands of graves.

While at Andersonville, visit the **National Cemetery**, the prison, and **Providence Spring House**, which the Women's Relief Corps built in 1901 as a tribute to the site where, during a downpour on August 9, 1864, a spring began to flow. Prisoners thanked "Divine Providence" for the fresh water. Today, this historic site is a memorial not only to the men who were imprisoned and who died at Andersonville, but also to all Americans ever confined as prisoners of war – the only such national park.

You might also consider visiting some of the many historic sites associated with key figures in the war. There are at least four sites dedicated to the life and career of Abraham Lincoln, including **Lincoln Birthplace National Historic Site** in Kentucky, **Lincoln Boyhood National Memorial** in Indiana, **Lincoln Home National Historic Site** in Illinois, and the **Lincoln Memorial** in Washington, DC.

In Virginia, **Arlington House** is a memorial to Robert E. Lee, who lived here with his wife before the outbreak of the war. The estate was later confiscated by the Federal government and is now part of Arlington National Cemetery. Lee's adversary, Ulysses S. Grant, is remembered at **Grant National Historic Site** in Missouri, where he resided in the years before the war. He and his wife are interred at **General Grant National Memorial** in New York City.

● *An extended list of Civil War sites appears in Travel Tips at the end of this book.*

Left, Confederate soldiers carr the "Stars and Bars" at a Civil War reenactment Right, General Warren Statue, Gettysburg National Military Park

NATIONAL PARKS

A vacation in the national parks? It's as American as apple pie. Mention the parks to most people and they think of the outsized landscapes of the American West like the Grand Canyon, Yellowstone, Yosemite. But the East and the Midwest have their share of national parks, too. As a matter of fact, more than half of the sites in the National Park System are to be found east of the country's legendary dividing line, the Mississippi River.

Their official designations vary. Some are called national monuments or recreation areas. Some are national seashores, rivers, historic sites or battlefields. Ranging in size from less than one-tenth of an acre (Thaddeus Kosciuszko National Memorial) to more than 1.5 million acres/607,000 hectares (Everglades National Park), they include everything from the heavenly Skyline Drive in Virginia to the depths of Kentucky's Mammoth Cave. They are, as one Park Service official proposed, a "vignette of primitive America" and a treasure house of American history.

There are many ways to experience the parks. Visitors interested primarily in "windshield tours" will find scenic byways with some of the grandest views in America. There are also much longer corridors, such as the Blue Ridge Parkway, running like green ribbons through unspoiled country.

For many, just gazing at these landscapes is gratifying enough. Most visitors don't venture more than a hundred yards from their cars. But there are some people who want more. And for them the Park Service has designed a network of trails that includes everything from a 2,000-mile (3,200-km) traverse of the Appalachian Mountains to a relaxing stroll on a paved nature trail.

To make sense of it all, the parks provide a wide range of interpretive programs: campfire talks and nature walks; canoe trips and bicycle tours; cruises, wildlife excursions and living-history demonstrations. And most importantly, there is the hard-working corps of park rangers, any one of whom can help you find your way out of the wilderness or into the nearest bathroom.

Still not enough things to do? How about white-water rafting through the New River Gorge? Mountain biking at Big South Fork? Bird-watching in the Everglades? Exploring a sea cave at Pictured Rocks? Kayaking at Acadia? Horseback riding at Buffalo River? Fishing in the Great Smoky Mountains? Scuba diving in the blue sea off the Virgin Islands?

These places have been set aside because they are a precious part of America's natural and cultural heritage. They are gifts that Americans give to themselves and the world. Enjoy them with care and wonder.

Preceding pages: Cape Hatteras Lighthouse, Outer Banks, North Carolina; gristmill, Great Smoky Mountains National Park; covered bridge, Valley Forge National Historical Park, Pennsylvania. Left, hiking in Virginia's Blue Ridge Mountains.

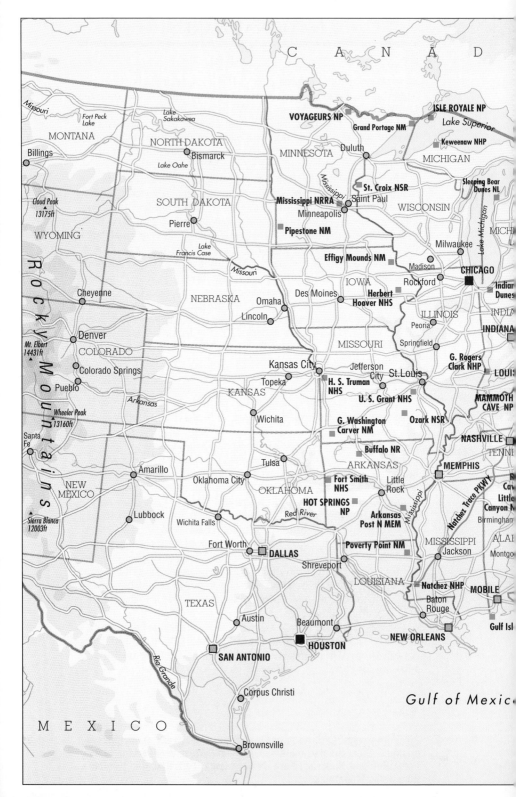

C A N A D A

VOYAGEURS NP
ISLE ROYALE NP
Lake Superior
Grand Portage NM
Keweenaw NHP

Missouri
Fort Peck Lake
Lake Sakakawea
Duluth
MICHIGAN

MONTANA
NORTH DAKOTA
Bismarck
Lake Oahe
MINNESOTA
Sleeping Bear Dunes NL

Billings

St. Croix NSR
Mississippi
WISCONSIN
MICH

Cloud Peak 13175ft
SOUTH DAKOTA
Mississippi NRRA
Saint Paul
Minneapolis

WYOMING
Pierre
Pipestone NM
Milwaukee

Lake Francis Case
Effigy Mounds NM
Madison
CHICAGO
Indian Dunes

Missouri
Rockford
IOWA
Herbert Hoover NHS
INDIA

Cheyenne
NEBRASKA
Omaha
Des Moines
ILLINOIS
INDIANA

Denver
Lincoln
Peoria

Mt. Elbert 14431ft
COLORADO
MISSOURI
Springfield

Colorado Springs
Kansas City
Jefferson City
St. Louis
G. Rogers Clark NHP
LOUIS

Pueblo
Topeka
H. S. Truman NHS
U. S. Grant NHS
MAMMOTH CAVE NP

Wheeler Peak 13160ft
Arkansas
KANSAS
Wichita
G. Washington Carver NM
Ozark NSR
NASHVILLE

Santa Fe
Buffalo NR
TENNI

Amarillo
Tulsa
ARKANSAS
MEMPHIS

NEW MEXICO
Oklahoma City
Fort Smith NHS
Little Rock
Natchez Trace PKWY
Ca
Little Canyon N

Sierra Blanca 12003ft
Lubbock
OKLAHOMA
HOT SPRINGS NP
Mississippi
Birmingham

Wichita Falls
Red River
Arkansas Post N MEM
MISSISSIPPI
ALA

Fort Worth
Poverty Point NM
Jackson
Montg

DALLAS
Shreveport
Natchez NHP
MOBILE

TEXAS
LOUISIANA
Baton Rouge
Gulf Isl

Austin
Beaumont
NEW ORLEANS

San Antonio
HOUSTON

Corpus Christi
Gulf of Mexic

MEXICO

Brownsville

Rio Grande

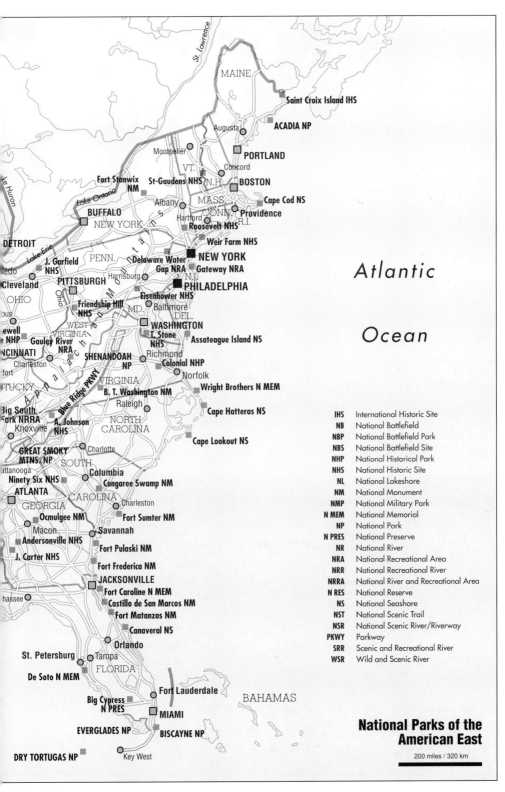

National Parks of the American East

St. Lawrence

MAINE

Saint Croix Island IHS

Augusta
ACADIA NP

Montpelier
PORTLAND

VT.
Concord

Fort Stanwix NM
St-Gaudens NHS
N.H.
BOSTON

Lake Ontario
Albany
MASS.
Cape Cod NS

BUFFALO
NEW YORK
Hartford
CONN.
Providence
R.I.
Roosevelt NHS

DETROIT

Weir Farm NHS

Lake Erie

J. Garfield NHS
PENN.
Delaware Water Gap NRA
NEW YORK
Gateway NRA

Cleveland
PITTSBURGH
Harrisburg
N.J.

OHIO
Ohio
PHILADELPHIA
Eisenhower NHS

Friendship Hill NHS
MD.
Baltimore
DEL.

WASHINGTON
T. Stone NHS
Assateague Island NS

ewell NHP
WEST VIRGINIA
Gauley River NRA

CINCINNATI
SHENANDOAH NP
Richmond
Colonial NHP

Charleston
Norfolk

TUCKY
VIRGINIA
Wright Brothers N MEM

B. T. Washington NM
Raleigh

Blue Ridge PKWY
Cape Hatteras NS

Big South Fork NRRA
A. Johnson NHS
NORTH CAROLINA
Cape Lookout NS

Knoxville

GREAT SMOKY MTNS. NP
Charlotte

attanooga
SOUTH

Ninety Six NHS
Columbia

ATLANTA
Congaree Swamp NM

GEORGIA
CAROLINA
Charleston

Ocmulgee NM
Fort Sumter NM

Macon
Savannah

Andersonville NHS
Fort Pulaski NM

J. Carter NHS

Fort Frederica NM

JACKSONVILLE
Fort Caroline N MEM

hassee
Castillo de San Marcos NM
Fort Matanzas NM

Canaveral NS

Orlando

St. Petersburg
Tampa
FLORIDA

De Soto N MEM

Fort Lauderdale
BAHAMAS

Big Cypress N PRES
MIAMI

EVERGLADES NP
BISCAYNE NP

DRY TORTUGAS NP
Key West

Atlantic

Ocean

IHS	International Historic Site
NB	National Battlefield
NBP	National Battlefield Park
NBS	National Battlefield Site
NHP	National Historical Park
NHS	National Historic Site
NL	National Lakeshore
NM	National Monument
NMP	National Military Park
N MEM	National Memorial
NP	National Park
N PRES	National Preserve
NR	National River
NRA	National Recreational Area
NRR	National Recreational River
NRRA	National River and Recreational Area
N RES	National Reserve
NS	National Seashore
NST	National Scenic Trail
NSR	National Scenic River/Riverway
PKWY	Parkway
SRR	Scenic and Recreational River
WSR	Wild and Scenic River

National Parks of the American East

200 miles / 320 km

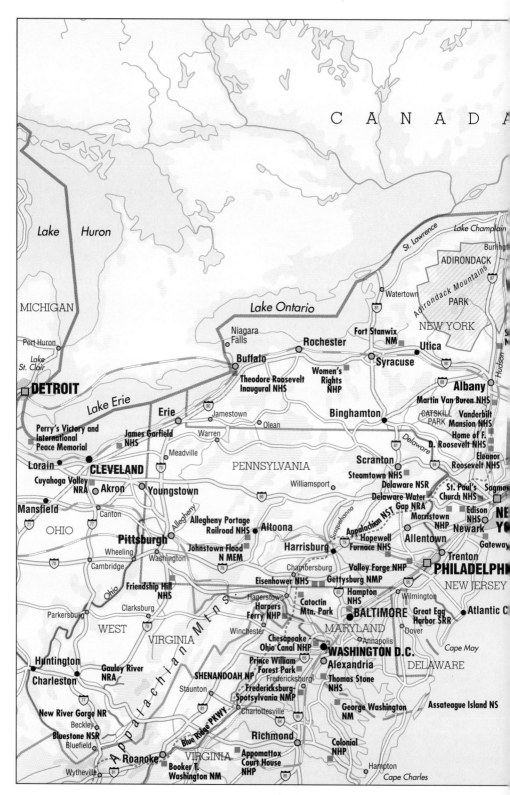

CANADA

Lake Huron

MICHIGAN

Port Huron

Lake St. Clair

DETROIT

Lake Erie

Lake Ontario

Niagara Falls

Buffalo

Theodore Roosevelt Inaugural NHS

Rochester

Women's Rights NHP

Fort Stanwix NM

Syracuse

Utica

Lake Champlain

St. Lawrence

Burlingt[on]

ADIRONDACK

Watertown

Adirondack Mountains

PARK

NEW YORK

Albany

Martin Van Buren NHS

Erie

Jamestown

Olean

Binghamton

CATSKILL PARK

Vanderbilt Mansion NHS

Home of F. D. Roosevelt NHS

Delaware

Eleanor Roosevelt NHS

Perry's Victory and International Peace Memorial

James Garfield NHS

Warren

Meadville

PENNSYLVANIA

Williamsport

Scranton

Steamtown NHS

Delaware NSR

Delaware Water Gap NRA

St. Paul's Church NHS

Sagmo[re]

NE[W] Y[ORK]

Lorain

CLEVELAND

Cuyahoga Valley NRA

Akron

Youngstown

Mansfield

Canton

OHIO

Allegheny

Allegheny Portage Railroad NHS

Altoona

Susquehanna

Morristown NHP

Edison NHS

Newark

Appalachian NST

Pittsburgh

Wheeling

Washington

Cambridge

Johnstown Flood N MEM

Harrisburg

Hopewell Furnace NHS

Allentown

Gateway

Trenton

PHILADELPH[IA]

NEW JERSEY

Chambersburg

Valley Forge NHP

Ohio

Friendship Hill NHS

Parkersburg

Clarksburg

WEST VIRGINIA

Hagerstown

Harpers Ferry NHP

Winchester

Eisenhower NHS

Gettysburg NMP

Hampton NHS

Catoctin Mtn. Park

BALTIMORE

MARYLAND

Wilmington

Dover

Annapolis

Great Egg Harbor SRR

Atlantic C[ity]

Cape May

DELAWARE

Huntington

Charleston

Gauley River NRA

Staunton

Appalachian Mtns.

SHENANDOAH NP

Chesapeake & Ohio Canal NHP

Prince William Forest Park

Fredericksburg

Fredericksburg-Spotsylvania NMP

WASHINGTON D.C.

Alexandria

Thomas Stone NHS

George Washington NM

Assateague Island NS

New River Gorge NR

Beckley

Bluestone NSR

Bluefield

Charlottesville

Richmond

Roanoke

Blue Ridge PKWY

VIRGINIA

Booker T. Washington NM

Wytheville

Appomattox Court House NHP

Colonial NHP

Hampton

Cape Charles

THE NORTHEAST

Its mountains are cloaked in a mantle of forest, its shores washed by the Atlantic, its rivers run swift and cold. America's Northeast is a rich and varied land.

The crown jewel is Acadia National Park off the northern coast of Maine. This is where the Atlantic rages against the fractured shore of Mount Desert Island and the great boreal forest creeps to the sea. Nearby, the bald summit of Cadillac Mountain – the highest peak on the eastern seaboard – catches the first light of dawn, while the trails and carriage paths that wind along its base come alive with birdsong, humming insects and early-morning hikers.

The coast puts on a different face at Cape Cod National Seashore, some 100 miles (160 km) southwest of Boston. Here the granite cliffs of Acadia are replaced by shifting dunes and eroded bluffs. Bordered by wide, sandy beaches and several lovely seaside towns, the national seashore is a favorite summer destination. But this is more than a seaside resort. Protected within its 42,000 acres (16,997 hectares) are vital wetlands, glacial ponds, isolated woods and a stunning variety of bird life.

You'll discover a different side of the Northeast at Delaware Water Gap National Recreation Area, just 90 miles (145 km) from New York City on the New Jersey–Pennsylvania border. The park is named after a scenic notch cut into the Appalachians by the Delaware River. More than 35 miles (56 km) of the river are protected within the park, as are the lovely waterfalls, shady woods and many historic sites along its banks.

A river of a different sort is protected in the rugged highlands of West Virginia. Once stripped of its natural beauty by mining and logging, the New River Gorge National River is now a mecca for all kinds of outdoors enthusiasts, including rock climbers, river runners, hikers and mountain bikers.

● *For a key to the symbols used in this map, please see page 119.*

Map labels

St. John

Mt. Katahdin
5267ft

Appalachian NST

MAINE

Calais
Saint Croix Island IHS

Bangor

ONT

Berlin

Augusta

ACADIA NP
Mt. Desert Island

NEW HAMPSHIRE
Lebanon

Saint-Gaudens NHS

Concord

Portland

Manchester

Longfellow NHS

Lowell NHP

Saugus Iron Works NHS

te Man NHP

Salem Maritime NHS

J.F.Kennedy NHS

gfield

BOSTON

Adams NHS

y NHS

Worcester

F.L.Olmsted NHS

Cape Cod NS

field

Providence

rtford

Roger Williams N MEM

Chatham

N.

R.I.

laven

Long Island

land NS

Atlantic Ocean

Northeastern National Parks

125 miles / 200 km

ACADIA

In September 1604 a tiny pinnace flying the fleur-de-lis of France sailed along the Gulf of Maine, exploring the shores of a land shrouded in fog and mystery. It was not the first vessel to ply these uncharted waters.

Six hundred years earlier, Viking long ships had parted the mists, passing through like ghostly apparitions and leaving only riddles in their wake. Later, European soldiers of fortune searched this coast for a mythical land of riches they called Norumbega. Instead, they found the home of the Abenaki Indians, a place they called the "Land of the Frozen Ground."

Under the command of the famed explorer Samuel de Champlain, the little pinnace of 1604 sailed along the wild, solitary shore of a land the French knew as *Acadie*. Thick forests of spruce and fir crowned bold craggy headlands. Gleaming granite islands jutted from the depths, some rising over a thousand feet above the sea, others merely breaching the surface like the backs of whales sleeping in the swells.

Landing on one of the larger islands, Champlain remarked upon the bare, sloping mountain tops, and called the place *L'Isle des Monts Déserts*, "the Island of bare mountains." A little to the west, Champlain named another island *L'Isle au Haut*, "the High Island," for the dramatic way it thrust above the sea. Centuries later, these two islands became the bulk of what is now **Acadia National Park**.

Acadia is a small park by western standards, measuring only 108 sq. miles (280 sq. km) and defined by a roving boundary weaving in and out of private holdings and incorporating portions of offshore islands and a distant peninsula, Acadia is nonetheless one of the jewels of the National Park System. Here is a natural province of unmatched beauty, a land of astonishing contrasts, a place where rugged mountains and cold northern forests march down to the sea.

Diversity is the theme, and the charm, of Acadia. The park is a rare crossroads of mountain and ocean, of northern and temperate climates, of civilization and wilderness. Here, a short walk will take you from the tidal zone to the alpine zone, from the calm waters of glacial lakes to the roiling Atlantic, from quiet carriage paths to busy roads, from the boutiques of Bar Harbor village to the silent boreal forest. In Acadia, the sweet fragrance of balsam fir blends with the salty sting of the sea. In one day you may see white-tailed deer, beaver, red fox, sea urchin, porpoise, bald eagle, herring gull and any one of several species of whale.

Mount Desert Island, constituting the bulk of Acadia, lies just off the northern coast of Maine, the portion of the state called "Down East." The term confuses landlubbers until they learn that ships heading east from Boston and Portsmouth had the advantage of sailing downwind on the prevailing westerly breeze.

Perhaps even more remarkable than its name is the actual length of this

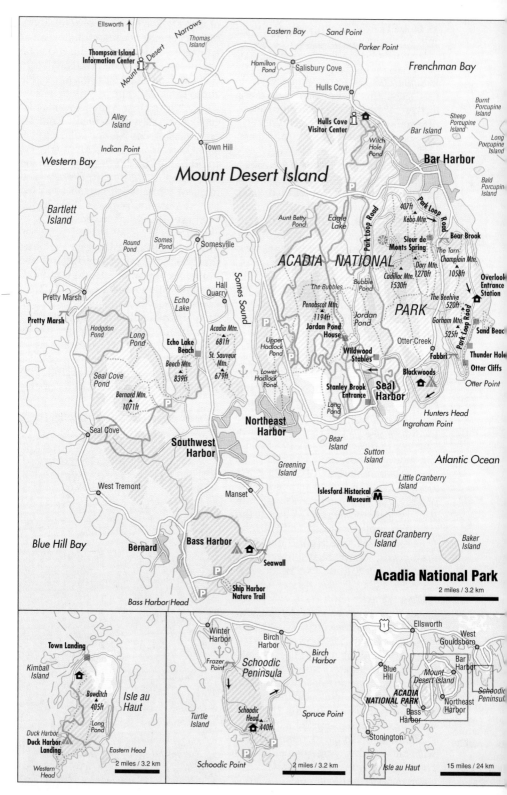

Acadia National Park

2 miles / 3.2 km

coastline: Maine possesses half the nation's Atlantic shore. Though only 200 miles (322 km) across from east to west, this vagrant shoreline winds in and out of a bewildering maze of peninsulas, necks and islands for some 2,500 miles (4,000 km) – a distance roughly equivalent to the span between New York and Salt Lake City.

Acadia, with its deep bays and inlets and, in Somes Sound, the only fjord on the Atlantic Coast, is typical of this meandering strand and of the raw beauty of rock and sea. Creation of this extraordinary landscape began about 500 million years ago. Molten rock miles beneath the earth's surface squeezed upward into fractures in the overlying strata. The eruption cooled and expanded beneath the surface, creating a huge dome of pink, subterranean granite. Two hundred million years of erosion wore away the overlying deposits and gradually uncovered a granite ridge known as the **Mount Desert Range**.

Then, about 20,000 years ago, the last great continental glacier advanced from Canada, carving the Mount Desert Range into a series of ridges separated by wide U-shaped valleys, cracking giant stone blocks from the mountain and sculpting the sheer cliffs along the ocean front. Some of the troughs filled with fresh water and became lakes or ponds. Others filled with sea water and became arms of the ocean. And as the ice sheet withdrew, giant boulders, called glacial erratics, were strewn about the landscape, some left stranded high atop mountains, balancing precariously on the slopes.

The rusticators: In the 19th century, Mount Desert Island was discovered by painters Thomas Cole, Frederick Church and other members of the Hudson River School, whose images of unspoiled nature lured wealthy "rusticators" from Boston and New York. During the Gilded Age, many of the country's richest families – Vanderbilts, Rockefellers, Morgans, Astors – built extravagant summer homes on the island. In keeping with the vacation atmosphere, they referred to their elegant, fully staffed, 50-room mansions as "cottages."

But the lavish parties and general gaiety of the times did not hide the fact that the island's natural beauty was being compromised by unfettered development. Several wealthy summer visitors, including Boston millionaire George Dorr, Harvard president Charles Eliot and industrialist John D. Rockefeller, Jr, joined in an effort to preserve the island's natural character. Together they donated a 6,000-acre (2,400-hectares) patchwork of coastal lands, lakes, mountains and forest that eventually formed the heart of the first national park east of the Mississippi River. Originally christened Sieur de Monts National Monument, and then Lafayette National Park, Acadia was renamed and expanded several times and now totals some 40,000 acres (16,000 hectares).

Then, in 1949, a forest fire devoured most of the opulent mansions and hotels. The fire also changed the natural landscape by opening large clearings in the uniformly thick spruce-fir forest that had covered the island. Light-loving trees such as birch and aspen quickly

ce-covered branches near a rocky stream.

colonized the gaps in the forest, adding color and contrast to the scene while providing browse for increased populations of white-tailed deer, beaver and other hardwood-forest dwellers. The forest slowly healed, but the Gilded Age was gone forever.

Rock and sea: Most visits to Acadia begin with a tour of the **Park Loop Road**, a curvy, 27-mile (43-km) drive that clings to the cliffs high above the Atlantic. The one-way drive offers glorious views of the sea, offshore islands and rocky, spruce-cloaked headlands. The loop starts at the **Hulls Cove Visitor Center**, where you can take in natural-history exhibits and an introductory video, pick up maps, books and brochures, and check on the day's schedule of ranger-led tours. If possible, start the drive early in the morning – you'll avoid traffic tie-ups and see the rugged, oceanfront cliffs glowing in the fiery orange light of dawn.

For more information on the park's natural history, make your first stop at the **Sieur de Monts** area about 2 miles (3 km) from the visitor center, where you'll find the **Acadia Wild Garden**, **Nature Center** and **Abbe Museum**. The Wild Garden is maintained by the Park Service and the Bar Harbor Garden Club and features nearly all the native plants that grow on the island. An easy path meanders through the 1-acre site, passing examples of the many ecological communities to be found in the park. Nearby, the Nature Center offers exhibits on the area's flora and fauna, including several designed for children, and the Abbe Museum features local Native American artifacts from thousands of years ago to modern times.

Back in the car, it's a short drive to the 2-mile (3-km) **Ocean Trail** which leads down to **Sand Beach**, the largest on the island and one of the most expansive on the Maine coast north of Portland. A swim in the ocean is bracing, to say the least; the waters off Sand Beach rarely top 55°F (13°C).

A little farther down the trail you'll come to **Thunder Hole**, where incoming surf funnels into a rock crevice and,

Reeds reflected in Eagle Lake.

with nowhere else to go, shoots skyward with a loud boom.

Just beyond is **Otter Cliffs**, pink granite crags that rise vertically from the sea – a favorite of local rock climbers. The trail dead-ends at **Otter Point**, which juts into the Atlantic like a granite thumb. Looking out on the sea, you'll notice color-coded buoys bobbing in the water and maybe a few lobstermen pulling in their catch. The buoys mark the location of the traps; the colors identify the owner.

For a more challenging hike, try the steep 1-mile (2-km) loop around the 520-foot (160-meter) granite mass of the **Beehive**, which branches south to **Gorham Mountain** and north to 1,058-foot (322-meter) **Champlain Mountain**. The trail starts across the road from the Sand Beach parking lot.

A bit farther along, the Park Loop Road jogs around the southern end of **Jordan Pond**, where you can stop for an Acadia tradition: tea and fresh popovers on the lawn of the **Jordan Pond House**. While you're relaxing on the grass, look across the lake to the **Bubbles**, two handsome, symmetrical granite hills rising above the north end of the pond. The great fire of 1947 cleared the summits of the vegetation that once hid the peaks from view.

Several trails are worth exploring here. The easy **Jordan Pond Nature Trail** gives a good introduction to the area's geology and history. The 3-mile (5-km) **Jordan Pond Shore Path** is a peaceful stroll along the pond's edge. Side trails on the northern end of the pond make steep climbs to the tops of **South Bubble** and **Penobscot mountains**.

Back in the car, you go about 5 miles (8 km) to a winding spur road that leads to the treeless, boulder-strewn summit of 1,530-foot (466-meter) **Cadillac Mountain**, the highest peak on the Eastern seaboard. On a clear day – and particularly on a clear morning – the **Summit Trail** offers breathtaking views of **Frenchman Bay**, **Bar Harbor**, **Somes Sound**, the **Cranberry** and **Porcupine islands** and the ocean beyond.

If you would rather walk than drive, you can hike the mountain on a number

irch trees in windswept meadow.

of trails. The most strenuous is the 7½-mile/12-km (a one-way hike) **South Ridge Trail**, which passes through a cool hardwood and coniferous forest near **Blackwoods Campground** before toiling to the summit across long slabs of bare pink granite.

The **North Ridge Trail** is more moderate but still very challenging; the trailhead is near the beginning of the Park Loop. A third route, the 2½-mile (4-km) **Gorge Trail**, starts on the Park Loop Road near **Kebo Mountain** and offers you the option of scaling Cadillac Mountain or its slightly less strenuous neighbor, **Dorr Mountain**.

Yet another option for experienced hikers is to start at the **Sieur de Monts Spring**, make a slight detour to see beaver dams near a rockbound little lake known as the **Tarn**, and then head up the stunning but extremely steep and winding **Dorr Mountain Trail**; a connecting route near the summit leads down the western slope of Dorr Mountain and straight up the east side of **Cadillac Mountain**.

Carriage paths: Once you've toured the Park Loop Road, step back in time and enjoy the park at a more leisurely pace, as John D. Rockefeller, Jr, urged his guests to do. Rockefeller, who considered automobiles "infernal machines," designed and built a 57-mile (92-km) network of carriage paths on Mount Desert Island. The paths, he believed, provided enjoyment of the natural beauty without compromising the environment. Recently restored, the trails are a terrific way to explore the island and enjoy the ocean views, interior lakes, forests, mountains and waterfalls.

Portions of the carriage paths are open to bicyclists, horseback riders and, in winter, cross-country skiers. Rides in traditional horse-drawn carriages are offered by **Wildwood Stables** near **Jordan Pond** in summer and autumn. Ask for a map at the visitor center as well as information on the carriage-path bridges. Rockefeller had 16 of these stone bridges handcrafted to match their rustic settings; they are truly works of art.

Lichens are a symbiotic growth of algae and fungus.

For a taste of the carriage paths, try the short loop from Hulls Cove Visitor Center to **Witch Hole Pond**. If you like what you see, consider a half-day, 6-mile (9.5-km) stroll around **Eagle Lake** or a 2-mile (3-km) jaunt to the waterfall near **Upper Hadlock Pond**. The paths form an interconnecting web as far south as **Seal Harbor**, so hikers and bicyclists can design routes that fit their own interests and endurance.

The western lobe: To see a quieter, less crowded side of the park, follow Highways 233 and 198 across the eastern half of the island and then turn left on Highway 102. It's about 4 miles (6 km) to **Echo Lake Beach**, one of the best places in the park for a refreshing swim, although the beach may be crowded on a hot day.

Just beyond the parking lot, you can hook up with an interesting network of trails that loop through nearby woods and meadows, or take a long and strenuous day hike to the top of 839-foot (256-meter) **Beech Mountain**, where a fire tower affords lovely views of glacially-

Somesville, Mount Desert Island.

formed **Long Pond**, **Echo Lake** and beyond. You can also pick up the **Acadia Mountain Trail**, which starts on Highway 102 about a half-mile (1 km) north of the Echo Lake Beach turnoff. The path makes a tough 2½-mile (4-km) climb to the summit with magnificent views of the island's western lobe. For longer hikes, a side trail follows the shore of Somes Sound at **Valley Cove** and intersects an equally challenging route to the top of neighboring 679-foot (207-meter) **St Sauveur Mountain**.

Continue south on Route 102 through the small town of **Southwest Harbor** and then bear left onto Route 102A to **Seawall**, named after a natural sea wall created by the action of waves on rock and sand. Just beyond **Seawall Campground**, the **Ship Harbor Nature Trail** is a self-guiding, 1⅓-mile (2-km) loop that skirts the boundary between the forest and rocky shore.

From here, it's just a short drive to **Bass Harbor Head Light** at the southernmost tip of Mount Desert Island. Perched on the craggy, and often

fogbound shore, the lighthouse has been guiding sailors through these treacherous waters since 1858.

Island hopping: If you feel the lure of the sea, consider a cruise led by a Park Service naturalist. While out in the waves and among the islands, keep your eyes open for porpoises, dolphins, seals, bald eagles, ospreys and sea birds such as black guillemots, common eiders and double-crested cormorants. Check at the **Hulls Cove Visitor Center** for details and cruise schedules.

To the southwest, you can catch a ride on a mail boat to **Isle au Haut**, a 4,700-acre (1,900-hectare) island, half of which is owned by the Park Service. The boat departs from **Stonington**, a little town on **Deer Isle** about 90 minutes from Bar Harbor. Visitors to Isle au Haut usually feel very much out at sea, and the campsites at **Duck Harbor** offer great views of the ocean. From here, you can hike 18 miles (29 km) of trails through the woods and along the shore, pick wild blueberries, enjoy the solitude, scan the ocean for whales and porpoises, and investi-

gate tide pools for sea urchins, sponges, mussels, crabs, sea stars and many other marine creatures.

Guided cruises are also available to tiny **Baker Island**, inhabited in the mid-1800s but now left to ospreys, gulls, seals and other sea animals. A lighthouse built in 1855 remains on the island. Boats depart daily in summer from **Northeast Harbor** on the eastern side of Mount Desert Island.

If your time is limited, consider a shorter cruise around the **Porcupine Islands** in Frenchman Bay. Boats leave daily from Bar Harbor in the summer and autumn months.

Connected to the mainland but as wild and uncrowded as the islands, the **Schoodic Peninsula's** rocky headland is pounded by the Atlantic in a dramatic show of spray and foam. The peninsula is about an hour's drive from Bar Harbor. A one-way, 6-mile (9½-km) scenic drive follows the rocky promontory with a short spur to the tip of **Schoodic Point**. Visitors can also hike 440-foot (134-meter) **Schoodic Head**, or drive an unpaved road to a parking area near the summit and then walk to the top.

Finally, no trip to Acadia would be complete without a visit to **Bar Harbor**. The little village buzzes with activity day and night during the summer. Visitors stroll along the two main shopping streets, frisbees fly across the village green in the center of town, and people sit on shady park benches, eating ice cream cones and watching the world go by. At night, all you need to do is listen for your favorite music or sniff out your favorite foods and make your way to their source.

While in Bar Harbor, walk down Main Street to Frenchman Bay. At low tide, you can walk across to little **Bar Island** on the exposed sandbar that gave the town its name. Keep an eye on the time – you'll have about 90 minutes to explore the island before the tide returns and floods the bar. If you get stranded, enjoy the enforced opportunity to relax and the adventure of being stranded on a desert island, if only for a while. And don't worry, the tide will go out again in 10 hours or so. It always has.

Left, Maine possesses half the nation's Atlantic shore. **Right** low tide in the Seawall area.

CAPE COD

Henry David Thoreau described it best: "Cape Cod is the bared and bended arm of Massachusetts; the shoulder is at Buzzards Bay; the elbow, or crazy-bone, at Cape Mallebarre; the wrist at Truro; and the sandy fist at Provincetown."

Geologically speaking, this is brand new territory. It was only about 15,000 years ago that glaciers, acting like giant bulldozers, piled up a great ridge of sand, silt and rubble here – what geologists call a terminal moraine. As the glaciers melted, sea level rose, all but drowning the newly created mound of debris. But the moraine, now free of its icy burden, rebounded and gradually surfaced even higher above the waves.

Ever since that time it has continually been reshaped by wind and water. Every footfall, every wave and gust of wind, transforms the landscape, eroding the cliffs along the Atlantic coast and re-depositing much of the sand farther down the cape, out toward Provincetown.

Like a great hook, the cape thrusts farther into the Atlantic than any other portion of the continental United States: 31 miles (50 km) east, then another 31 miles to the north. As Thoreau put it, "A man may stand there and put all of America behind him."

Created in 1961, **Cape Cod National Seashore** encompasses more than 40,000 acres (16,187 hectares) of the outer Cape. Dominated by the sea, this is a surprisingly diverse region of pounding surf, towering dunes, fertile marshes, solitary stands of beech and white cedar, and glacially-formed kettle ponds fringed by pitch pine and oak forests. Foraging for food on the beaches and wetlands are a variety of shore birds – terns, egrets, herons, gulls, cormorants, the endangered piping plover. You may catch sight of small mammals such as raccoons, foxes, squirrels and opossums in the woodlands, as well as deer and even an occasional coyote. Giant whales are often sighted offshore in spring, summer and fall.

Unlike larger parks, the seashore is interspersed with private holdings and several lovely villages. An evening stroll along one of the working harbors or an afternoon on the circus-like streets of Provincetown make an interesting complement to the seashore's natural beauty.

European explorers arriving in the latter years of the 16th century found the inhabitants – Wampanoag Indians – cultivating corn and beans and harvesting the sea. Bartholomew Gosnold sailed by the great sandy peninsula in 1602 and noted that the waters were rich in codfish; hence came the peninsula's name. It was here that the Pilgrims made their first stop and drew up the Mayflower Compact, the early constitution that blossomed into the Commonwealth of Massachusetts. From Provincetown, the Pilgrims then sailed across Cape Cod Bay to settle at Plymouth.

Other immigrants from other places came much later to scratch a living from the sandy soil, ply the waters for lobster, cod, scallops, clams, bluefish and other marine life; and occasionally salvage small fortunes from nearly 3,000 ships

that foundered on the cape's treacherous shoals.

Tracking the shore: The best place to start exploring the seashore is the **Salt Pond Visitor Center** in **Eastham**. It has an ample selection of maps, books and exhibits on the cape's natural and human history as well as information on ranger-led tours, hiking, biking, horseback riding, boating and other activities.

The 1-mile (1½-km) **Nauset Marsh Trail** starts at the visitor center and descends to **Salt Pond**, a depression hollowed out by glaciers during the last Ice Age. Salt Pond once contained fresh water, but the sea carved a connecting channel, and today Salt Pond is filled twice daily by nutrient-rich ocean tides that nourish oysters, mussels, quahogs and fish. Shore birds, including a large population of terns, congregate here to feast on the bounty of marine life sustained by the marsh. Farther on, the trail climbs through a woodland of red cedar, pitch pine and oak to an overlook above **Nauset Marsh**, first charted by French navigator Samuel de Champlain in 1605.

The trail reenters the forest and crosses an abandoned farmstead before intersecting **Buttonbush Trail**, a half-mile (1-km) self-guiding nature walk that is specially designed to help the visually impaired.

To the north of Nauset Harbor are **Coast Guard Beach** and **Nauset Light Beach**, where one of the cape's several picturesque lighthouses stands guard above the roiling surf. Here writer Henry Beston spent "a solitary year in the company of the ocean" in the late 1920s. Beston's cottage, consisting of "two rooms and a fireplace," was the setting for *The Outermost House*. Unfortunately, the cottage was destroyed in a violent nor'easter in the winter of 1978.

The **Nauset Bicycle Trail**, a paved 1½-mile (2-km) path, runs from the visitor center to Coast Guard Beach. Pedestrians may use the path, but bicycles have the right-of-way. A shuttle bus leaves from the nearby Little Creek parking lot for Coast Guard Beach from late June to early September.

A short drive from the visitor center,

Cape Cod takes its name from the codfish that once flourished in its waters.

on the southeast side of Nauset Marsh, is the **Fort Hill** area. These plains were once heavily forested, but European settlers stripped the trees and cleared the land for farming, an activity that continued until the 1940s, when the fertile topsoil was finally depleted. The settlers raised rye, corn and hay and planted orchards and vegetable gardens, and allowed livestock to graze in the rich pastures.

But the destruction of the forest, combined with overcultivation and erosion, finally diminished the productivity of the land. The farms were abandoned, and today a forest of red cedar is slowly reestablishing itself, reclaiming former fields and pastures.

To experience the Fort Hill area, take the **Fort Hill Trail**, a 1.5-mile (2-km) path which starts near the historic **Penniman House**, a grand Victorian built by a wealthy whaling captain, Edward Penniman. From an overlook you can see the former farm fields, trimmed with stone walls and bordered by red cedars, sweeping down to Nauset Marsh.

Farther down the cape (toward Pro–vincetown), **Marconi Beach** is another spectacular swimming and strolling beach beneath a towering sandy cliff overlooking the Atlantic. Above the beach, high atop the escarpment, is **Marconi Station**, where Guglielmo Marconi set up his giant transmission towers, making it possible for President Theodore Roosevelt, in 1903, to exchange the first transoceanic wireless message with Edward VII in England.

Near Marconi Station is the **Atlantic White Cedar Swamp Trail**. About 1¼ miles (2 km) long, this boardwalk trail weaves through an unusual forest of Atlantic white cedars – normally a southern, sun-loving tree that invades swamps and bogs along the coast after natural or human-caused disturbances.

The Atlantic white cedars moved into the sheltered low-lying area behind the sand escarpment after the end of the last Ice Age, colonizing the depression carved out by the great ice sheet. The cedars grow so thickly together, their canopy virtually blocks the sky, and it is

reating a
and
culpture at
Nauset Light
each.

always cool in the cedar swamp – even on the hottest days. The white cedar wood is light and resistant to decay and was highly prized by early settlers. They used it in the building of homes, farm structures, boats, casks for whale oil, fence posts and other necessities.

On the bay, **Wellfleet** is considered one of the most charming fishing villages on the cape. The shady, tree-lined streets wander past classic Yankee homes, shops and churches; several restaurants serve fresh seafood; and numerous art galleries are open to the browsing public. Be sure to stroll down to **Wellfleet Harbor**, where you can watch the fishing boats tie up and unload their catch.

Along the north side of Wellfleet Bay is **Great Island**. Here, the vigorous walker will enjoy an 8-mile (13-km) round-trip hike through shady pine forest, over dunes, and eventually out to the very tip of Great Island at **Jeremy Point**, a sandy spit extending well out into Cape Cod Bay. Along the way, you'll pass the site of the **Great Island**

Tavern where 250 years ago whalers and fishermen repaired for food, drink and entertainment. Great Island was once completely ringed by water but became connected to the mainland by a sandspit that developed around 1830.

North of Wellfleet, in the vicinity of **Truro**, the land becomes progressively wilder, more open and barren. Here, giant sand dunes and scrubby pitch pine and bear oak give the landscape an almost deserted feeling. East of the little crossroads of Truro, the half-mile **Pamet Cranberry Bog Trail** offers a look at the little red berry that has played such an important role in the cultural and economic history of the cape.

Typical of Cape Cod cranberry bogs, the Pamet Bog was created in the 1880s in a former red maple swamp. The swamp was clear-cut, and the stumps and roots were removed from the peaty soil. Ditches were dug around the perimeter and across the expanse of the bog to flood it in winter to protect the cranberry plants from frost, cold and desiccating winds. Flooding also helped

Lobstermen use buoys to identify their traps.

protect the flowering buds in spring and sheltered the berry crop in autumn. Today, a boardwalk helps keep visitors high and dry.

The last best place: In North Truro, where the cape narrows to only a mile or so across, is **Pilgrim Heights**. Here, at a spring along the ¾-mile (1-km) **Pilgrim Spring Trail**, is where the Pilgrims replenished their water supply after landing in November 1620.

Also at Pilgrim Heights is the **Small Swamp Trail**, a ¾-mile (1-km) loop winding through pitch pine to a sandy ridge overlook. From here you can gaze out over a freshwater marsh, cut by a meandering stream and bordered by a wall of shoreline sand dunes. Beyond the dunes, forming a dramatic backdrop, is the blue Atlantic.

Many visitors feel that the cape saves the best for last. At the fist of the cape are the **Province Lands**, where the scrub forest dwindles away to shifting dunes, which in turn surrender to the sea. Beneath the surface the sandy bars form dangerous, ship-wrecking shoals. More

vessels have been lost off this stretch of the cape than anywhere else along the Atlantic Coast.

Access to the Province Lands is from **Race Point Road** in Provincetown. The road passes the **Beech Forest** area on the left. Prior to European settlement, beech forests were common on the cape. These hardwood forests were the climax stage of forest succession in this environment, but they were largely depleted by logging and grazing during the 17th and 18th centuries. The Province Lands Beech Forest is one of the few remaining examples of a fully mature forest community on the cape.

The **Beech Forest Trail** is a 1-mile (2-km) loop through the forest, sand dunes and around two freshwater dune ponds. Unlike most Cape Cod kettle ponds, which were formed by giant blocks of melting glacial ice, these ponds were formed when the wind scoured shallow depressions that exposed the water table.

Three lighthouses guard the Province Lands: **Race Point Light**, **Wood End**

great blue heron scouts for a meal.

Light and **Long Point Light**. And two beautiful sweeping white-sand beaches, **Race Point Beach** and **Herring Beach**, surround the very tip of the cape.

At Race Point Beach is the National Seashore's **Old Harbor Museum**, with exhibits describing the storied past of the US Life-Saving Service, precursor to the Coast Guard, whose members saved countless shipwreck victims in the 19th and early 20th centuries. The museum is housed in an old Life-Saving Service station that the Park Service floated from Chatham in 1977.

Back from the shore, nestled among the great sand dunes, is the **Province Lands Visitor Center**. Exhibits, films, lectures and ranger-led activities are scheduled here in spring, summer and fall. The visitor center observation deck offers a great view of the ocean, and with the aid of binoculars the sharp-eyed visitor may be able to see whales off Race Point.

From the visitor center, an 8-mile (13-km) paved biking trail winds among dunes, beech forest and freshwater

ponds. Also in the Province Lands area are three horseback riding trails: **Sunset Trail**, **West Trail** and **Herring Cove Trail**. Ask at the visitor center about horse rentals and guided rides. All of these trails offer spectacular views over the Atlantic and eastward into Cape Cod Bay.

Quaint and gaudy: "In my end is my beginning," wrote T.S. Eliot. It seems to apply to **Provincetown**, that curious melange of history and contemporaneity at land's end. Here is where the 252-foot (77-meter) **Pilgrim Monument** was erected in 1910. Where America's great dramatist Eugene O'Neill and his fellow Provincetown Players launched their experimental theater productions early in the 20th century. Where the traditional sweet breads of Portuguese descendants mix with the freewheeling and colorful – and, yes, often gaudy – attractions of a vibrant gay community that has been a fixture here for a couple of generations.

Tourists, artists, fishermen and some 3,500 year-round residents mingle on **Commercial Street** and environs in an eclectic milieu of 19th-century clapboard and 20th-century modern that can justifiably be called unique.

On a par with observing the passing crowd is a surging interest in whale-watching. The once-bustling New England whaling industry collapsed late in the 19th century when chemicals and manufactured substitutes replaced whale products. Although some whale stocks were severely depleted during the whaling era, and despite the fact that major environmental threats persist, several North Atlantic species are recovering, and they are regularly spotted off the coast of New England during the months of June through October.

Commonly, baleen whales such as the finback (second in size only to the blue whale), humpback and minke whales are seen from whale-watching vessels. On rare occasions, a blue whale – the largest of all animals – can be seen. And while scanning the surface, the attentive observer may also spot other marine animals, including seals, sharks and numerous species of ocean birds.

Left, pedaling through the park. Right, the cape offers excellent surf fishing.

DELAWARE WATER GAP

What a pleasant surprise. Just 90 miles (145 km) from the crowded streets of New York City is a place where stressed-out city dwellers can climb a mountain, paddle a canoe, enjoy the cool spray of a waterfall and watch a hawk soar over the treetops.

It's not the Great Northwest. It's **Delaware Water Gap National Recreation Area**, a 70,000-acre (28,300-ha) preserve of forested mountains, glacial lakes, fertile flood plains and a sprinkling of historic sites from the early years of Indian and European occupation.

"The Gap," as it is known around these parts, takes its name from a dramatic notch cut by the Delaware River into the **Kittatinny Mountains**. The river flows for about 37 miles (60 km) through the recreation area, gently sliding between the rocky, glacially-carved slopes of the Kittatinnies in New Jersey and the **Pocono Plateau** in Pennsylvania. Along the way, it captures scores of tributaries, many of which cascade down shady hemlock ravines in thunderous veils of water.

One of the few undammed rivers in the Northeast, the Delaware is a haven for canoeists and kayakers. Here they can spend a day or two paddling its calm waters, fishing for shad, walleye or smallmouth bass, and exploring its wooded banks and islands.

The park is laced with hiking trails, including a 25-mile (40-km) stretch of the **Appalachian Trail**, which follows the crest of the Kittatinny Ridge. Although surrounded by developed areas, there is still plenty of space here for a solitary walk in the woods where the only company you're likely to have are white-tailed deer, squirrels, a curious fox or an occasional black bear or coyote.

In spring and again in autumn, when a variety of raptors migrate through the region, it's not uncommon to spot hawks patrolling the skies, or to see an osprey dive to the river and snatch up a fish. Great blue herons wade in the shallows, blue jays jabber in the forest, and a variety of songbirds, including vireos, warblers and gnatcatchers, enliven the woods and meadows. Bald eagles arrive in winter, roosting along the river's edge and fattening themselves on fish and other birds.

Into the breach: The Delaware Water Gap is situated in the southern tip of the recreation area. You can get a good feel for the place just off Interstate 80 at the **Kittatinny Point Visitor Center**. It is set in a shady spot on the east bank of the river, with the twin domes of **Mount Tammany** and **Mount Minsi** rising on either side. From this vantage point, it's easy to see how the water did its work. As the ridge rose, the river cut through layers of shale, slate and sandstone that had been deposited millions of years earlier at the bottom of an ancient sea. Glaciers finished the job. They rounded off the peaks on both sides of the river, exposed bare slabs of limestone and littered the slopes with glacial "erratics" before retreating north about 10,000 years ago. The result is a notch in the earth's surface about 1,600 feet (489

Preceding pages: fern and fallen leaves on Kittatinny Ridge. Left, frost on maple-leaf viburnum. Right, a pair of young raccoons.

meters) deep through which the Delaware River flows in a lazy S.

To get a closer look at the Gap, consider a 3-mile (5-km) hike on the Appalachian Trail along the west slope of Mount Tammany. You can pick up the trail at the **Dunnfield Creek Natural Area**, just across the highway from the visitor center (ask a ranger to direct you to the nearby underpass). The white-blazed trail follows a cool, shady section of **Dunnfield Creek** before making a steep 3-mile (5-km) climb to **Sunfish Pond**, a lovely, glacial tarn atop the Kittatinny Ridge. The slope-shouldered bulk of **Mount Mohican** lies just beyond, with magnificent views of the river and surrounding valley.

Several side trails branch off the Appalachian Trail. One of them is the 1¾-mile (3-km) **Blue Dot Trail**, which veers right about a half-mile from the parking area to the top of Mount Tammany. Along the way, you'll pass dense stands of pine, poplar and hickory, as well as streams splashing down smooth limestone outcroppings. You may even see a hawk or turkey vulture gliding on the warm columns of air that curl up the mountainside.

It's a tough climb, but well worth the effort. The view of the river (and, more prosaically, the highway) slipping through the Gap is quite spectacular. Get a slightly different perspective on the scene by following the **Red Dot Trail** down the opposite side of the mountain for a 3½-mile (6-km) loop.

To see the Gap from the opposite side of the river, take Interstate 80 across the toll bridge and follow signs to Route 611 South. Three roadside overlooks – **Resort Point**, **Point of Gap** and **Arrow Island** – offer good views. If you feel like hiking, pick up the connection to the Appalachian Trail at **Resort Point Overlook** and head for the summit of Mount Minsi, 2½ miles (4 km) away. At 1,463 feet (446 meters), it's just slightly shorter than its neighboring mountain across the Delaware.

Back on the New Jersey side, **Old Mine Road** follows the river north from the visitor center through **Worthington**

Dog tired.

State Forest (almost completely surrounded by the recreation area), passing several trailheads, campgrounds, put-ins and picnic areas along the way. About 8½ miles (14 km) from the visitor center, stop at **Van Campen Glen Recreation Site** for a picnic lunch and a relaxing walk along **Van Campen Brook**, which tumbles over a pair of nearby waterfalls before joining the Delaware. The quarter-mile path to the lower falls leads through a cool, shady valley where pencil-straight hemlocks tower over a thick pad of forest duff sprouting ferns, mosses and gangly rhododendrons. The larger, upper falls can be reached from the **Upper Glen Parking Area**, about a half-mile north on Old Mine Road. You can also follow the brook in the opposite direction to the **Watergate Recreation Site** and beyond.

Window on the past: Just north on Old Mine Road, at the intersection of Route 602, is **Millbrook Village**, a tiny farming settlement established in 1832. Visitors are welcome to explore about 20 restored or reconstructed buildings, including a church, blacksmith shop, gristmill and several homes. Costumed interpreters reenact daily 19th-century life on summer weekends and during the **Millbrook Days Festival** held in early October.

Old Mine Road winds north along the river toward the recreation area's other major historic sites. The handsome old **Van Campen Inn** is nestled among woods and cornfields on an unpaved section of the road about 6½ bumpy miles (10 km) from Millbrook Village. Built in 1746, the stately, stone-fronted structure was host to early-American luminaries, like John Adams, who were traveling between New England and Philadelphia.

A right turn off Old Mine Road onto Route 615 leads to **Walpack Center**, a one-street town that was all but abandoned in the 1970s to make room for a reservoir that would have swallowed up about half of the recreation area. Thanks largely to campaigns by local residents and conservationists, construction of such a dam was blocked and the Dela-

ocky terrain.

ware River continues to run freely. Directly north, the **Peters Valley Craft Center** offers instruction in traditional and contemporary arts at a quaint crossroad village. Thousands of art-lovers flock to the tiny village every July for the annual **Peters Valley Craft Fair**. The **Peters Valley Craft Store and Gallery** are open daily.

This section of the recreation area also offers some of the best hiking. Just north of Millbrook Village, a side road winds along up the Kittatinny Ridge to the **Blue Mountain Lakes Parking Area**, where a network of trails and unpaved roads connects the twin Blue Mountain Lakes with secluded **Hemlock Pond**, **Crater Lake**, **Long Pine Pond**, **Beaver Swamp** and the Appalachian Trail. The loop around the Blue Mountain Lakes is an easy 2-mile (3-km) hike, with plenty of secluded spots for a quiet day of fishing.

A slightly more ambitious outing is the 4-mile (6-km) round-trip to Hemlock Pond, a placid little tarn hemmed in by the forest. About a half-mile beyond Hemlock Pond is Beaver Swamp. Look for a large stand of ghostly-white snags killed by the beavers' system of dams and ponds. You won't see beavers in the daytime – they tend to be nocturnal – but with a little hunting you should be able to spot one of their dams or dome-shaped lodges. A second connecting trail – the orange-blazed **Hemlock Pond Trail** – leads east from Hemlock Pond up a steep quarter-mile ridge to the Appalachian Trail near the edge of Crater Lake. From here you can circle the lake, follow the Appalachian Trail north out of the recreation area, or go south to Long Pine Pond.

Old Mine Road continues north along the foot of the Kittatinny Ridge to New York, past roadside meadows splashed in summer with bold black-eyed Susans and tiger lilies and with autumn clusters of Queen Anne's lace and downy goldenrod. Two bridges cross the Delaware in this northern section of the park, including **Dingmans Bridge**, a rickety old thing built at the turn of the century. The last privately-owned bridge on the

The remains of an old farmstead at Peters Valley.

river, it is a tangible link to the olden days along the Delaware.

Across the river: The Pennsylvania side of the recreation area tends to be busier and more developed. The big attractions here are the waterfalls, which are larger, more dramatic and easier to get to than those on the New Jersey side. Among the most picturesque and easiest to reach is 130-foot (40-meter) **Dingmans Falls**, which shed a great curtain of water down a rocky chute. The falls are an easy half-mile walk from the **Dingmans Visitor Center** through a cool, hemlock-shaded ravine that is filled, in summer, with showy rhododendron blossoms. Along the way, you'll pass **Silver Thread Falls**, which send a lacy ribbon of water down a narrow fissure.

You'll find equally splendid falls at the nearby **George W. Childs Recreation Site**, which has a series of three cascades, and **Raymondskill Falls**, about 7 miles (11 km) north off Route 209. Both areas can be reached on well-marked paths; wooden stairs and bridges have been installed on the steepest sections of the trails.

The most dramatic cascades in the area are outside the recreation area at **Bushkill Falls**, a privately-owned park billed as the "Niagara of Pennsylvania." Often crowded, Bushkill is certainly not the place for a quiet day in the woods. If you don't mind sharing the scenery with a swarm of other visitors, it makes a worthwhile side trip. A fee is charged at the gate, and an awful lot of stair-climbing is required to cover the entire site.

Elsewhere on the Pennsylvania side, the Pocono Environmental Education Center offers summer nature camps for kids and families. A network of mostly moderate trails leads through the surrounding forest and hemlock ravines.

Camping in the park is limited to two privately managed sites – Dingmans and Walpack Valley campgrounds – and a campground in **Worthington State Forest**. Camping is permitted at designated sites along the Delaware River for overnight canoe trips and along the Appalachian Trail.

Hobblebush grows along a mountain stream.

NEW RIVER GORGE

It's been called the "Grand Canyon of the East." A mile (1½ km) wide and about 1,400 feet (427 meters) deep, the New River Gorge gapes in the mountains of West Virginia, where some 62,000 acres (25,091 hectares) of land are protected within the site called **New River Gorge National River**.

Despite its name, the New River is among the oldest in the world. Like a liquid buzzsaw, its powerful waters have cut into the earth's surface for more than 65 million years as the mountains – an extension of the Appalachians – rose around them. The result is a sheer-walled, gracefully curved canyon of astonishing proportions, its rocky slopes softened by a cloak of hardwood forest and by the patches of mist that often drift between its rims.

White water is the byword here. "River rats" from all over the world flock to the New River to test their mettle against its churning eddies, boulder fields and black holes. With a vertical drop of 750 feet (229 meters) in only 50 miles (81 km), the New offers some of the most exciting kayaking and rafting in the region.

But the New River isn't only for experienced river runners. There are long stretches of calm water punctuated by less difficult rapids that are perfect for amateurs or canoeists who are more interested in a quiet day of paddling, fishing (smallmouth bass, muskellunge, walleye, catfish and carp are abundant) or simply taking in the scenery.

There are also several outfitters in the region (call park headquarters for a current list) who offer one- or two-day guided trips. Rafters get a close-up view of the gorge, learn basic river skills and help navigate the craft.

Nor is the New River Gorge only for boating. A variety of outdoors enthusiasts, including hikers, mountain bikers and rock climbers come to the park to take advantage of its unique recreational opportunities, or simply to escape into a solitary patch of forest.

It wasn't always so lovely here. Only 50 years ago, the gorge was choked with slag, smoke, coal dust and the insistent clatter of sawmills, trains and machinery. More than a dozen coal-mining towns crowded the narrow river banks, hundreds of coke ovens belched toxic gases, mine shafts honeycombed the canyon walls, and timber companies, with an eye for ready money, denuded the surrounding forest.

Mining was a particularly backbreaking and dangerous job. Miners knew that their lives were at stake every time they entered a shaft. In one disaster, 13 miners were killed in a methane-gas explosion in 1905. A witness said that a plume of fire shot clear across the canyon. An 11-man rescue team entered the mine immediately after the blast, only to be killed by a second explosion. The victims of that accident, as well as of many others, are buried in the park on tiny **Red Ash Island**.

Few signs remain of the gorge's industrial past. The **C & O Railroad** still runs along the river, although much less frequently than it did 50 years ago. The

receding ages: mountain iker at edge f gorge, New liver Gorge ridge in the istance. **Left,** appelling own Beauty Mountain. **Right,** wild urkey.

Park Service has renovated a railroad depot in the old town of **Thurmond**, a National Historic District about 7 miles (11 km) from **National River Headquarters** in the northern section of the park. The depot now appears as it did during its heyday in the early 1900s.

Otherwise, all that remains of the mining towns and the people who lived and worked in them are skeletal structures debilitated by rust and vandalism, foundation stones overgrown with vines and grasses, slag heaps slowly being reclaimed by the river and forest, and abandoned mine shafts now colonized by bats, opossums and other creatures.

Off the road: Approaching the park from the north, you will find that the best place to begin your visit is just outside of **Fayetteville** at the **Canyon Rim Visitor Center**. Park rangers, a slide show, exhibits, books and a variety of free pamphlets will help organize your journey. A quick look at a map will tell you that, unlike many other national park areas, New River Gorge National River isn't really designed for motor-

ists. Because the park is long and narrow with no main thoroughfare, you must drive out and around the boundaries to get from one end to the other. And while there are several roads in the park with lovely views – including **River Road**, **McKendree Road** and **Route 41** – there isn't a scenic drive per se. In order to really see the gorge, you need to leave the car behind.

You can start just outside the Canyon Rim Visitor Center on the **Canyon Rim Boardwalk**. It leads to an observation platform with a dramatic view of the **New River Gorge Bridge** which, at a length of 3,030 feet (924 meters), is the longest single-arch steel bridge in the world. Just across the road from the visitor center is an easy 1-mile (1½-km) walk on the **Laing Loop Trail**, which passes through several habitats, including an oak-hickory forest, beech-maple forest and rhododendron thicket, to an open field where it's not uncommon to spot white-tailed deer grazing in the morning or evening.

It's a short drive south on Highway 19

Poison ivy sprouts near Sandstone Falls.

across the New River Gorge Bridge to winding, narrow **Fayette Station Road**, where you can pick up two other interesting trails. The first is the **New River Bridge Trail**, which is only 1½ miles (2 km) long but extremely steep and rocky, with a few exposed areas at the tops of cliffs; the views of the gorge and bridge are quite spectacular.

The other is the **Kaymoor Trail**, which starts about 2 miles (3 km) farther along Fayette Station Road. The trail entails a moderate, 4-mile (6-km) round-trip to the old **Kaymoor** mining town, where a few derelict structures still stand in mute testimony to the gorge's industrial past. A short spur trail leads down the slope to the remains of beehive ovens, once used to reduce raw coal to hot-burning coke. Here as elsewhere, abandoned mines and other structures are extremely dangerous. Do not attempt to enter them.

From Kaymoor, hikers can pick up the **Cunard–Kaymoor Trail** which roughly parallels the river for about 7 miles (11 km) past former mine sites.

The trail follows an old mine road and is very popular with mountain bikers, who can extend the trip for another 6 miles (10 km) by making a connection with the **Southside Junction–Brooklyn Trail**. This route follows an old railroad bed past the ruins of mining towns and across trestles with excellent views of the river. (Bikers are cautioned to walk bikes over all trestle bridges.)

Hikers and bikers may share another trail a bit farther south. The trailhead is at the end of **Minden Road** just outside the little town of **Oak Hill**. The **Thurmond-Minden Trail** runs for about 3 miles (5 km) along an old railroad grade. Along the way, you'll have excellent views of Thurmond, a former railroad town that stands across the river.

The early 1900s were boom years in Thurmond. Back then, the bustling little town handled more freight than many other much-larger cities. Today, however, it's virtually a ghost town. Although about a dozen people still live in Thurmond and the **Thurmond Depot** has been restored with historic furnish-

view of the New River, one of the oldest rivers in the world.

ings and exhibits, most of the old buildings are empty and decaying.

Continuing south, the **Grandview** area offers a visitor center, amphitheater, playground, picnic shelters, restrooms and several easy-to-moderate hiking trails, most less than a mile long. Just across the road from the visitor center, for example, is a short trail to the main overlook, where you'll be treated to sweeping vistas of the New River as it meanders through the canyon at **Horseshoe Bend**. Along the way to the overlook, you can pick up **Canyon Rim Trail**, which follows the lip of the gorge for about 2 miles (3 km) along the highest cliffs in the park. The shorter but more difficult **Castle Rock Trail** winds along the base of the cliff past several fascinating rock formations and coal deposits. The two trails intersect, making a convenient 1-mile (1½-km) loop.

For a more remote backwoods experience, consider a long day hike on **Glades Creek Trail**, which starts at the end of **Glades Creek Road** (four-wheel-drive recommended) about 6 miles (10 km) outside **McCreery**. The 5½-mile (9-km) route follows a New River tributary into one of the best wildlife-watching areas in the park.

Connections may be made with a number of side trails, including a steep 1-mile (1½ km) climb to lovely **Kates Falls** and a 4-mile (6 km) loop through the densely wooded **Polls Plateau**. These side trails may not have signs, so be sure to obtain a map and talk to a park ranger before starting out.

You can end your hike at **Big Branch Trail** in the southern tip of the park. The trailhead is on River Road across from the **Brooks Falls Day Use Area**. A moderate loop, at just under 2 miles (3 km), the route follows a lively stream as it flows through a thick woodland and tumbles over a 30-foot (9-meter) waterfall toward the New River. About 3 miles (5 km) farther north, River Road dead-ends at the **Sandstone Falls parking area**, where an easy half-mile trail leads to one of the park's most impressive sights. Standing between 10 and 25 feet (3–7½ meters) high and some 1,200

The river is a mecca for canoeists and kayakers.

feet (366 meters) wide, **Sandstone Falls** creates a thunderous wall of cascading water that stretches across the river.

There are plenty of other options for hikers and mountain bikers as well as several horseback-riding trails. The park is still being developed for visitors, so consult a ranger about trail conditions, access points and recent changes before heading out. Primitive camping is permitted in some areas, and campsites with water and other amenities are available in nearby state parks. Caution: hunting is permitted within the national river, so wear blaze orange or other bright colors during hunting season.

White-water adventure: For those with the inclination, one of the best ways to see the New River Gorge is by boat. Several companies in the area run float trips in sturdy, self-bailing rafts. The season runs from April to October, although May and June are considered prime time because that's when the waves are the biggest.

River runners divide the New River into two sections – Upper and Lower.

The **Upper New**, a 13-mile (21-km) stretch from McCreery to Thurmond, is considered the tamer of the two runs, and this is where most rafting companies offer special "family trips." These move at a leisurely pace and sometimes feature hands-on nature lessons. The Upper New is also popular with private boaters, especially canoeists.

The heaviest rapids are found on the **Lower New**, the 15-mile (24-km) stretch from Thurmond to Fayetteville. It is in this part of the gorge where the river is at its most fierce. Most of the rapids are rated between class III and V+ on the international scale of difficulty (class I being flat water and class VI being considered extremely dangerous and virtually unnavigable). As the river flows over rocky slabs and ledges, it forms enormous wave trains that routinely swell to 10 or 12 feet (3–4 meters) during periods of high water.

With this in mind, truly adventurous rafters plan their trips for the spring runoff when the river is at its highest. If they're really lucky, they'll catch it after

Rafting below the New River Gorge Bridge, the world's longest single-arch steel span.

a long soaking rain. In that case, be prepared for the ride of your life! River guides report waves towering as high as 24 feet (7 meters), the river's highest navigable level.

Gauley and Bluestone rivers: If you're in the mood for more river adventure, consider visiting two other nearby National Park areas – **Gauley River National Recreation Area** and **Bluestone National Scenic River**.

Unlike the wild and ancient New River, the Gauley is preposterously modern. Located about 10 miles (16 km) north of the Canyon Rim Visitor Center, it is a dam-release river that, like some outsized appliance, is "turned on" with the flick of a switch. For most of the year, the Gauley lies dormant within a man-made basin known as **Summersville Lake**. When the dam is closed, the mighty river trickles out in levels suitable only for fishing and for inflatable "duckie" boats.

Fortunately, Summersville Lake has to be drained every fall. When the water is released – usually on weekends from

early September to mid-October – the Gauley is open for business. And what a business it is! On any given weekend morning, hundreds of rafts are piled in the parking lot below the dam. Buses and trucks are bumper to bumper. Up to 8,000 river runners ply the rapids each weekend.

The 26-mile (42-km) segment from the Summersville Dam to the town of **Swiss** is what the fuss is all about. Most of the rapids are rated class III or better. The most serious white water is concentrated in the **Upper Gauley**, a 9-mile (14-km) segment from the dam to **Panther Creek**. That stretch has five class V+ rapids.

Because most of the land along the Gauley is privately owned, other forms of recreation are limited. In summer, there is some fishing and low-water rafting, though it's nothing like the high-water adventure of the fall season.

Hikers who visit the Gauley area spend most of their time in **Carnifex Ferry Battlefield State Park**, adjacent to the recreation area a few miles down the road from Summersville Dam. The park has trails that lead down to one of the Gauley's most spectacular rapids: **Pillow Rock**. During the fall rafting season, the shoreline is thronged with photographers and spectators who cheer successful runs and wipeouts alike. This practice is known as "vulturizing."

For an entirely different experience, consider exploring **Bluestone National Scenic River**. Though it's only a few miles south of the New River Gorge, the Bluestone is light years away from the hustle and bustle of the New and Gauley.

A gentle river known more for its scenery than its rapids, the Bluestone is the perfect place for a peaceful nature walk. The 8-mile (13-km) **Bluestone Trail** is a favorite haunt of regional birders. Kingfishers, great blue herons and wild turkeys are frequently sighted.

Primitive camping is permitted at Gauley River National Recreation Area near the put-in site at the dam. Overnight stays are not permitted at Bluestone National Scenic River, but campgrounds are available at nearby **Pipestem** and **Bluestone** state parks.

Getting a closer look a the river's edge.

TROUBLE IN PARADISE

There's trouble in the parks. Acid rain at Acadia, traffic jams at Great Smoky Mountains, development along the Blue Ridge Parkway, contaminated water at Mammoth Cave, habitat loss in the Everglades, poaching at Shenandoah, crumbling facilities, neglected historic sites, crime, overcrowding, pollution, low morale. Sometimes it seems that the parks are under siege.

Some problems are internal – a chronic lack of funds for park maintenance, substandard ranger housing, the need to clean up old mines and dispose of industrial waste, and conflicts with various user groups such as mountain bikers, rock climbers, horseback riders and hunters who want to utilize parklands for their own purposes.

But the most serious threats come from outside the parks, often from commercial developers or industry. In Virginia, for example, park supporters in 1994 narrowly headed off a proposal by the Walt Disney Company to build a massive theme park just 3 miles (5 km) from Manassas National Battlefield and 30 miles (48 km) from Shenandoah National Park. In southern Florida, the Everglades continue to be choked by the influx of agricultural chemicals and the diversion of fresh water despite efforts to remediate the situation. Mercury poisoning is particularly harmful to wildlife, including the endangered Florida panther, the last of which retreated to neighboring Big Cypress National Preserve.

At Great Smoky Mountains and Shenandoah national parks the problem is a tiny invader – the balsam woolly adelgid – a non-native insect that was introduced to the United States from Europe. The little bugs have a big appetite for Fraser fir, one of the main components of the region's spruce-fir forest. About 90 percent of the Fraser fir in the Great Smokies have been killed by the insects and the situation is worse at Shenandoah. How this will effect other species dependent upon the trees remains to be seen.

The problem is compounded by air pollution, particularly the build-up of ground-level ozone (not to be confused with the beneficial kind higher in the atmosphere) and acid rain – both products of automobile emissions and industrial smokestacks. From the Great Lakes to the Everglades, the magnificent views that are often associated with the national parks have been increasingly blurred by a yellowish haze.

Finally, and perhaps most ironically, one of the biggest problems facing the parks is the growing number of visitors. The parks have become victims of their own popularity. The situation is especially difficult in the East where the parks tend to be smaller and the crowds larger. Acadia, for example, is one of the smallest national parks but gets more than 4 million visitors a year. Great Smoky Mountains – the most visited park in the nation – receives well over 8.5 million. Traffic jams are now quite common during the summer season at many parks, and campsites are often fully booked months in advance.

The problems may seem daunting, but there are a lot of committed and hardworking people who are looking for solutions. In addition to the Park Service itself, there are watchdog organizations such as the National Parks and Conservation Association, the Audubon Society, the Wilderness Society and the Sierra Club who keep an eye on the health of the parks and lobby the government for their protection.

Ultimately, though, the responsibility for the parks rests with the people who use them. These are precious places. They deserve our care and protection. ∎

Pollution threatens many parks.

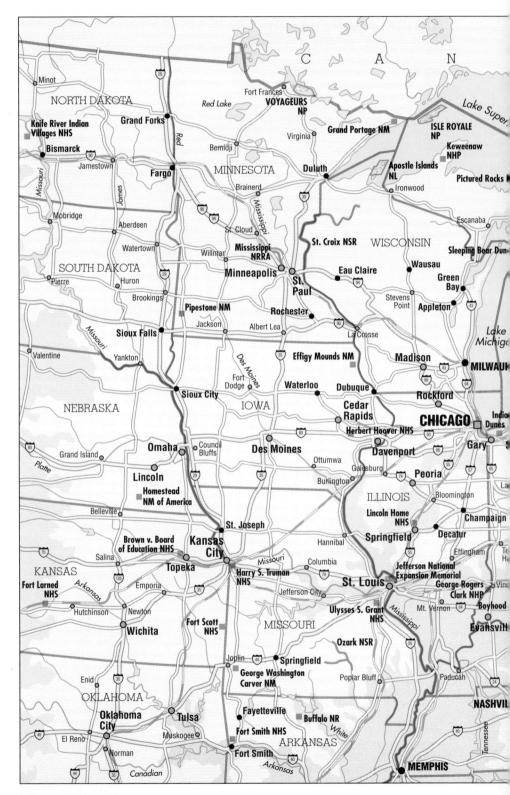

Midwestern National Parks

125 miles / 200 km

D A

Mackinaw City

Lake Huron

CHIGAN

Standish

Saginaw

Port
Huron

Flint

Lansing

DETROIT   Lake Erie

Perry's Victory and
national Peace Memorial

James Garfield
NHS

Toledo   Lorain

Findlay   Cuyahoga Valley
NRA

t Wayne   Mansfield   Akron   Pittsburgh

Lima   OHIO

COLUMBUS

Dayton   Dayton Aviation
Heritage   Hopewell Culture
NHP   NHP

APOLIS   Chillicothe

Cincinnati

Ohio   William Howard Taft
NHS

ille   Frankfort   Huntington   New River
Gorge NR

Lexington   Bluestone NSR

Abraham Lincoln   KENTUCKY
Birthplace NHS

MOTH
NP   Cumberland
Gap NHP

th Fork   Andrew Johnson
NRRA   NHS

ed WSR   Knoxville   Asheville

ESSEE   GREAT SMOKY
MOUNTAINS NP

Chattanooga

Lake
Ontario
Rochester

Niagara Falls

Theodor Roosevelt   Buffalo
Inaugural NHS

NEW YORK
Jamestown

Erie   Warren

PENNSYLVANIA

CLEVELAND

Youngstown   Altoona
Allegheny Portage
Railroad NHS

Johnstown
Cambridge   Washington   Flood
N MEM
Friendship Hill
NHS

WEST
Parkers-   VIRGINIA
burg

SHENANDOAH NP

Charleston   Staunton

Gauley River
NRA

VIRGINIA

Roanoke

Booker T.
Washington NM

Wytheville

Guilford Courthouse
NMP

Statesville   Greensboro

NORTH
CAROLINA

Carl Sandburg Home   Charlotte
NHS   Kings Mtn. NMP

Greenville   SOUTH CAROLINA

Appalachian NST

Blue Ridge PKWY

Tennessee

THE MIDWEST

A wide range of landscapes and ecosystems are to be found in the midwestern parks. From the wind-battered shores of the Great Lakes to the swift rivers of the Ozark Mountains, the parks are a gateway to the region's natural treasures.

Both Voyageurs and Isle Royale national parks are set in the great North Woods. Named after the fur traders of French-Canadian extraction who paddled through the region in the late 17th and 18th centuries, Voyageurs is a maze of lakes and forests in the remote northeastern corner of Minnesota. This is one of the least trammeled parks in the lower 48 states. There are no public roads inside the park and no car-camping facilities. Visitors must enter by boat or airplane or else on foot.

Isle Royale National Park is even more secluded. Set on an island in Lake Superior, the park is home to a wide range of North Woods wildlife, including moose, beavers, bald eagles and gray wolves. There are no public roads in this park either; the only way to enter it is by boat or seaplane.

Four other parks are on the Great Lakes, too, each a "vignette" of the area's diverse ecology. Both Indiana Dunes and Sleeping Bear Dunes national lakeshores feature a changing landscape of sand dunes, bluffs and beaches on the windswept edge of Lake Michigan. Farther north, Apostle Islands and Pictured Rocks preserve a portion of the dramatic cliffs, sea caves and rugged backcountry of Lake Superior's wild islands and shoreline.

In an entirely different part of the region, two parks protect wild and scenic rivers in the Ozark Mountains. Buffalo National River in Arkansas and Ozark National Scenic Riverways in Missouri are both favorites among canoeists and kayakers and offer the opportunity for a firsthand look at the Ozarks' natural and cultural history.

● *For a key to the symbols used on this map, please see page 119.*

VOYAGEURS

In Minnesota, at the southern edge of the North Woods – that great coniferous forest belt that spans the continent from Labrador to Alaska – lies Voyageurs National Park.

Two centuries ago this fur-rich country on the Minnesota–Ontario border was a thoroughfare for trappers, traders and Native American hunters in their birch-bark canoes. The French-Canadians became especially famous for their canoe skills and endurance as they paddled and portaged 3,000 miles (4,828 km) from Montreal to the Canadian Northwest, and it is for these travelers, or *voyageurs*, that the park is named.

The *voyageurs'* route of travel through the maze of lakes, islands, streams and rivers was so established by 1783 that the treaty ending the American Revolution specified that the international boundary should follow the "customary waterway" between Lake Superior and Lake of the Woods. **Voyageurs National Park**, created in 1975, lies along a 56-mile (90-km) stretch of that waterway. Its four large lakes – **Rainy**, **Kabetogama**, **Namakan** and **Sand Point** – cover almost 39 percent of the 219,000-acre (88,600-hectare) park and feature 1,600 islands, plus thousands of secluded coves and bays. The sparkling water, archipelagos and pink and gray rocky shores have inspired some to call this remote area "the Aegean Sea of the North Woods."

Woods and water: The solitude, the scenery, the very rhythm of travel in the park evoke the spirit of the days when Ojibwa, explorer and fur trader threaded these waters. Sigurd Olsen, the dean of North Woods naturalists, aptly described the enjoyment of a place like Voyageurs: "I often think… how swiftly time passes in the out-of-doors, where there is never a moment without something new; dawns and sunrises with mists moving out of the bays. The sifting of clouds, the way light plays with water and trees, the sound of bird calls. The sight of flowers, the movements of animals, the magic of dusk and the last slanting rays of color."

Glaciers are responsible for the character of the park. They have covered the area at least four times in the past million years and only recently (10,000 years ago) receded to reveal the ancient rock of the Canadian Shield, up to 2.7 billion years old – some of the oldest exposed rock formations in the world. The depressions left behind became lakes, bogs, marshes and streams; a land laced with water perfect for the development of the canoe.

No one knows when the birch-bark canoe came into use. The Algonquin tribes perfected the art of building a vessel that weighed less than 300 pounds (136 kg) yet could transport up to 5 tons of crew and freight. All the building materials came from the forests: the ribs were made of white cedar, which was easy to carve; the root fibers of black spruce were used to sew together the bark covering and for pitch to seal the seams; the bark of the yellow and paper birch formed the shell.

The canoe opened up North America to western expansion, according to Ralph Frese, a Chicago historian and builder of *voyageur* canoes. "Movies and popular fiction portray horses and covered wagons as having the most impact, and that simply isn't true." Canoes supported the development of the continent's biggest industry from the mid-17th century on into the 19th century: the fur trade. In 1795, the birch-bark canoes constructed by Indians on the southern shore of Rainy Lake were cited by the British as indispensable to maintaining control of western Canada.

A boat is still vital here; there are no public roads and no car-camping facilities anywhere in the park. Access to Voyageurs' backcountry requires crossing a "middle-country" of water, which may be reached from four entry points. Surrounding communities and resorts offer a variety of accommodations and services.

Unless you're bringing your own canoe or motorized boat, an extended visit to the park's interior requires advance transportation planning. For visitors arriving without their own gear, park

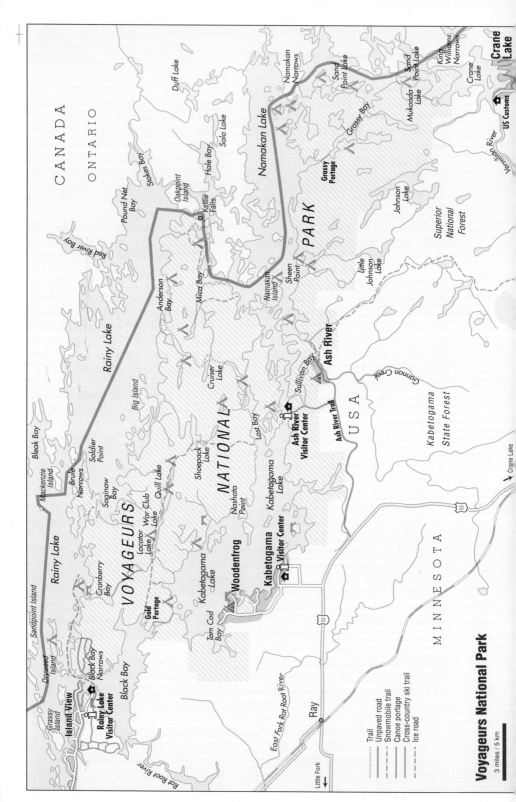

Voyageurs National Park

3 miles / 5 km

Trail
Unpaved road
Snowmobile trail
Canoe portage
Cross-country ski trail
Ice road

concessionaires and outfitters offer canoes, camping equipment, even guides. Once inside the park, there are more than 100 designated campsites scattered along the park shores, each equipped with a table, a fire ring, a tent pad and an open-air privy.

Paddle and portage: The westernmost entry point is the **Rainy Lake Visitor Center**, located 12 miles (19 km) east of **International Falls** via Highway 11. This is the only visitor center open all year. From late June through August, costumed guides offer visitors a chance to paddle a replica of a *voyageur*'s canoe. The park also offers interpretive trips in conjunction with concession cruises. Programs cover the area's geology, wildlife, history and, on the evening star watch trips, astronomy. Reservations for the boat programs are recommended, but walk-ins are taken on a space-available basis. There are special programs for kids from 7 to 12.

Houseboat rentals are another intriguing option for enjoying Voyageurs. Fully equipped for an extended stay, the boats are actually floating cottages. From your deck, or anywhere in the park, you may see flocks of mergansers, cormorants and Canada geese, a bald eagle perched on a snag, a great blue heron wading in the shallows, or, on the open water, an osprey fishing.

Would-be *voyageurs* can easily paddle their own or a rented canoe onto **Rainy Lake** and imagine the life of the men for whom the park is named. The real *voyageurs* were uniformly slight, weighing around 150 pounds (68 kg) and standing 5½ feet (nearly 2 meters) tall. Yet the strength, stamina and good humor of these colorful French-Canadians is legendary.

Every summer these hired canoemen twice paddled the 60-mile (97-km) length of Rainy Lake. It was but one short stage of their 4,000-mile (6,437-km) round-trip from the Canadian northwest to the shores of Lake Superior.

During the short season available for travel in the north, one group could not make it across the continent and back in one year. But two groups – one moving east with the pelts of beaver, otter, fox and other mammals collected during the winter, and one moving west from Montreal with goods for payment and trade – could meet, or rendezvous, in the middle. This great gathering took place in what is now **Grand Portage**, Minnesota, on the shores of Lake Superior.

The men repeatedly risked their lives in rapids and put up with the swarms of black flies and mosquitoes that are the curse of the north country. But the most amazing feats of endurance came when it was time to portage, or carry, tons of gear and the boats between navigable stretches of water. Each man was expected to haul no less than two 90-pound (41-kg) bales on each trip, and often he carried three. It was not uncommon for the men to die of hernia injuries on the journey. But if the tales are to be believed, the *voyageurs* scoffed at the occupational risks and challenged each other to see who could carry the most weight in the fastest time. One "winner" carried 820 pounds (372 kg) for one mile (1½ km).

The crews typically paddled for 18

Lakeside pebbles.

hours a day, stopping once an hour for a brief pipe break. Distances were measured by the number of pipes they smoked. At the end of a hard day of paddling, they had a long evening of gathering wood for camp, repairing the canoes, storytelling and singing around the fire.

Wildlife watching: You need not be a marathon paddler, or be particularly athletic, to enjoy Voyageurs' lakes. Those looking for just a few hours of canoe travel should check in at the **Kabetogama Visitor Center**, off Highway 53 in the southwest section of the park. Park naturalists offer outfitted canoe trips to the nearby islands and bays of **Kabetogama Lake**. Other interpretive trips from this center are offered in conjunction with a concession boat and take visitors past nesting bald eagles and towering pines.

To anglers, Kabetogama Lake is synonymous with walleye. From mid-May into the fall, the lake buzzes with fishing boats, but for those more interested in wildlife above the water than below,

Voyageurs won't disappoint. In fact, all the animals that the original *voyageurs* would have seen remain here except the wolverine and woodland caribou. Encounters with beavers, deer, river otters and loons are common, and the park is home to a population of about 200 black bears and a small number of moose.

This is one of the only places in the continental United States where the eastern timber wolf has managed to survive. About 30 to 40 wolves cruise through Voyageurs on a regular basis, but the chances of seeing one of these elusive animals is slim. You're more likely to hear the wolf's lonesome howl on a moonlit night.

A good place from which to embark on a wildlife-watching tour is the **Ash River Visitor Center**, in the south-central region of the park. To get there, take Highway 53 to County Road 129 (the **Ash River Trail**), then go about 11 miles (18 km). It has more limited hours and services than the other two visitor centers, but there are also nature programs, including a short but challeng-

A snapping turtle hisses at intruders.

170

ing hike to a beaver pond. Their dams, lodges and cuttings are common features of the North Woods landscape. The ponds that form behind the dams create excellent habitat for creatures such as frogs, fish, minks, otters, moose and waterfowl.

Most of the park's 32 miles (52 km) of trails are on the **Kabetogama Peninsula** and are part of the **Cruiser Lake Trail** system, which connects eight campsites and touches the shores of seven inland lakes. The trail includes both short loops and an approximately 10-mile (16-km) one-way cross-peninsula route, which takes you to the park's "high country."

The trail is easy to follow as it winds through marsh and bog, southern boreal forest, over ancient beds of gneiss and granite, and through scrub-oak barrens. Along the way you'll come to **Cruiser Lake**, the highest lake in the park, at 1,246 feet (380 meters).

From Cruiser Lake the trail continues north to Rainy Lake, passing over windswept ridges with unspoiled views of the surrounding country, including Canada only 10 miles (16 km) away. During late July and early August, the open ridges are also the best place to find blueberries, *if* you beat the voracious black bears to the feast.

Boat rentals or water taxis from one of the resorts will get hikers to the Cruiser Lake trailhead at either **Lost Bay** (close to the Ash River Visitor Center) or on Rainy Lake at **Anderson Bay**. Plan to spend at least one night camped at Anderson Bay. Here the lake is oriented so that the sunsets are unusually long and colorful. Darkness brings a cacophony of nocturnal sounds – a chorus of frogs, the yodeling of loons, the call of a barred owl, the slap of a beaver's tail… and those mysterious sounds of rustling and a low moan. Is it a bear, or is it the wind?

Old logging roads (which are used for hiking today) are found throughout the park and surrounding state and national forests. They hearken back to the era when the lumber industry replaced the fur trade, and the lumberjack replaced

An owl in mid-flight.

the *voyageur* in the legends of the north country.

It's said that the mythical lumberjack Paul Bunyan could level a forest when he sneezed. And sneeze he did. In 1905, some 2 billion board feet (600 million meters) of lumber were cut in Minnesota alone. Twenty years later the yield was one-fifth as large. And then all that remained were the trails of the loggers. At Voyageurs, some of the more inaccessible islands and an occasional grove of white or red pines escaped the saw, but for the most part the mature forest has been replaced by pioneering aspen and birch, and second-growth spruce, balsam and fir.

Trees are only a small part of the diverse plant life in the park. More than 300 plant species have been recorded. Spring flowers begin blooming in May, with golden marsh marigolds, trout lilies, trillium and wild iris being especially profuse and riotous. A variety of berries can be had for the picking, including strawberries, raspberries, huckleberries and dewberries. Wild rice, a staple of Native Americans, can be found in **Cranberry Bay**, about 5 miles (8 km) east of the Rainy Lake Visitor Center (harvesting is prohibited without a permit).

Pictures from the past: Cranberry Bay with its extensive marshes is also a canoe route to the interior of the Kabetogama Peninsula. A moderate 1½-mile (3-km) portage leads off the bay to a chain of small lakes such as **Locator**, **War Club** and **Quill**. Anglers who portage a canoe will be rewarded with northern pike, rock bass, yellow perch and largemouth bass. This area, thick with beaver signs, is the best place in the park to see moose.

At the far southeast end of the park, 25 miles (40 km) northeast from Orr on Highway 23, is **Crane Lake**, the fourth access point. For canoeists looking for an easy and protected trip, a loop taking from three to five days, with only one portage, can be made from here.

The route goes north through **King Williams Narrows**, across Sand Point Lake, and into the southeast corner of

Frozen lakes offer excellent snowmobiling

Namakan Lake. The entry to the lake, the **Namakan Narrows**, is just over 1 mile (1½ km) long and less than 100 yards across at many points.

The towering cliffs of the Canadian side of the narrows are the site of Ojibwa pictographs. Some are hard to spot, but on one of the tallest rock faces you should recognize a stick figure of a man about 4 feet (1 meter) above the water. Stay alert as you round the cliff and you'll see a reddish moose, about 15 feet (4½ meters) above the water line. Dozens of known pictographs are scattered throughout the border lakes area of the North Woods. Mostly, their meaning and age are unknown. Perhaps they depict spiritually or historically important events. Or perhaps they're graffiti. Whatever their intent, they act as a greeting from another time and culture.

Beyond the Namakan Narrows is a maze of inviting, tree-lined islands, very popular for camping. You make the return loop by paddling west and south, with a half-mile (1-km) portage (flat but wet) into **Grassy Bay**, surrounded at its

northern terminus by towering cliffs and craggy shores.

At **Kettle Falls**, on the eastern end of the Kabetogama Peninsula, a dam controls the water levels of Namakan and Kabetogama Lakes, and a concessionaire operates an automated portage between Rainy and Namakan Lakes for boats less than 21 feet (6 meters) long.

On a rise overlooking the dam sits the historic **Kettle Falls Hotel** built in 1910. Over the years the region's healthful atmosphere was advertised as especially soothing for those with hay fever, and notables such as Charles Lindbergh and John D. Rockefeller, Jr, have been guests at the hotel. Today, guests will find the accommodations still rustic, but hardly primitive. Recently the structure was refurbished and villas were added. The hotel operates seasonally and is accessible only by boat and floatplane. Transportation can be arranged by the hotel for an additional fee; or you can schedule your visit to coincide with a regular stop by the park's concessionaire boat, or include it on your own boating route

oing the rty work camp.

around the park. Both lodging and meals require advance notice.

For experienced and fit canoeists, a 75-mile (121-km) clockwise paddle around the Kabetogama Peninsula, beginning at any of the visitor centers, may be the park's ultimate adventure. Only two short portages are necessary on this journey of five or six days, but you'll probably want to stretch your legs more often than that, so plan an eight-day visit (that way, you'll have a rain-layover day built in). The circuit requires some short open paddles on Rainy Lake, where waves of 2–3 feet (½–1 meter) can build quickly on windy days. Usually, however, the waters are relatively calm, allowing unhindered views of the rocky coastline along Rainy's south shore, some of the most spectacular in the park. Fewer motorboats or other campers and generally good weather make May, late September or early October the best times of year for this trip.

Just to the east of the park is an additional 16,000 sq. miles (41,440 sq.

km) of premier canoe country. **Quetico Provincial Park** protects much of the wilderness on the Canadian side of the *voyageurs'* trail. On the American side, the **Boundary Waters Canoe Area** (part of **Superior National Forest**) is designated wilderness, which means that there are no roads, and motors are restricted. The entire 220-mile (350-km) route from Grand Portage, where **Grand Portage National Monument** is located, to Rainy Lake is nearly as wild today as in the fur-trading heyday. The journey can be made by canoe in about a month – or less if you want to be authentic and paddle 18 hours a day. From the town of Ely, Minnesota, there are many lake and river accesses to the *voyageur* route that would shorten the trip. If you don't want to paddle, you can hike the 8½-mile (14-km) portage trail in the national monument.

Winter is a force to be reckoned with here, but it doesn't keep adventurous visitors away. "There are excellent ice fishing opportunities here," according to Ron Meer, Rainy District naturalist. "When we evaluated visitor use of the park, we discovered ice fishing may be as popular as snowmobiling."

A 7-mile (11-km) ice road from Rainy Lake Visitor Center to Cranberry Bay, plowed to let cars and trucks into the park interior, receives most of the ice fishing action, but a growing number of anglers prefer to cross-country ski or snowshoe into the backcountry, where they can ice fish on secluded lakes. All of the park is open to fishing in winter, but selected zones are closed to motorized traffic to protect sensitive wildlife species such as gray wolves and bald eagles.

Day skiing is best on the **Black Bay Ski Trail** within the park or the nearby **Ash River Recreational Trail** in **Kabetogama State Forest**; both trails are groomed and tracked. Terrain around the inland lakes tends to be rugged – better for snowshoes rather than skis.

For snowmobilers, the park maintains marked trails on the frozen surface of Rainy, Kabetogama and Namakan lakes. A network of trails is maintained outside the park by snowmobile clubs.

Left, an early-morning frost. **Right**, pileated woodpecker

ISLE ROYALE

As islands go, **Isle Royale** is large: 45 miles long and 9 miles wide (14 by 73 km). As national parks go, it is small: a mere 571,000 acres (231,000 hectares) within boundaries that extend 4½ miles (7 km) offshore. What enhances the wilderness here is its location. The park is situated in the northwest corner of the largest (in terms of surface area) freshwater lake in the world, Lake Superior.

Isle Royale is one of only a few national parks in the lower 48 states that is accessible solely by boat or floatplane. This heightens the sense of isolation and adventure for those who make the effort to get here. The island is about 22 miles (35 km) off Minnesota's lakeshore and 56 miles (90 km) from Michigan's **Upper Peninsula**. The nearest landfall is 15 miles (24 km) away at a place called **Caldwell Point** in Canada.

Visitors won't find overwhelming vistas or majestic natural features, aside from the shoreline and lake, and there's no particular point to which everyone flocks. The objective of most visitors is not a place but an experience – getting away from the modern world. There are no roads on the island; services include just one lodge, two stores and a few ranger stations. The park can be explored only "by boot or boat."

"The wilderness here," says North Woods writer Jeff Rennicke, "is found in the storm waves that batter the shorelines and in the ancient silence of the cedar swamps, in the claw marks of glaciers scratched into bedrock and in the slap of a beaver's tail on the water. Here is a quieter, simpler kind of wilderness. Nature working with a finer brush."

Across the Great Water: In other parks, visitors often drive through in a few hours; Isle Royale's average visitor stays three or four days. It's a place that requires planning and preparation in order to be enjoyed fully. Regularly scheduled ferry services operate during the park's season, which is from mid-May to mid-October. (Isle Royale is the

only national park to close in winter.) Mainland towns served by the ferries are **Grand Portage** in Minnesota and both **Copper Harbor** and **Houghton** in Michigan. Vessels are large and carry boats up to 20 feet (6 meters) long as well as passengers. Ferry rides range from three to eight hours one way, depending on departure and arrival points. The park can be reached by floatplane in 30 minutes, but a flight misses part of the adventure of entering the wilderness by crossing *Kitchigami*, "the Great Water," as it is called by the Ojibwa.

Douglass Houghton, an early geologist, described the boat trip as "vexatious" and "more of an adventure than the average person would want to undertake." Technology and forecasting capabilities have improved since his time (Houghton himself drowned in the lake), but today's ferry schedules are occasionally delayed for a day or more because of weather, and it won't hurt to take prophylactic measures to avoid seasickness.

Approaching the island on a calm

Preceding pages: bull moose. Left, driftwood at Rock Harbor. Right, red fox.

day, one sees the water sparkle, the trees and rocks shimmer. In a gray rain or misty fog, a shadowy outline comes and goes. It appears to be the legendary floating island of ancient myth.

From a barren rock exposed after the last Ice Age, a complex ecosystem has evolved. Fourteen species of mammals reached the island, including beaver, red fox, deer mice and bats, and the most frequently sighted red squirrel. Caribou, lynx and coyote, found here before the turn of the century, have all disappeared, but two new mammals have arrived.

Moose appeared around 1900, either swimming from the mainland or venturing over the ice. With no natural predators and thick browse, the population outgrew its food supply and then starved in ongoing cycles. During the cold winter of 1948-49, timber wolves crossed the frozen lake and have since become part of a balanced ecosystem. The wolves help keep the moose population in check, which in turn helps protect vegetation from overbrowsing.

Wildlife other than mammals have also become part of Isle Royale's ecological chain. Two species of snakes and more than 200 species of birds have been observed in the park. Gulls, geese, ducks, various woodpeckers and songbirds delight even the casual birdwatcher, but it's the loon that seems to epitomize the North Woods realm. Its strange cry is often heard on the inland lakes and along coves and bays.

Forest now cloaks most of Isle Royale's rock. The modifying influence of the lake keeps summers cool and winters mild – perfect conditions for white spruce and balsam fir, the species that predominate on the edges of the island and much of the interior. Where forest fires have opened an area, the subclimax mix of quaking aspen and paper birch, with a willow and cherry understory, are found. Swamps and lowlands support black spruce, white cedar and balsam fir along with some larches. Sugar maple and yellow birch grow on the interior uplands. And dry locations along ridges support small stands of northern red oak and white, red and jack pines. The more than 200 small islets that form Isle Royale's archipelago support their own species of plants, some of them rare and endangered.

Getting around: Some 15,000 visitors come to Isle Royale every summer. Many stay on cabin cruisers, preferring to fish offshore for lake trout. Others get dropped off by ferry boat at various locations around the island to hike or backpack some of the 165 miles (265 km) of trails, many of which interconnect, making it easy to make trips of a day or a week. The paths are filled with history and natural beauty. Old fishing and logging camps and copper mining pits lie nearly hidden among the broken shoreline and peaceful forests. Camping permits may be obtained at ranger stations or on the Park Service ferry, and designated campsites must be used.

Most visitor activity is clustered around either end of the roughly east–west elongated island. On the east end of the island is the **Rock Harbor Visitor Center** and the **Rock Harbor Lodge**. The complex includes a hotel,

Bald eagles contesting over a perch.

housekeeping cabins and a marina. The concessionaire rents motorboats and charters cabin cruisers and fishing trips. Reservations at the lodge need to be made in advance. The campground here has a one-night limit. From Rock Harbor you can hike 3 miles (5 km) to **Three Mile Campground**, or arrange a water taxi to take you to another site. It's best to arrange schedules before arriving.

The trails on the eastern end of the island offer a wide variety of scenery and range in difficulty from easy to strenuous. The **Stoll Loop Trail** begins east of the Rock Harbor Lodge and ends at **Scoville Point** 2 miles (3 km) away. The trail is named for journalist Albert Stoll, Jr, who wrote a series of articles for the *Detroit News* in the 1920s promoting national park status for the island. This status was formally granted in 1940. Stoll Trail winds between forest and shoreline, with views of craggy cliffs and forested islets in the harbor. Exhibits along the way describe the natural and cultural history of the area.

It's possible to combine paddling and hiking from Rock Harbor Lodge by renting a canoe there. **Mott Island**, the site of park headquarters, is a three-hour paddle away. From the beach on the east side of the island, a 2½-mile (4-km) circular hiking trail begins and ends near Mott Harbor. The trail passes coves with idyllic views of Rock Harbor, and you can sunbathe on the smooth rocks along the shore.

People not up to paddling can visit the **Rock Harbor Lighthouse** and **Edisen Fishery** via the concessionaire boat. The lighthouse was built in 1855 to guide boats into the harbor during the mining era. There are also guided day trips to **Raspberry Island** where a short hike along a nature trail will give you a good introduction to plants and other features of inland bog ecology.

At the western end of Isle Royale on **Washington Harbor** is the **Windigo Information Center**. In the 1890s, Windigo was the site of the town of Ghyllbank, which included a two-story office building, stores and homes for 135 people who were there for copper

mining. Miles of roads were built, but no profitable amounts of copper were found. In the 1900s, investors decided to attract tourists with a resort on nearby **Washington Island** that featured a bowling alley and dance hall. Now Windigo hosts only the information center and a store with showers, laundry, canoe and motorboat rentals, marina fuel and sandwiches along with the usual assortment of camping supplies.

Washington and **Grace Creeks** on this end of the island are good for trout fishing. For a long day hike or a short overnight outing from Windigo, the **Huginnin Cove Loop Trail** covers a wide variety of scenery and habitat. The trip takes from four to eight hours, and you have to battle some thick underbrush before getting into the open with views of Washington Harbor. The numerous beaver ponds along the trail are perfect habitat for moose.

Huginnin Creek Campground, right off the lakeshore on the island's northwest side, has limited campsites. The eastern arm of the loop winds back

through marsh where purple wild iris, yellow pond lily and wild calla may be in bloom. Farther along, you see evidence of the mining era – steel rails, old log cabins and exploration pits, now covered by thick vegetation.

Going with the grain: By using water taxis and the scheduled ferry service, you can arrange to hike the island from end to end on one of the long ridge trails: the **Greenstone** or the **Minong**. From these ridges you get a feel for the geological forces that formed the island. More than a billion years ago, huge lava flows periodically covered the area. In between flows, sandstone and conglomerate layers were deposited from the erosion of the surrounding mountains. The pressure that created the Superior Basin caused the land to tilt. The action of wind, water and glaciers during the last million years eroded the softer layers into long narrow valleys, while the harder layers remained as parallel ridges running the length of the island. The north face of the ridges are steep, while the south sides are gently sloping. Hiking from south to north is going "against the grain" and takes more work than heading in the other direction.

Greenstone Ridge Trail runs the entire length of the park for 42 miles (68 km), from **Lookout Louise** on the easternmost point to Windigo (Washington Harbor) on the west. Because of transportation schedules, most people start the hike from Rock Harbor. The wide and well-marked trail offers moderate hiking over open ridges, along patches of thick thimbleberry bushes, through dense forests and over (thanks to Park Service planking) bogs.

Along the way hikers climb to the highest point in the park, **Mount Desor** at 1,394 feet (425 meters) – 794 feet (242 meters) above the lake – but with the thick foliage of sugar maple and birch all around they often don't realize their accomplishment – having climbed the highest point on the largest island in the largest lake in the world.

Minong Ridge, north of the Greenstone, stretches for 27 miles (44 km) between **McCargoe Cove** and Windigo. It's more difficult than other trails and

Isle Royale can be reached only by boat or floatplane.

not as well marked. Repeated up-and-down sections traverse boggy areas that are not planked. Its difficulty makes it less traveled, but a fit and prepared hiker will have abundant opportunity for wildlife watching – especially moose sightings – and the chance to stay at three of the park's nicest shoreline campgrounds. Moose cows with calves and bulls in rut can be very dangerous.

The only other wildlife on the island that might cause trouble are mosquitoes and black flies; they peak in May or June and are present in smaller numbers throughout the summer. It's always a good idea to bring plenty of repellent just in case.

At McCargoe Cove on the east end is evidence of hundreds of Indian mining pits. As many as 6,000 years ago people risked their lives to reach the island by canoe in order to dig out the precious pure copper. They used the malleable metallic element to form tools and ornaments and for trade. Isle Royale's copper, distinctive for its silver content, has shown up in artifacts among tribes in Texas and Florida. For some reason, indigenous people had given up mining by the time of the first European explorations. In 1844, the Chippewa relinquished their claim to the island, allowing white miners to move in. "Modern" copper mining took place off and on until 1899.

At its height, the **Minong Mine** near the head of McCargoe Cove housed 150 workers and their families. Horses pulled cars along a rail that ran between the shore and the mines. But the effort was unproductive and by the end of the century the town was gone.

By combining the various sections of the long ridge trails with cross-island routes, loop trips of up to two weeks can be done on either end of the island. The most remote loop trip is **Feldtmann Ridge**, starting and ending at Windigo. Don't be surprised if you hear or see signs of wolves.

For experienced paddlers in good condition, there are a couple of inland water routes involving portages that get you farther away from the foot traffic of

Brown bats huddle together on a cave ceiling.

the trails. The **Indian Portage Trail** runs from McCargoe Cove on the north to **Chippewa Harbor** on the south. This is purported to be the same route used by early Native Americans in their birch-bark canoes. The 20-mile (32-km) crossing can be made with canoe or kayak, or those with no boat can follow hiking trails around the lakes. Camping on small lakes such as **Chickenbone**, **Livermore**, **LeSage** or **Richie** gives you a chance to watch for wildlife coming to drink at dawn and dusk.

Fishing on the inland lakes is best done from a boat, and some anglers like to carry in a small rubber raft instead of a canoe. Fish are found in all except 12 of the 42 named inland lakes. Species like trout, yellow perch, walleye and pumpkinseed sunfish are common, but northern pike is the most widespread. No fishing license is needed for inland lakes and streams (a Michigan license is required in all Lake Superior waters).

The northeast end of the island, known as **Five Fingers**, is a boater's paradise with secluded coves, protected waters and fjord-like inlets. The four campgrounds in **Duncan Bay**, **Belle Isle** and **Merritt Lane** have deep-water docks for power boats. An additional three campgrounds accommodate paddlers. Most of the lakeside campsites in the park have screened-in shelters, especially nice in the drizzling rain or when bugs are out in force. Otherwise, a good tent is a must – to protect against insects as well as Great Lakes storms. Also necessary on any overnight outing is a backpacking stove for cooking, although there are a few sites where open-air campfires are allowed.

Located right in the middle of Lake Superior's shipping lanes, Isle Royale has been described as a "graveyard for ships." During certain periods, the island seemed to be especially treacherous. In the three years from 1884 to 1886, three ships were wrecked. One of them was the *Algoma*, the first steel-hulled vessel to work the lake. It could accommodate 840 passengers, but during November 1885 it was carrying fewer than 50 on its run to Thunder Bay. During a fierce storm the ship ran onto the reefs only 30 yards from **Mott Island**. The hull split and whole sections of the *Algoma* and its passengers where swept away. A small band desperately clung to the shattered boat on a tiny shoal. Exhausted and only a stone's throw from shore, some could not hold on and were washed into the frigid lake. Only the captain and 11 passengers survived. Although four lighthouses were eventually erected, five more ships were lost between 1924 and 1935.

Experienced divers can explore the 10 major wreck sites that have been located and marked by the Park Service, creating a unique underwater museum displaying maritime technology from the 1870s to the mid-1900s. At some wreck sites, like the *America* in Washington Harbor or the *Emperor* near **Canoe Rocks**, scuba divers can swim the passageways and gaze at staterooms and pieces of the past, imagining what turmoil must have preceded the ghostly silence. The cold, clear water of Lake Superior has preserved artifacts in outstanding condition.

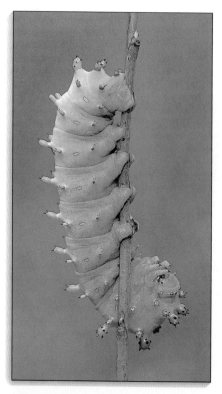

Cecropia moth larva.

CALL OF THE WOLF

Pity the poor wolf. It is the most misunderstood creature in the animal kingdom. *Canis lupus*, the gray or timber wolf, has figured prominently in fairy tales and folklore, but the real wolf is another story.

One of the most common misconceptions is that wolves have been exterminated in all but the most remote areas of the mountainous West, Alaska and northern Canada. Not so. In fact, of the lower 48 states, Minnesota has the greatest wolf population, more than 2,000 divided into about 260 packs, including about 30 individuals that move in and out of Voyageurs National Park. A small population is also found at Isle Royale National Park in Michigan, and a related species, the red wolf, has been reintroduced into the southern Appalachians at Great Smoky Mountains National Park and other refuges.

Nor is it true that wolves are bloodthirsty, indiscriminate killers. They are indeed expert hunters. They stalk large prey as a pack, using cooperative strategies to isolate and kill animals such as caribou, deer or moose that are often much larger than themselves. They tend to cull young, old or debilitated members of the herd and, as an apex predator, they help keep the population of the prey animals in check.

Nor are wolves a threat to humans, as most tall tales would have us believe. According to Shaun Chosa, assistant curator at the International Wolf Center in Ely, Minnesota, "A healthy wild wolf has never attacked a human in North America. Ever." Most reports of wolf bites actually involve captive animals or "wolf-dog" mixed breeds that people try to train as watchdogs, a particularly bad idea, Chosa says, because wolves tend to be shy by nature.

Highly social animals, wolves live in packs of between two and 20 individuals that may range over an area of some 25 to 115 sq. miles (65–298 sq. km) or more. An alpha male and female dominate the pack and are the only animals to breed, although the others help to feed and look after the pups. The dominant pair usually leads the hunts. As Terry Lindsay, naturalist at Isle Royale, explains, "they often actually kill the prey," which at Isle Royale is mostly moose. "There are times when an alpha male and female will single-handedly – or single-pawedly – take down an animal." Chunks of meat are usually brought back to the pups

or swallowed down and regurgitated when the adults return to the den.

Hierarchy within the pack is maintained by a complex system of body postures and "ritual" interactions. Fights may break out among pack members who challenge the hierarchy, and sometimes an animal may be driven out. These lone wolves will then look for their own territory where they can establish a new pack. Meetings between packs may also lead to an attack, and it's not uncommon for an animal to be killed or wounded in the encounter.

Visitors at Voyageurs and Isle Royale are unlikely to see wolves, although they may come across tracks or scat. "Sightings are rare," says Lindsay, "but it's not uncommon to hear them." On a recent foray on the island, he was awakened before dawn by a "ruckus of howls and yips and carrying on."

Howling seeems to serve a number of purposes. It helps identify and protect the animals' territory, and locate distant members of the pack. It may also stimulate the pack's urge to hunt or summon members to a rendezvous.

One thing is certain: the call of the wolf is one of the most distinct and haunting sounds in nature. Once heard, it will never be forgotten. ■

Canis lupus, the gray or timber wolf.

LAKESHORE PARKS

The Great Lakes are the largest expanse of fresh water on earth. And every American schoolchild is supposed to know their names: Superior, Michigan, Huron, Erie and Ontario. Millions of people live within a day's drive of them, and each year thousands visit.

How were they created? By the forces of four Ice Ages. The lakes have been called "glacial gifts." When the glaciers finally retreated about 10,000 years ago, a landscape of newly formed valleys and rivers emerged from beneath the ice. Where the glaciers had been thickest and the depressions greatest, five great lakes formed, covering nearly 95,000 sq. miles (246,000 sq. km).

In the United States, it is the four parks administered by the Park Service that attract the most attention. Two national lakeshores are on Lake Michigan and two are on Superior, places where aquatic and terrestrial wilderness meet.

Indiana Dunes: Right beside the steel mills of Gary, Indiana, within an hour's drive or train ride of Chicago, lies a 14,000-acre (5,666-hectare) expanse of dunes, bog and woodland. The area is protected within **Indiana Dunes National Lakeshore** and adjacent **Indiana Dunes State Park**. With easy access from Interstates 80, 90 and 94, the parks can be included in plans that call for cross-country travel or a visit to the Chicago area.

In 1916, Stephen Mather, the first director of the National Park Service, wanted to save the Indiana Dunes as Sand Dunes National Park. His call went unanswered. Forty years later, the poet Carl Sandburg joined the effort to create a national park. "Those dunes are to the Midwest what the Grand Canyon is to Arizona and the Yosemite to California," Sandburg wrote. "They constitute a signature of time and eternity; once lost, the loss would be irrevocable." The effort was successful; the national lakeshore was established in 1966.

Though the dunes aren't particularly high – most are 50–70 feet (15–21 me-

ters), with some blow-out dunes considerably higher – they stretch inland for up to 2 miles (3 km). It is what lies beyond the dunes, in the glacial moraines, that tells the story of the region's creation. The **Valparaiso Moraine**, about 16 miles (26 km) south of Lake Michigan, marks the southern terminus of the last glacier to cover Indiana. Lake levels changed periodically as the glacier receded. Four dune ridges mark the successive location of beaches from 14,000 years ago to the present. The farther away from the lake, the older the dune. The untrained eye would not recognize the older dune formations, covered as they are with vegetation and the soil that has formed from centuries of plant growth and decay.

Most of the park's points of interest can be easily reached from Highway 12 paralleling the lakeshore. East of **Burns Harbor**, it runs along the **Calumet Dunes**, the site of a trail used by early explorers and Native Americans to travel between the settlements that would become Chicago and Detroit. The **Ly-co-**

ki-we Trail near the visitor center is a good place to view the oldest dune formation, the **Glenwood Dunes**, which formed at the lake's edge about 14,000 years ago, and to compare it to its successor dunes, the Calumet, which are about 12,000 years old. These and other dunes on the lakeshore were created by sand washing up on Lake Michigan's southern shore and lifted inland by prevailing winds. Obstructions such as plants, fences, hills, even one's own body lying on the beach, slow the wind and cause it to drop its sand load. Eventually a dune becomes stabilized as vegetation grows. The forest has slowly covered the older dunes as Lake Michigan's shoreline moved north.

Indiana Dunes State Park, at the end of Highway 49, is a good place to view recent dunes. You can hike its system of trails, including a rugged 1½-mile (3-km) climb to **Mount Tom**, which at 192 feet (59 meters) above the lake is the highest dune in the area.

The **Bailly-Chellberg Homestead**, 5 miles (8 km) west of the lakeshore

visitor center (near park headquarters), concentrates on the area's human history. The 2-mile (3-km) **Little Calumet River Trail** takes you past a ravine where you can imagine the life of the Indian village that flourished on the banks of the river between 200 BC and AD 500. In 1822, Joseph Bailly, a French-Canadian, chose this site for a trading post because two major Indian trails met here. The house and grounds are open to visitors.

Lying in the cold embrace of US Steel on the west and Midwest Steel on the east, the **West Beach** unit protects a 2-mile (3-km) stretch of sandy beach and extensive recent dune formations. In June the prickly-pear cactus blossom.

Dr Henry Cowles, a botanist who conducted much of his research at Indiana Dunes in the early 1900s, is credited with observing and demonstrating more clearly than any other the principles of ecology by studying how plant communities transform a bare sand dune into a site for a living forest. In dynamic succession, the plants that colonize a dune change from pioneering grasses and shrubs to cottonwood, then pine, followed by oak and finally the beech–maple plant community. **Succession Trail** in the West Beach area lets the visitor observe some of these dynamics.

If you're spending the night near the dunes, both the towns of **Chesterton** and **Michigan City** have plenty of beds. Camping is available in both the national lakeshore and the state park.

Sleeping Bear Dunes: On the east side of Lake Michigan, about a 5-hour drive from Indiana Dunes, is "America's biggest sandpile" – **Sleeping Bear Dunes National Lakeshore**. Situated at the base of the **Leelanau Peninsula** in the northwest corner of lower Michigan, Sleeping Bear Dunes National Lakeshore was federally authorized in 1970 and protects 71,000 acres (28,700 hectares). Here, steep slopes tower 450 feet (137 meters) above the lake's blue water. The Sleeping Bear Dunes formation is among the largest in the world. Only those in Colorado, the Sahara Desert and Saudi Arabia outrank it.

For the most part, the park lies along **Indiana Dunes in winter.**

a 35-mile (56-km) stretch of Michigan Highway 22 that winds around the lakeshore. Roughly halfway between the north and south limits of the park's mainland section is the visitor center at **Empire**. A slide program, exhibits and a bookshop provide an introduction to the area.

For an overview of the dunes, head north from Empire on Highway 22 to Highway 109. From there it's about a mile to the **Pierce Stocking Scenic Drive**, a 7-mile (11-km) route that takes you to the bluffs above Lake Michigan. The one-way loop is marked with numbered signs, and an interpretive brochure is available at the entrance. Panoramic vistas are offered from various stops along the way. **Glen Lake**, which is visible on the inland side of the dunes, used to be part of Lake Michigan, but a sandbar has separated the two bodies of water. From an overlook 450 feet (137 meters) above Lake Michigan, you'll view the park's shoreline stretching in both directions. You'll also be able to gaze on the hulking mass of the Sleep-

ing Bear Dunes Plateau, covering about 4 sq. miles (10 sq. km).

There are two kinds of dunes in the park: beach dunes (created, as you might expect, from beach sand) and perched dunes (created from glacial sands atop plateaus). Sleeping Bear Dunes is an example of the latter. Ojibwa legend has it that a mother bear and two cubs were driven into the lake by a forest fire. The mother bear swam to safety and climbed ashore to await the cubs. Too exhausted to make the crossing, the cubs drowned a few miles from land. The Sleeping Bear Dune represents the waiting mother bear. Her two cubs can be seen in the form of **North** and **South Manitou Islands**, 7 miles (11 km) off **Sleeping Bear Point**. Tranquil and secluded, the islands are under federal protection.

From Pierce Stocking Drive, proceed north on Highway 109. Along the way there's a chance to climb a dune (strenuous, but rewarding), swim in Glen Lake or pitch a tent at **D.H. Day Campground**. From the hamlet of **Glen Haven**, a spur road leads west to the **Mari-**

Canadian geese tracks in Empire Bluffs, Sleeping Bear Dunes.

time Museum. The museum documents the role of the US Life-Saving Service, which later became the US Coast Guard, in assisting shipwreck victims during the late 19th and early 20th centuries. Risking their own lives in treacherous storms, these crews of six to eight boatmen had an astounding 99 percent success rate in their rescue attempts.

The dunes are still very much a work in progress. As recently as 1931, the Coast Guard buildings had to be moved from Sleeping Bear Point to the museum's present location because migrating dunes threatened to cover them. Shifting sands also cover trees or whole tracts of woodlands. When the dunes move on, "ghost forests" of dead trees are exposed, stark reminders of the dunes' passing.

From the town of **Leland**, 5 miles (8 km) northeast of the park, you can take a passenger ferry to **South Manitou Island**. Travel time one-way is about 90 minutes; the boat docks for four hours and returns. Campers can remain and arrange for transportation back to the mainland another day. South Manitou has been important in both human and natural history. In the mid- to late 19th century, the island was a source of wood for steamships. But not all the trees were cut: a grove of huge white cedars remains. One of the giants measures 17½ feet (5 meters) in circumference and is estimated to be more than 500 years old. **North Manitou** is the larger and more primitive of the two islands, a place where backpackers and hikers can explore 15,000 acres (6,080 hectares) of wilderness. Ferry services from Leland are available from mid-May to mid-November, weather permitting.

The section of the park south of Empire doesn't have the same spectacular dunes, but the **Aral Dunes** along **Platte Bay** are fascinating. Miles of trails wind through the beech-maple forest and past lakes and meadows. The **Platte** and **Crystal rivers** also offer opportunities for leisurely float trips and fishing. Canoes can be rented.

Pictured Rocks: Northeast of the town of **Munising** in Michigan's **Upper Pe-**

Left, Hygrophorus mushrooms. Below, Cattail leaves.

ninsula is **Pictured Rocks National Lakeshore**. It hugs the southern Lake Superior shoreline for more than 40 miles. Only 3 miles (5 km) at its widest point, the park contains an impressive variety of scenic features. Most notable among them are the **Pictured Rocks** – 15 miles (24 km) of richly colored sandstone cliffs that rise abruptly from Lake Superior. The rock walls have been sculpted by wind and water into caves, columns, arches and great jutting headlands. For centuries, Ojibwa Indians hunted these forests of hardwoods, pine, spruce, hemlock and fir, and fished the waters. To them this was the land of "thunder and gods," so named for the booming sound of waves crashing into the caves of the Pictured Rocks cliffs. No wonder Pictured Rocks was designated the United States' first national lakeshore in 1966.

The linear park can be explored from either direction. If you came into the Upper Peninsula from Sleeping Bear Dunes, you'll reach the town of **Grand Marais** at the eastern edge of the park

first. Follow Highway H58 directly into the park. The road is unpaved, narrow and winding, so allow plenty of time to travel slowly and enjoy nature's handiwork. The views of Lake Superior are impressive, but as with many national parks in the Midwest, much of the beauty and wonder is to be found on a smaller scale: the sunlight shimmering through the thick forest canopy; the carpets of marsh marigolds at the edges of beaver ponds; and the sounds – bird songs by day, and the calls of loons, frogs and owls by night.

The first stop along the way is **Grand Sable Dunes**. The perched dunes cover 4 sq. miles (10 sq. km) and rise nearly 300 feet (91 meters) above the lake. Behind them is **Grand Sable Lake**, an example of a "kettle" lake, formed when a giant block of glacial ice became isolated and melted in its hollow. Coniferous forests are found close to the beach, but for the most part, deciduous hardwoods dominate. The habitat of dunes and mixed woods supports a number of rare and threatened plant species, in-

*elow,
taghorn
umac.
ight, a
maple
eedling and
round cedar.*

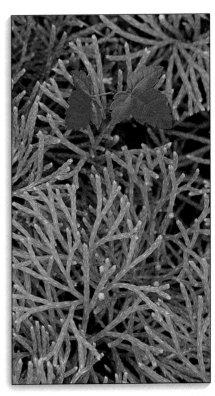

cluding orchids that bloom in the spring and early summer.

Farther west, **Twelvemile Beach** is a good spot for a picnic or a hike along the sand and pebble shore. A campground with water, picnic tables, grills and toilets is also available for a fee on a first-come, first-served basis. The road then continues south out of the park through **Lake Superior State Forest**. This North Woods semi-wilderness is home to white-tailed deer, beaver, coyote and black bear, plus many species of migratory birds and the recently reintroduced peregrine falcon.

Take a side trip off H58 by swinging north 3 miles (5 km) to **Little Beaver Lake Campground**. Nestled in the park's midsection, it's a good spot to begin an easy 5-mile (8-km) hike; the **Beaver Basin Loop Trail** is an especially welcome walk on a hot sunny day. While circumnavigating **Big** and **Little Beaver Lakes**, you'll pass a stand of white pines that are 250 to 300 years old, and skirt sea caves that were carved when the water level was higher.

In the western part of the lakeshore, **Miners Castle Overlook** has a view of a sandstone monolith rising as tall as a 9-story building. Legend has it that in the 1600s a French Jesuit missionary and explorer celebrated Mass for American Indians on top of the rock and that a cross is carved on one of the formations. Nearby, just a half-mile off **Miners Castle Road**, is **Miners Falls**, a 75-foot (23-meter) cascade that plummets into a dark canyon below.

The town of Munising marks the end of the park drive, but there's still a lot to see. From **Munising Falls Interpretive Center**, a paved trail leads visitors behind a 70-foot (21-meter) waterfall. Also from town, boat tours take visitors out for a loon's-eye view of the "pictured rocks." Lake Superior may seem benign as you leisurely pass shapes named **Grand Portal**, **Indian Head**, **Flower Vase** and **Painted Cove**, but the shore between Munising and Grand Marais has been dubbed "the graveyard coast" because of the many ships that rest beneath the water. A dozen shipwrecks, as well as huge, colorful rocks and weed beds teeming with fish, are protected as part of the **Alger Underwater Preserve**. It can be visited by well-prepared, experienced scuba divers using commercial charter services.

Pictured Rocks also offers a spectacular environment for backcountry hiking and camping. The park contains approximately 80 miles (128 km) of easy-to-moderate hiking trails. The main backcountry trail, the **Lakeshore Trail** (a component of the **North Country National Scenic Trail**), is 42 miles (68 km) long. Fifteen miles (24 km) of the Lakeshore Trail are atop towering cliffs with dramatic views of the largest body of fresh water in the world. Located at intervals of 2–5 miles (3–8 km) along the Lakeshore Trail are 13 campgrounds and eight group sites. Each has a set capacity; open camping is not allowed. Reservations can be made for group sites; all others are available on a first-come, first-served basis.

Summer holiday weekends and mid-July to mid-August are the busiest times of the year at Pictured Rocks. Late spring

A cross-country skier explores an icy sea cave at Apostle Islands.

and early summer bring a great profusion of wildflowers as well as the black flies and mosquitoes that make life miserable for warm-blooded creatures. Fall is a pleasant time for a backcountry trip when crowds and insects are replaced by gorgeous autumn colors.

Apostle Islands: Clustered off the tip of the **Bayfield Peninsula**, and described as "an emerald necklace on blue velvet," northern Wisconsin's Apostle Islands occupy a 720-sq. mile (1,865-sq. km) area of Lake Superior. French missionaries named the islands after the disciples of Christ, but there are actually 22 islands, not 12, in the archipelago. Twenty-one of the islands, plus an 11-mile (18-km) strip of mainland shoreline, are now part of the **Apostle Islands National Lakeshore**.

The islands are between 1 and 16 miles (1½ and 26 km) from shore. They are rugged and uncrowded, ranging in size from 3-acre (1-hectare) **Gull Island**, home only to gulls and other nesting birds, to 10,054-acre (4,067-hectare) **Stockton Island**, with a sizable population of black bears. The park has secluded white sand beaches, over 20 miles (32 km) of strikingly eroded cliffs, 22 documented shipwrecks, six 19th-century lighthouses, abandoned fishing camps, and a history rich with the lore of Native American and French *voyageurs* – not to mention sweeping vistas of the big lake. The islands are heavily wooded with maple, aspen, birch, pine and spruce, providing habitat for deer, fox, marten and other small North Woods mammals and birds.

The gateway to visiting the Apostle Islands is the small town of **Bayfield** on Lake Superior's **Chequamegon Bay**. Bayfield is less than two hours from Duluth, Minnesota, and six hours north of Madison, Wisconsin. The **National Lakeshore Visitor Center** is housed in the old **Bayfield County Courthouse**, built in 1893, and now on the National Register of Historic Places.

The easiest way to see the archipelago is to take an excursion boat. "The Grand Tour" is a four-hour nonstop cruise through the Apostles featuring views of

he Great akes are the orld's reatest xpanse of esh water.

lighthouses, sea caves and 20 islands. If you have more time, hiking and sightseeing tours of the closer islands are offered every day. In addition to scheduled service, charter boats and water taxis can be arranged.

The islands are similar in vegetation and wildlife, but each offers some special feature. For example, tiny **Devils Island** (318 acres/129 hectares) is the most remote. It has only one campsite. If you manage to get here, you'll find yourself alone at the tip of Wisconsin. **Oak Island** (5,078 acres/2,055 hectares) is more accessible. Rising 480 feet (146 meters) above the lake, it is the highest of the cluster and is primarily undeveloped except for widely placed backcountry camping areas and 11 miles (18 km) of hiking trails. Stockton Island is also a good choice for an overnight visit. The largest of the islands in the park, its exposed bedrock has been shaped into graceful arches, caves, columns and cliffs; there are also sand-and-pebble beaches. The **Tombolo Loop Trail** (4 miles/6 km) leaves from

the camping area and winds through a variety of habitats – towering pines, old and new bogs, a lagoon, sand dunes and ancient beach ridges.

The islands themselves deservedly get most of the attention, but don't neglect to visit the mainland section of the national lakeshore. This strip of coast, never more than a mile or so wide, extends for 11 miles (18 km) from **Little Sand Bay** on the east to **Squaw Bay** on the west. The **Little Sand Bay Visitor Center** is 13 miles (21 km) north of Bayfield. In summer, excursion boats leave from here for tours of **Sand Island** with its colorful cliffs and historic lighthouse, as well as tours closer to shore to view the magnificent **Squaw Bay Sea Caves**.

The caves, 4 miles (6 km) east of the tiny village of **Cornucopia**, represent one of the most beautiful features of the national lakeshore. It's possible to kayak into some of these caves and pass beneath arches of sandstone. A Bayfield outfitter offers paddling instruction, sea kayak rentals, and both short and extended Apostle Islands kayak tours.

There are no Park Service campgrounds on the mainland unit of the national lakeshore, but backcountry camping is allowed all year on 18 of the islands. Permits are required. Camping on most islands ranges from developed sites (often near docks) to undesignated locations away from developed areas. Camping is also available on nearby state and **Chequamegon National Forest** lands, plus private campgrounds. Bayfield has a number of motels and bed-and-breakfasts.

The national lakeshore can be visited year-round. May and June offer solitude, spring flowers and migrating birds, but can be cool and foggy. Weather in July and August is great, but there are more people to contend with. September and October are beautiful and uncrowded, but can be stormy. Most winters it's possible to ski, snowshoe or hike across frozen Lake Superior to the inshore islands. The sea caves on Sand Island and along Squaw Bay are particularly interesting, with spectacular icicles hanging from the ceilings.

Left, an inside look at Pictured Rocks. **Right**, winter moonrise near Lake Superior.

196

OZARK RIVERS

This isn't a typical national park. What the federal government protects in this Ozark Mountain hideaway are certain rivers. The **Ozark National Scenic Riverways** consists of 100 (160 km) miles of the **Current River** and 34 miles (54 km) of its main tributary, the **Jacks Fork**. They are the first US rivers to be permanently safeguarded from damming and development, thanks to an Act of Congress in 1964. With an adjacent buffer zone, the Riverways protect 80,000 acres (32,400 hectares) of water and rock, hills and valleys, in this part of southern Missouri, a couple of hours' drive from St Louis.

Ecological crossroads: Rising to 2,800 feet (853 meters), the Ozarks are one of the few elevated regions between the Appalachians and Rocky Mountains. Biologically, the region is a meeting place of eastern forests and western prairie. Because of its elevation, several plants that are usually associated with more northern climates flourish here, as do southwestern species such as armadillos and tarantulas.

Forests of oak and hickory interspersed with sun-dappled glades stand atop limestone cliffs that were deposited by ancient seas as much as 500 million years ago. The ancient outcrops, says writer Richard Rhodes, give the landscape an air of "great weather-beaten age, conveying a feeling that these hills have seen it all, not once but a thousand times, and serenely accept change as a constant fact of life." Here, Rhodes writes, is a "rough and sturdy land, not smoothed and softened by glacial scouring like lands farther north, not clothed with rich topsoil like the alluvial land to the south, but bare bones, plainness itself, tough and permanent."

Below the surface, thousands of caves have been carved out of the limestone by rainwater made slightly acidic by carbon dioxide in the soil and atmosphere. Springs gush from the rocks. In fact, the largest concentration of springs in the world are found in the Ozarks –

not, as you might think, because there's so much water, but because there's so much rock. Although the average rainfall is only 40 inches (102 cm) a year, it percolates quickly through the porous limestone and drains into fissures – reappearing as springs and seepages.

In the late 19th century, full-scale logging began removing the virgin oak and pine forest, and this continued until World War I. Countless loads of timber were hauled to midwestern lumberyards. The once clear rivers filled with silt, and gravel washed down from the hills. The remaining wildlife was hunted and scattered until only remnant populations survived in a few passed-over tracts. Today, second-growth trees are healing the landscape – oak, pine, hickory, gum, dogwood and redbud on the hills, sycamore, cottonwood, maple and birch closer to the water.

While the wildlife population is not what it used to be – black bears, wolves, cougars and bison are all extinct here – there still remains a wide diversity and abundance of animals. Early-morning

Preceding pages: mustard flowers and Villines Cabin, Buffalo National River. Left, Alley Spring Mill on the Jacks Fork River. Right, maple leaf floating among pine needles.

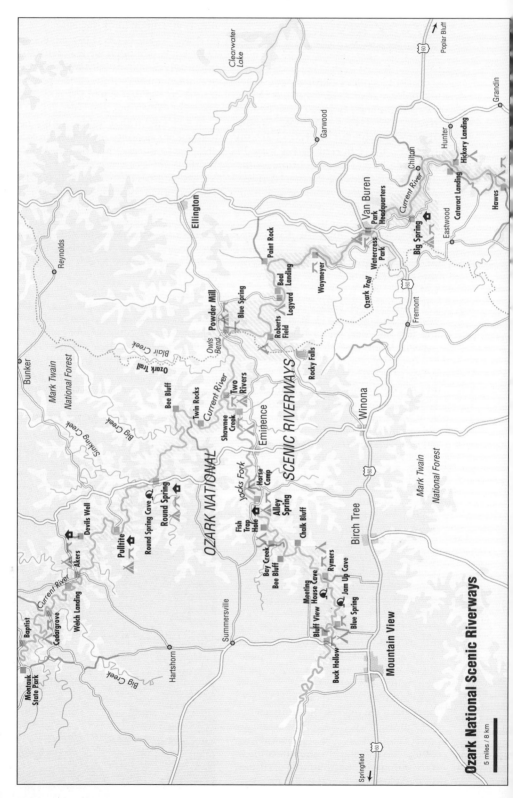

Ozark National Scenic Riverways

5 miles / 8 km

mists hang in the air as rising campers watch minks, raccoons, beavers and other small mammals at streamsides. Deer, bobcats and foxes might be spotted by sharp-eyed canoeists. Forty-three species of mammals inhabit the area, and, not surprisingly with the number of caves, thirteen of the species are bats. Birds, too, find the varied habitat to their liking; 300 different types, from bald eagles and ospreys to tiny Carolina wrens and gnatcatchers, have been recorded within the park.

Wild ride: One of the wildest canoe rides in mid-America is offered at the **Jacks Fork**, a smaller and more serpentine river than the Current. From the farthest upstream put-in at **Buck Hollow**, a trip of 90 miles (145 km) can be made to the southern edge of the Riverways at **Hawes** on the Current River. Trips of various lengths can be made by using a variety of access points.

Lots of concessionaires in the Riverways area rent canoes. A float down either river is highlighted by cold springs, mysterious caves, moss- and lichen-covered bluffs up to 200 feet (61 meters) high, and the accompanying variety of plants and animals that thrive in this riverine habitat.

One of the first things you'll notice about any Ozark stream is its clarity. The hard rock bottom of chert or flint lets the stream roll clear except after the hardest rains. Smallmouth bass, rock bass, carp, sunfish and even trout near the cold springs hover in the eddies or swim under your bow. The deep-blue pools of the Jacks Fork and Current are perfect for exploring with a mask and snorkel, or for lazily casting a line.

About 6 miles (10 km) below Buck Hollow, there's a hairpin turn as the river approaches **Jam-up Bluff and Cave**, a feature accessible only from the river, with a pool and waterfall inside. About 18 miles (29 km) downstream from Jam-up is the site of **Alley Spring**, the seventh largest spring in Missouri. With an average discharge of 81 million gallons (307 million liters) every day – enough to supply the needs of a mid-sized city – the spring transforms the Jacks Fork from a seasonal trickle to a robust, year-round river. Alley Spring is a half-mile (1 km) downriver from the campground of the same name. Special programs are held at the Park Service amphitheater, and you can visit a one-room schoolhouse and an historic roller mill that grinds corn and wheat.

The Jacks Fork continues another 14 miles (22½ km) to the Current River. From the confluence at **Two Rivers Campground** and canoe launch, it's another 7 miles (11 km) to **Owls Bend**, where Highway 106 crosses the river. Nearby, accessible by road and trail, is **Blue Spring**, kept in the shadows by overhanging trees and towering cliffs. The Indian name for this artesian pool meant "spring of the summer sky," referring to its striking azure hue.

Granddad gusher: Thirty miles (48 km) downstream, and a few miles south of the Highway 60 bridge at **Van Buren** (where Park Headquarters is located), you'll find **Big Spring**, the granddaddy of Ozark gushers. One of the two largest single orifice springs on the continent, Big Spring discharges 276 million gal-

Juniper perched on a rock ledge in the Ozark Mountains.

lons (1,045 million liters) of water per day into the river. An estimated 65,000 tons of calcium carbonate (limestone) is carried away with the effluence every year, enough to excavate a good-sized cave on an annual basis. The park has an interpretive area here offering programs on quilting and the art of building johnboats (a long, flat-bottomed skiff). Johnboat rides are also available, allowing you an opportunity to travel the waterway as many of the locals do. Ask at the ranger station for specifics.

The Current River and the section of Jacks Fork below Alley Spring can be paddled most of the year; the upper Jacks Fork is usually runnable only in spring. The smooth water can be fast-flowing, and parts of the Jacks Fork are narrow and winding, but neither river has rapids or ledges, so they are suitable for novices. Always discuss river conditions with a ranger before starting out. Summer weekends are hectic; avoid them unless you're interested in a paddling party. Choose spring or fall, or summer weekdays.

Although the Ozark Riverways are not a typical national park, there are ranger talks and special programs at many sites. Seven campgrounds offer car-camping facilities; many springs and caves are accessible from parking areas and require only short hikes. Park rangers lead a 1-mile guided tour of **Round Spring Cave** located on the Current.

Buffalo National River: About 150 miles (241 km) southwest, the Buffalo National River tumbles down the north face of the **Boston Mountains**, the most rugged section of the Ozark region, before crossing the **Springfield Plateau** and emptying into the **White River**, a journey of 150 miles (240 km).

The Buffalo's location in northwest Arkansas makes it both accessible and remote. The river is within a two-hour drive of **Little Rock**, and more than 10 million people live within 250 miles (400 km), but the solitude of the valley is demonstrated by the fact that only eight auto bridges span the river, and some of them are just one lane wide.

Boating, fishing and hiking are the

Patrolling the Current River at Ozark National Scenic Riverways.

main activities along the Buffalo. Canoe rentals and outfitting are available in many locations, including **Ponca**, **Jasper**, **St Joe** and **Yellville**. Motors (up to 10 horsepower) are permitted below **Erbie Ford** only, so touring by johnboat is limited to the middle and lower sections. Float trips can be arranged for almost any duration – ranging from a half-day outing to a 10-day wilderness expedition.

The upper portion of the river is the most challenging for paddlers. From the tiny village of Ponca downstream 50 miles (80 km) to **Woolum Ford**, the Buffalo is an intimate, feisty stream that loops back and forth between prairie meadows and precipitous bluffs. Names on the map like **Close Call Curve**, **Crisis Curve** and **Wreckin' Rock** indicate that this section is for those with some experience.

Immediately after the put-in, sheer 200- to 300-foot (60–90-meter) cliffs swallow the river. **Big Bluff**, the tallest limestone cliff in the Ozarks at more than 500 feet (152 meters) high, is about a half-day's paddle from Ponca. A few miles farther on, a flat rock ledge signals the take-out for the trail to **Hemmed-in Hollow**. A half-mile (1 km) scramble up a narrow, dead-end canyon leads to a 173-foot (53-meter) waterfall, the highest of its kind between the southern Appalachians and the Rockies.

After **Pruitt**, where a Park Service **information station** is located, the river alternates between calm, clear pools and periodic riffles, then gradually widens as the bluffs begin to dwindle. Between Carver and Woolum, the Buffalo offers a near-wilderness experience.

The middle and lower sections of the Buffalo generally contain enough water to float throughout the year. Campsites along the way are numerous and scenic. The main dangers of the Buffalo are downed trees and flash floods; the river has been known to rise more than 25 feet (8 meters) in one day.

Long-distance hiking is possible in the 11,300-acre (4,573-hectare) **Ponca Wilderness Area**. An 18½-mile (30-

Horseback riders ford the Buffalo River.

km) trail between Ponca and Pruitt criss-crosses the river, providing panoramic overlooks of the Ozark backwoods. The trail passes Big Bluff and Hemmed-in Hollow, and includes historic sites such as the **Parker-Hickman log house**, built around 1840, and two cemeteries dating from the Civil War. There are plenty of opportunities for day hikes, too. The **Lost Valley Trail** in the historic **Boxley** area is only a 3-mile (5-km) round-trip, but it passes waterfalls, cliffs, a large bluff shelter and a natural bridge as it follows a creek bed up to a cave. The cave, about 200 feet (61 meters) long, ends in an opening with a 35-foot (11-meter) waterfall.

Spring is the best time to see the profusion of wildflowers and flowering shrubs. Rhododendron, azalea, redbud and laurel present a palette of color against a canvas of burgeoning green. But the growing season is long here, and there are an estimated 800 to 1,000 flowering plants, starting in January with witch hazel and ending in late fall when Indian pipes appear in the woodlands.

Located farther west than the Ozark National Scenic Riverways, the Buffalo River is home to more "southwestern" species. Armadillos, road runners and tarantulas co-exist with wild turkeys, white-tailed deer, raccoons, opossums, bobcats, minks, black bears and beavers. Elk populations have slowly increased since their introduction in 1981.

Typical of the bird life are the spindly-legged great blue herons, crow-sized pileated woodpeckers, and sleek ospreys that accompany river travelers. In addition, four species of poisonous snakes make their home in the park: the copperhead, water moccasin, canebrake rattlesnake and pygmy rattlesnake. Rest easy – it is extremely unlikely that you will encounter any of them.

Like the Ozark National Scenic Riverways, this park is set up for boaters. Still, those who enjoy driving the hills and hollows can find access to many sites of interest. Fourteen campgrounds in the park are accessible by car and are open on a first-come, first-served basis. The only park-managed cabins are found at **Buffalo Point**, 20 miles (32 km) south of Yellville and a few miles off Highway 14.

The **Tyler Bend Visitor Center** (midway in the park off Highway 65) and ranger stations at other locations offer seasonal interpretive programs, Ozark craft and folk music, and guided hikes and canoe floats.

Also within the park is the **Indian Rockhouse**, one of the largest prehistoric bluff shelters in the Ozarks; and the **Rush Mining District**, an area active from the 1880s to the 1960s but now a ghost town on the National Register of Historic Places.

While you're visiting the area, the **Ozark Folk Center** in **Mountain View** (southeast of the river on Highway 14) is worth a trip. Artisans demonstrate traditional crafts and music and promote understanding of the region's culture and history. Also near Mountain View, the US Forest Service maintains **Blanchard Springs Caverns**, a large underground cave system reached by elevator. It has lights and walkways, but otherwise has been left undeveloped.

Hiking Goat Trail at Buffalo National River.

PHOTO TIPS

National parks are legendary for stunning landscapes and wildlife. A little advance preparation, plus a moment of reflection before tripping the camera's shutter, will ensure that your photos capture the beauty and grandeur of these magnificent natural areas.

The best pictures are not necessarily products of cameras with the most "bells and whistles." When shopping for a camera, compare several models until you find one that is comfortable, not confusing, to operate. If you own a camera but use it infrequently, shoot a roll of film before going off on vacation to refamiliarize yourself with its operation.

Most single-lens reflex cameras are equipped with a 50mm-55mm lens, appropriate for family photos and simple landscapes. Add breathtaking scale to panoramic vistas with a wide-angle lens of 28mm or 35mm. These lenses allow sharp focus over great distances (known to photographers as "depth of field"). With a wide-angle lens, it is possible to include flowers, an interesting tree or an unusual rock formation in the foreground for perspective.

To capture details, move in close. This helps eliminate cluttered backgrounds and fills the frame with color or action. A macro lens (100mm-105mm) is ideal for flower or butterfly close-ups. A short telephoto lens (150mm-200mm) pulls deer, alligators or large birds into prominence. Pack a longer telephoto (300mm-500mm) to stalk elusive species such as bears or songbirds.

Camera movement is the most common cause of blurry photos. As a rule of thumb, you can't hand-hold a camera at a shutter speed slower than the reciprocal of the lens length. For example, you could palm a camera with a wide-angle lens at 1/30 second, but with a long telephoto in hand, you should shoot at 1/500 second or faster. Mounting the camera on a sturdy tripod and tripping the shutter with a cable release eliminates most shakiness.

Film choice depends upon how you wish to display your results. For color prints, choose negative films. To project slides, and perhaps print some of the best, opt for transparency films. Purchase a few extra rolls, as well as fresh camera batteries.

Photography records patterns of light on film. Whether your camera is automatic or manual, film "sees" light differently than the human eye. For example, a camera won't capture the entire range of tones in a sunny, midday scene. When bright sky and highlights are properly exposed, shadows will be dark and featureless. Conversely, if enough light strikes the film to bring out the details in the shadows, sunlit spots will be badly overexposed. Avoid these problems by shooting between sunrise and 9am or between 4pm and sunset, the so-called "magic hours" of dawn and dusk when the landscapes are illuminated by warm, glowing light. Overcast days provide even light excellent for close-ups and portraits. By bracketing – or taking extra shots at various exposures – you should be able to produce a perfectly-lit shot.

Pleasing photographs display a strong center of interest. They send a clear visual message why the photographer chose that place or time to trip the shutter. As you aim your camera, pause to consider the composition. Horizontal lines impart a peaceful mood; diagonals suggest action. Read the landscape, study light, and look for interesting angles and perspectives.

Successful photos will enhance your memory of nature's wonders. Mastering your equipment, lighting and composition helps preserve vacations on film and provides enjoyment for years to come. ∎

Setting up a shot.

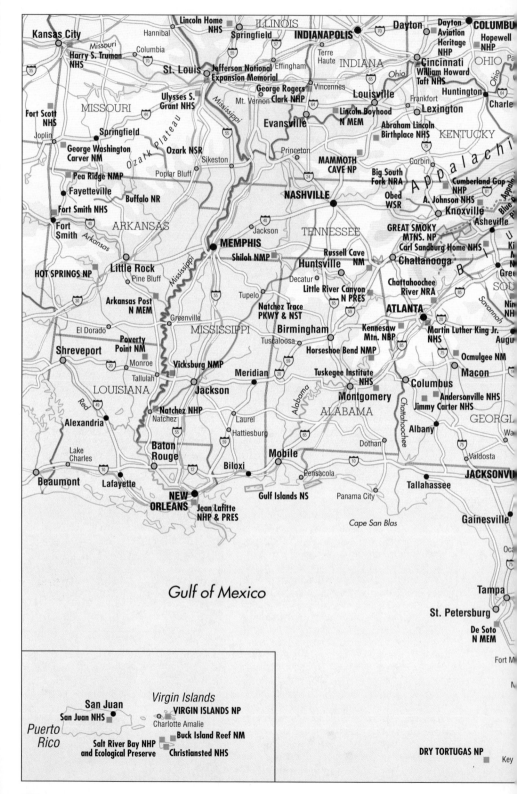

Kansas City

Harry S. Truman NHS

Missouri

Columbia

Hannibal

Lincoln Home NHS

Springfield

ILLINOIS

INDIANAPOLIS

Dayton

Dayton Aviation Heritage NHP

COLUMBUS

Hopewell NHP

OHIO

Pa

Fort Scott NHS

Joplin

MISSOURI

St. Louis

Jefferson National Expansion Memorial

Ulysses S. Grant NHS

Mt. Vernon

Effingham

George Rogers Clark NHP

Vincennes

Terre Haute

INDIANA

Ohio

Louisville

Lincoln Boyhood N MEM

Frankfort

Cincinnati

William Howard Taft NHS

Huntington

Lexington

Charle

Evansville

Princeton

Abraham Lincoln Birthplace NHS

KENTUCKY

Springfield

George Washington Carver NM

Pea Ridge NMP

Fayetteville

Fort Smith NHS

Ozark Plateau

Ozark NSR

Sikeston

Poplar Bluff

Buffalo NR

MAMMOTH CAVE NP

Corbin

Big South Fork NRA

Cumberland Gap NHP

A. Johnson NHS

Obed WSR

Knoxville

Asheville

Appalachi

Fort Smith

ARKANSAS

Arkansas

Jackson

NASHVILLE

TENNESSEE

GREAT SMOKY MTNS. NP

Carl Sandburg Home NHS

Ki

HOT SPRINGS NP

Little Rock

Pine Bluff

Memphis

Shiloh NMP

Russell Cave NM

Huntsville

Chattanooga

B

Decatur

Little River Canyon N PRES

Chattahoochee River NRA

Gre

SOU

Arkansas Post N MEM

Mississippi

Tupelo

ATLANTA

Nin NH

El Dorado

Greenville

MISSISSIPPI

Natchez Trace PKWY & NST

Birmingham

Tuscaloosa

Kennesaw Mtn. NBP

Martin Luther King Jr. NHS

Augu

Shreveport

Poverty Point NM

Monroe

Vicksburg NMP

Meridian

Horseshoe Bend NMP

Ocmulgee NM

Macon

Tallulah

LOUISIANA

Jackson

Tuskegee Institute NHS

Columbus

Andersonville NHS

GEORGI

Red

Natchez NHP

Natchez

Laurel

Montgomery

ALABAMA

Jimmy Carter NHS

Albany

Wa

Alexandria

Hattiesburg

Dothan

Valdosta

Lake Charles

Baton Rouge

Biloxi

Mobile

Pensacola

Tallahassee

JACKSONVI

Beaumont

Lafayette

NEW ORLEANS

Jean Lafitte NHP & PRES

Gulf Islands NS

Panama City

Cape San Blas

Gainesville

Gulf of Mexico

Oca

Tampa

St. Petersburg

De Soto N MEM

Fort M

N

San Juan

San Juan NHS

Puerto Rico

Virgin Islands

VIRGIN ISLANDS NP

Charlotte Amalie

Buck Island Reef NM

Salt River Bay NHP and Ecological Preserve

Christiansted NHS

DRY TORTUGAS NP

Key

THE SOUTH

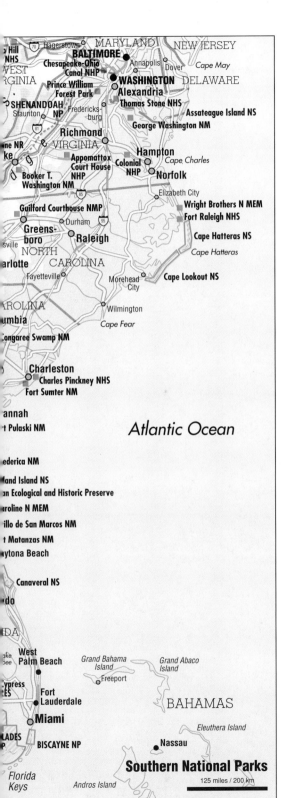

Southern National Parks

125 miles / 200 km

Hiking through the South in 1867, John Muir proclaimed it "the most favored province of bird and flower." Like Muir, millions of travelers have been enchanted by the profusion of living things in the region's mist-shrouded mountains, vast wetlands and balmy coast.

The most-visited park in the South – and, for that matter, the most-visited in the nation – is Great Smoky Mountains. Sprawling across a half-million acres on the Tennesee–North Carolina border, the Smokies boast the highest peaks in the East and some of the country's most diverse plant and animal life.

Connected to the Smokies by the Blue Ridge Parkway is Shenandoah National Park. Ensconced amid the Blue Ridge Mountains of Virginia, it runs along the jagged spine of the Appalachians and features leaping streams, emerald forests and gorgeous views of the valleys.

Along the Appalachians' western shoulder, Big South Fork National River and Recreation Area protects a stunning river gorge in the Cumberland Plateau, attracting white-water rafters, mountain bikers and hikers. Farther west, the steaming waters of Hot Springs bubble up from the Ouachita Mountains in Arkansas, and the bizarre passageways of Mammoth Cave – the world's longest mapped cave system – honeycomb a thick bed of limestone in Kentucky.

Down south, the Everglades sprawl across 1½ million acres (607,000 hectares) at the tip of Florida. Its saw-grass plains and mangrove swamps sustain a rich variety of life, including alligators, crocodiles, otters and 300 species of birds. Visitors can get a close-up look at the fragile coral reefs at nearby Biscayne National Park or explore the reefs of the Dry Tortugas, about 70 miles (113 km) from Key West. Marine life also abounds in the Caribbean, where about two-thirds of the island of St John is preserved at Virgin Islands National Park.

● *For a key to the symbols used on this map, please see page 119.*

SHENANDOAH AND THE BLUE RIDGE PARKWAY

Once upon a time, according to Cherokee legend, everything lived in the sky. When the sky became too crowded, a diving beetle plunged into the ocean and emerged with a ball of mud. The ball of mud grew enormously, but it was too soggy for anything to live on it. So a buzzard volunteered to fly close to the earth and dry it with his wings. The buzzard flapped and flapped but soon tired and fell from the sky. Its outstretched wings form the mountains we know as the southern Appalachians, home of **Shenandoah National Park**.

Unlike most national parks, Shenandoah was pieced together from private land, much of it damaged by logging, farming and erosion. Situated in Virginia's **Blue Ridge Mountains**, an eastern rampart of the Appalachian chain, the park is a long, narrow corridor of ridges and valleys clothed in dense forest and laced with leaping streams and waterfalls. Running along the backbone of the mountains is **Skyline Drive**, a 105-mile (169-km) scenic highway that serves as the park's main thoroughfare.

Twelve thousand years ago, Native Americans made forays up these forested ridges to gather chestnuts, hickory nuts, wild berries and medicinal plants. Hunters stalked deer, woodland elk and bison, often using fire to drive the animals from cover or to lure them into greening meadows recovering from recent burns.

The first European settlers preferred to farm rich bottomlands in the Virginia and North Carolina Piedmont. By the mid-1700s, as settlers proliferated and arable land dwindled, farmers began to clear the lower slopes of the Blue Ridge, named for the ever-present veil of thin blue haze that drifts between the peaks.

At first they "deadened" trees by stripping the bark around the base. After the leaves shriveled, sunlight penetrated to the forest floor. But the thin soil eroded easily, leaving rocky rubble where shortly before corn and beans had flourished. Although the mountains were sparsely populated, families often moved when the fields played out. By the early 1900s, much of the Blue Ridge had been cleared and there were few plots of fertile soil left to exploit.

The effort to create a national park in the Blue Ridge was launched in the 1920s, and construction of Skyline Drive was begun in 1931. Much of the work was done by the Civilian Conservation Corps, created by President Franklin D. Roosevelt to relieve unemployment during the Great Depression. After more than a decade of land acquisition and boundary disputes, the park was dedicated in 1936. More than 2,000 people still lived within the park, however, and relocation was no easy matter. Despite poor economic conditions, many families resisted pressure to move away from their beloved mountain homes.

A second major project – the **Blue Ridge Parkway** – was also started in the 1930s. Described by former Park Service director William Penn Mott, Jr, as "the most graceful road in America," the Blue Ridge Parkway stretches 469 miles (755 km) along the backbone of

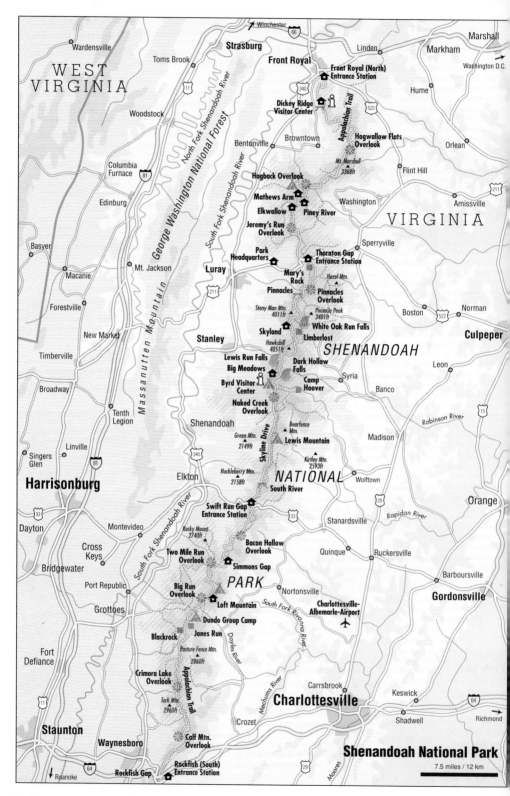

WEST
VIRGINIA

Wardensville
Toms Brook
Strasburg
Front Royal
Winchester
Linden
Markham
Marshall
Washington D.C.

Woodstock

North Fork Shenandoah River

George Washington National Forest

Front Royal (North)
Entrance Station

Hume

Columbia
Furnace

Edinburg

Bentonville
Browntown

Dickey Ridge
Visitor Center

Hogwallow Flats
Overlook

Appalachian Trail

522

Orlean

Flint Hill

Basyer

Macanie

Mt. Jackson

South Fork Shenandoah River

Mt. Marshall
3368ft

Hogback Overlook

Mathews Arm
Elkwallow
Piney River

VIRGINIA

Washington

211

Amissville

Forestville

Luray

Jeremy's Run
Overlook

Park
Headquarters

Sperryville

Thornton Gap
Entrance Station

Massanutten Mountain

New Market

211

Mary's
Rock

Pinnacles

Hazel Mtn.

Pinnacles
Overlook

Boston

Norman

522

Timberville

Stanley

Stony Man Mtn.
4011ft

Pinnacle Peak
3401ft

Skyland

White Oak Run Falls
Limberlost

SHENANDOAH

Culpeper

Broadway

Tenth
Legion

Hawksbill
4051ft

Lewis Run Falls
Big Meadows
Byrd Visitor
Center

Dark Hollow
Falls

Camp
Hoover

Syria

Leon

Banco

Robinson River

15

Singers
Glen

Linville

81

Naked Creek
Overlook

Shenandoah

Green Mtn.
2149ft

Skyline Drive

Bearfence
Mtn.

Lewis Mountain

Madison

Harrisonburg

Dayton

33

Montevideo

Elkton

340

Huckleberry Mtn.
2158ft

Kirtland Mtn.
2593ft

NATIONAL

South River

Wolftown

Orange

Cross
Keys

Bridgewater

South Fork Shenandoah River

Rocky Mount
2740ft

Swift Run Gap
Entrance Station

Bacon Hollow
Overlook

33

Stanardsville

29

Rapidan River

Port Republic

Two Mile Run
Overlook

Simmons Gap

PARK

Nortonsville

Quinque

Ruckersville

Barboursville

Grottoes

Big Run
Overlook

Loft Mountain

South Fork Rivanna River

Charlottesville-
Albemarle-Airport

Gordonsville

Fort
Defiance

Blackrock

Dundo Group Camp

Jones Run

Doyles River

Pasture Fence Mtn.
2860ft

Mechums River

Carrsbrook

Keswick

64

Crimora Lake
Overlook

Appalachian Trail

Turk Mtn.
2960ft

Charlottesville

Shadwell

Richmond

11

Staunton

Waynesboro

Calf Mtn.
Overlook

Crozet

Shenandoah National Park

64

Roanoke

Rockfish Gap

Rockfish (South)
Entrance Station

29

Moores

7.5 miles / 12 km

the Appalachian Mountains between Shenandoah and Great Smoky Mountains national parks, crossing the Virginia state border into North Carolina. Along the way are countless overlooks, historic sites, wayside exhibits, hiking trails and museums.

To make finding your way easier, both Skyline Drive and the Blue Ridge Parkway are marked by mileposts starting from their northernmost points. Together, these two scenic drives form the longest and one of the most stunning roads in the National Park System.

Daughter of the stars: The "windshield" views along Skyline Drive are stupendous, but the true essence of Shenandoah lies beyond the pavement. Consider for a moment just how far the park has come in so short a time. Only 60 years ago, these mountains were dominated by bare, eroded ridges and hardscrabble farms. Today, only about 5 percent of Shenandoah is developed; the rest is occupied by a mature and nearly continuous array of pines, oaks, hickories, hemlocks and tulip poplars.

The forest is crosshatched with more than 500 miles (800 km) of hiking and horseback-riding trails, including 95 miles (153 km) of the **Appalachian Trail** which roughly parallels Skyline Drive and then continues south along the Blue Ridge Parkway for about 100 miles (160 km) before veering west into **Jefferson National Forest**.

Southern Appalachian forests are remarkably diverse. There are about 25 dominant tree species here, exploiting a wide range of habitats from moist and shady to dry and sunny. Another two dozen trees are slightly less prolific but still common. Well over 1,000 types of flowering plants, mosses, ferns and countless fungi flourish. By early spring, visitors start their annual pilgrimage to the park to see the parade of wildflowers. Hepatica kicks off the season, blooming when the snow melts. By April, the woods are carpeted with trilliums, phlox, violets and spring beauties. Azaleas and mountain laurel bloom from mid-May to mid-June in the higher elevations. Catawba rhododendron follows in June.

Visitors flock to the ridges in October

when the foliage flames in a final burst of color. Gum, sourwood, dogwood, sumac and sugar maple are abundant and especially colorful along southern sections of the Blue Ridge, eliciting "oohs" and "ahhs" of delight from visitors around each new curve.

When settlers harvested the forests, bears, deer and turkeys were displaced from the Blue Ridge. But as their habitats recovered, wildlife – large and small – has returned.

White-tailed deer graze peacefully along the roadsides, barely raising their heads as cars pass. Does bring their spotted fawns into the open by midsummer. Gray squirrels and chipmunks skitter across the leafy forest floor in search of acorns and hickory nuts. Gray foxes prowl from dusk to dawn, as do striped skunks and their rarer spotted cousins. Woodchucks (also called groundhogs) gorge themselves on roadside grasses. Bears forage for nuts, berries and small animals. Combined, the parks shelter more than 200 species of birds throughout the year, including a

Hiking on a rainy day.

variety of warblers, woodpeckers, vireos, owls and hawks.

Doing the drive: If you visit Shenandoah from the north in the summer, you will enter a shady green tunnel of hardwoods upon leaving Highway 340 at **Front Royal**. Like a winding staircase, the pavement curves around the hills, then sprawls into a breathtaking overlook above the **Shenandoah Valley**. Nearby **Dickey Ridge Visitor Center** provides an introduction to Shenandoah's natural and human history with exhibits, books, free maps and pamphlets. Just across the road, for approximately 1½ miles, **Fox Hollow Trail** loops through old farmsteads reclaimed by pines and hardwoods.

By mile 21, you will be nearing an elevation of 3,400 feet (1,036 meters), and from **Hogback Overlook** on a clear day, you can count several bends in the **Shenandoah River** meandering through the verdant valley. About a mile south, several trails diverge from the **Mathews Arm Area**, including the nearly 4-mile (6-km) round-trip to **Overall Falls**. The double cascade has a drop of 93 feet (28 meters), but it slows to a trickle in dry weather. As with most trails, going downhill is easy. Allow double the time for the more arduous return.

For an easier hike, try the 3½-mile (5½-km) self-guiding **Traces Nature Trail**, which leads past a few remaining signs of early white settlement now being reclaimed by the forest. Farther south at mile 37, a steep 3-mile (5-km) round-trip leads to **Corbin Cabin**, a log home built in 1909 by George Corbin, whose family scratched a living from the soil in this isolated "holler."

At **Thornton Gap**, Highway 211 crosses Skyline Drive. To rise above the scene, park at **Panorama Restaurant** and hike the Appalachian Trail to **Mary's Rock**, named for the bride of one of the area's first settlers. The nearly 2-mile (3-km) ascent gains 1,210 feet (369 meters), but the 360-degree view is worth the effort. Continuing south, the rocky visage of **Stony Man** appears above the drive as milepost 39 comes into view. The trail to the 4,011-foot

Shenandoah means "daughter of the stars."

216

(1,227-meter) summit begins at the **Skyland** resort.

Touch the sky: During the 1890s, George Freeman Pollock, an enthusiastic promoter of the region, built Skyland on a 5,000-acre (2,000-hectare) tract at the head of **Kettle Canyon**. Most original buildings have been replaced, but the resort continues to provide lodging for hikers, horseback riders and those who simply want to relax in the cool mountain air. Across the drive, a 3½-mile (6-km) trail follows **Whiteoak Run** as it cascades down a series of six waterfalls. The first falls, an 86-foot (26-meter) plunge, is 2⅓ miles (4 km) away and 1,040 feet (317 meters) lower than Skyland.

Hikers can loop back through the **Limberlost**, a superlative grove of hemlocks, some of which are 400 years old. Pollock saved the cathedral-like setting in which sunbeams are filtered by misty air and sounds are muffled by a carpet of ferns and mosses by offering his neighbors $10 for every massive tree they did not cut down.

At 3,680 feet (1,122 meters), Skyland is the highest point on Skyline Drive. A few miles farther south are trailheads for 4,049-foot (1,234-meter) **Hawksbill**, the highest summit in the park, whose cloud-shrouded, windswept peak looms for miles. Three routes give hikers a choice – either short and steep or progressively longer with easier grades.

Continuing south, **Big Meadows** marks the halfway point on Skyline Drive with a campground, visitor center, naturalist programs and horseback riding. It is also home of the **Big Meadows Lodge**, a model of rustic elegance constructed of local chestnut in 1939.

It is not unusual to see deer among the waving grasses of the 300-acre (120-hectare) meadow at dawn or dusk. In late spring, brilliant male indigo buntings sing bubbly songs as they flit about in search of mates. Trails radiate east to **Dark Hollow Falls** and west to **Lewis Run Falls**. Dark Hollow, which requires a round-trip of 1⅓ miles (2 km), is the waterfall closest to Skyline Drive. The trail to Lewis Run is longer and steeper,

"Shelves" of fungus grow on a fallen log.

but the view of the tiered 90-foot (27-meter) falls is worth the extra effort.

It's a short drive to **Milam Gap**, where you can park the car and begin the 2-mile (3-km) jaunt to **Camp Hoover**, a mountain hideaway built by President Herbert Hoover to escape the pressures – and the summertime heat – of life in Washington, DC. Getting there can be a little tricky: follow the Appalachian Trail to the **Mill Prong Trail** and then turn onto the access road. A National Historical Landmark, the site is still occasionally used by government officials.

The rocky mile-long scramble to the top of **Bearfence Mountain** (mile 56.4) requires the use of knees and elbows in a few places. Once on top, you will be enticed by nonstop views urging you to linger and to catch your breath while pondering jagged greenstone rock outcrops that could well stop a bear.

Farther along, the **South River** picnic area at mile 62.8 is decked out in white trillium each spring. Lucky hikers may spot yellow lady slipper orchids along the 2½-mile (4-km) round-trip to **South River Falls**. Like most waterfalls, the mossy rocks are slick; several visitors have taken unfortunate side trips to the hospital emergency room because of them. Stay on the marked trails and pay particular attention to your footing in damp areas.

Loft Mountain is the southernmost campground along Skyline Drive. Rangers offer summer nature programs, and the self-guiding, 1⅓-mile (2-km) **Deadening Trail** explores forest succession from the clearing of fields by settlers to the return of locusts, hickories and oaks.

From Loft Mountain, you slowly descend to the terminus of Skyline Drive at Rockfish Gap. For a final streamside hike, try **Doyles River** or **Jones Run**. Both have pretty cascades, accessible from trailheads at mile 81.1 or 84.1. At mile 84.8, a 1-mile (2-km) round-trip to **Blackrock** showcases a vista overlooking the historic villages of **Grottoes** and **Port Republic** in the southern Shenandoah Valley.

Blue Ridge Parkway: To continue your mountain odyssey, cross Interstate 64 at

Overlooking the Blue Ridge Parkway.

Rockfish Gap and head south to **Humpback Rocks Visitor Center** on the Blue Ridge Parkway. Here, a reconstructed farmstead explores the lives of turn-of-the-century mountaineers.

Improved roads and electricity were slow to reach this rugged land. Families tended large vegetable gardens, putting potatoes, dried beans and jars of apple butter in the root cellar for safekeeping. They butchered and smoked several hogs each winter and supplemented their diets with squirrel, venison and other wild game. For entertainment, they sang ballads accompanied by banjos or guitars and repeated tales told by their parents and grandparents. Visitors with a few extra moments can hike a short distance south on the Appalachian Trail to "**The Rocks**," the landmark on the original wagon road that passed the farm.

At **James River** crossing (mile 63.8) are remnants of the **Kanawha Canal**. This antebellum water highway flowed west from Richmond for 200 miles (322 km), with mule-drawn barges bringing salt, bolts of cloth, guns and ammunition to mountain communities. The settlers sold cured meats, whiskey and tanned hides, which were transported to willing buyers downriver. A self-guiding trail begins at the visitor center.

The parkway climbs from its lowest point at James River southwest to **Peaks of Otter**. Here a visitor center, campground, lodge and restaurant nestle in a forest clearing that offers dramatic views of **Sharp Top** (3,875 feet/1,181 meters) and **Flat Top** (4,001 feet/1,220 meters).

The parkway skirts the eastern edge of **Roanoke**, a sleepy settlement that grew into a thriving community with the coming of the railroad in the 1880s. South of Roanoke lies **Mabry Mill**, with a water wheel where corn and buckwheat are ground. Sorghum making, apple butter cooking and blacksmithing are seasonally reenacted here. Demonstrations of weaving take place on a century-old four-poster loom at the **Brinegar Cabin** (mile 238), situated in the highland meadow known as **Doughton Park**.

Twenty miles (32 km) of hiking trails

High-elevation grassy bald.

GROWING UP IN THE PARKS

Martha Ellen Zenfell lived in Shenandoah National Park in the 1950s and early 60s. Her father was the park engineer.

When we moved to Shenandoah, we had to give our dog away, as no domestic pets were allowed. We were heartbroken, but adjusted pretty quickly because of the other animals around. The bears tended not to bother us, as they lived at the top of the mountain and we lived at the foot, but deer were very common; they used to come right up to our front yard at twilight. At certain times each year hunting was allowed on the public land very near park headquarters, so the deer would seek refuge with us. My mother was afraid to let us play outside during hunting season; whenever we did, we always had to wear red, so the hunters wouldn't shoot us.

We also had snakes and spiders. One day I went to retrieve a ball from a hole in our yard and discovered my hand was only inches away from a black widow spider, a nest of babies, and the remains of the spider's mate (she had eaten the rest).

Ugh! Another time, we found a huge snake, long and fat like a black rubber hose, curled up on the hot water tank in the basement. I wasn't crazy about those times.

But I loved all the others. We had the whole of the park and the Blue Ridge Mountains to play in. There weren't many children, only about six, but what we lacked in numbers we made up for in activity: we were outside from early morning to late dusk. The neighbors had a great big bell on their back porch that they rang when it was time for dinner. The sound used to travel for miles, it seemed, in the clear, mountain air, so whenever we heard the gong we knew it was time to go in. We would get really sad.

Every so often, we would find flint arrowheads and other relics in the ground, and the big oak tree at the bottom of our yard had a hatchet buried in the bark. We never knew if it was an authentic hatchet from Indian times or a more modern one, but the hatchet gave that tree a certain mystique, and it was always our favorite, especially when one of the park rangers built a two-story treehouse for us in it.

The other children were mainly boys, but I didn't let that stand in my way. I would put on the frilliest dress my mother would allow, then go out and climb the tallest tree or ride my bicycle backwards down the hill that was too scary for anyone else to attempt. We were daredevils, little savages, really, but always did well at school. Whenever there was a nature project, like identifying leaves, or documenting the habits of birds, the park naturalist would help us and we would get really good grades.

We always made our own decorations, too, embellishing the house at Christmas with pine cones and pine branches from our yard, or gathering wild violets at dawn to make into Easter corsages. Picking wildflowers probably isn't allowed now.

The event I remember most was the day our pet skunk arrived. The mother had been run over by a car, leaving behind four babies. Because they were too young to survive in the wild, the naturalist asked each family if they wanted a little skunk. When we all said yes, he took them to the vet to have them deodorized. We named ours "Romy" (short for Aroma), and he used to scurry around the house like a big, hairy cat. I took pictures of him to school and all the town kids were impressed. Romy was very sweet, but always preferred outdoors to indoors and didn't like being dressed up in dolls' clothes very much. Looking back, I guess it wasn't such a good idea to try and domesticate a skunk. ■

The author at Shenandoah.

radiate from the nearby campground. Deer frequent the grassy meadows at dawn and dusk. Farther south, **Northwest Trading Post** (mile 258.6) offers mouthwatering country hams, sourwood honey and an array of crafts.

All along the parkway you'll see examples of homemade fencing, including post-and-rail and snake-and-buck styles. Old-time rails were split from chestnut, a durable forest tree that was common in the Blue Ridge Mountains prior to 1920. Unfortunately a blight introduced from Asia spread rapidly through the East in the early 1900s, killing millions of stately chestnuts. The names **Chestnut Ridge** and **Chestnut Hill** are local reminders of trees that once dominated the surrounding forest. Other intriguing place names along the parkway include **Smart View** (a "right smart view" in early May when the dogwoods bloom), **Jumpinoff Rocks** and **Blowing Rock**, where prevailing upslope winds usually return hats sailed out over the edge of the bluff.

South of Blowing Rock, the skyline of western North Carolina is dominated by 5,964-foot (1,818-meter) **Grandfather Mountain**, named for the antiquity of its rock formations or for the face it's said to resemble. The peak is the centerpiece of a private recreation area adjoining the parkway. Many visitors hike here, and a few of the more daring indulge in the sport of hang gliding. A nearby 7½ -mile (12-km) section of the parkway was the last to be completed. It includes **Linn Cove Viaduct**, an engineering marvel that soars 1,243 feet (379 meters) across a rough chasm with minimal disturbance to the fragile vegetation below.

At mile 316.3, **Linville Falls** dramatically plunges 90 feet (27 meters) over stair-stepping rock ledges. Impressive at any season, the gorge glows with especially breathtaking bursts of gold and crimson in mid- to late October. Gemstones gleam in competing rainbow hues at the **Museum of North Carolina Minerals** (mile 331), which displays an amazing array of rocks.

The mountains become increasingly

contorted near **Mount Mitchell**, and the parkway follows several tunnels through the rugged ridges rather than traversing them. The 6,684-foot (2,037-meter) peak, the highest point east of the Mississippi River, lies within **Mount Mitchell State Park**, accessible from the parkway via Highway 128.

A 6-mile (10-km) stretch of the parkway rolls through windswept **Craggy Gardens**, a rhododendron thicket that reaches purple-flowering perfection in mid-June. Then the road descends and circles southeast of **Asheville**. The **Folk Art Center** (mile 382) offers traditional and contemporary crafts.

The imposing **Biltmore House**, a 255-room mansion completed by railroad heir George Vanderbilt in 1895, stands 2½ miles (4 km) north of the parkway off Highway 25. Vanderbilt sought the advice of the country's best foresters and encouraged them to manage his 100,000-acre (40,500-hectare) estate for renewable resources. Most of the Vanderbilt lands are now incorporated in **Pisgah National Forest**, visible from mileposts

390 to 425. **Cradle of Forestry Visitor Center** (on Highway 276 east of Wagon Road Gap) interprets the forest history of that era.

Flirting with heaven: The parkway flirts with the heavens in its final 60 miles (97 km). At mile 408.6, **Mount Pisgah**, site of an inn, campground and restaurant at the 5,000-foot (1,520-meter) level, offers stunning views.

The road continues upward, over **Richland Balsam** and on to **Waterrock Knob**, with a view that spans four states. The spruce-fir forests at these elevations share climatic conditions with the boreal forests of Canada. Numerous dead firs, however, stand in mute testimony to damage from the balsam woolly adelgid, an invasive forest pest from abroad that has proved to be a stubborn and destructive guest.

Panoramas at **Waterrock Knob**, **Heintooga Ridge** (mile 458.2) and **Big Witch Gap** (mile 461.9) include glimpses of the **Great Smoky Mountains**. From Big Witch Gap, the parkway descends into the town of **Cherokee**, heart of the Cherokees' **Qualla Reservation** and gateway to **Great Smoky Mountains National Park**.

For nearly 600 miles (970 km), Skyline Drive and the Blue Ridge Parkway provide a high road to mountain adventure. The roads are intended for leisurely motoring, not for serious point-to-point travel. The speed limit is 35 mph (56 kmph) on Skyline Drive and 45 mph (72 kmph) on the parkway, but with frequent stops and occasional tie-ups actual travel time dawdles from 20 to 30 mph (32–48 kmph).

At that rate, the entire 575-mile (925-km) trip requires a week. High-elevation areas with their frequently foggy conditions can slow the pace even more. Winter ice storms temporarily close portions of the route, and many facilities close in winter.

Food, gas and lodging are usually available at "crossovers," junctions where major highways intersect the scenic drive. If you are in a hurry, choose a parallel route, such as Interstate 81 through central Virginia or Interstate 40 in western North Carolina.

Left, wild strawberry. **Right**, a hungry but uninvited guest.

GREAT SMOKY MOUNTAINS

Everyone who comes to the Great Smoky Mountains, it seems, has a favorite trail, a favorite waterfall, a favorite flower or a special view. These comforting old mountains in North Carolina and Tennessee inspire strong attachments. Maybe it's the history of the place. This national park, one of the East's largest and the most visited in the country, was home to many people not so long ago.

Only about 60 years ago, the 500,000 acres (202,343 hectares) of **Great Smoky Mountains National Park** were carved out of private land. History here is close to the surface and still very much alive. People return to their old homes to reunite with families, fill a jug with clear spring water, lay flowers on the grave of a loved one, sing the old hymns, stitch a quilt or saw on a fiddle.

With the arrival of springtime, they keep their eyes open for ramps. What is a ramp? Well, it's a wild leek, stronger kin of the onion. And when they're ripe, mountain folk offer samples to anyone willing to try them. It's an unforgettable experience. A former Smokies resident says ramps can make Democrats smell like Republicans, and vice versa.

Rising well over 6,000 feet (1,829 meters), the Smoky Mountains also provide much-needed respite from steamy lowland summers.

Visitors are attracted to the flowers that sprout in incredible profusion from spring through summer, and to the mantle of green that softens the mountains' rocky contours. They seek the wild streams and waterfalls, clear impetuous water spilling over rocks with swallow-tail butterflies dancing in the mist; the excellent trails, including a 70-mile (112-km) stretch of the **Appalachian Trail**; and the black bears, bobcats, red wolves, white-tailed deer and other wildlife that use the Smokies both as refuge and as nursery ground.

Making the mountains: At the southern end of the Appalachian chain, the Great Smokies are the highest mountains in the East and among the oldest in North America. The basement rock, the crystalline gneisses and schists that underlie everything, were made into their present form about a billion years ago. Even geologists, who measure time quite differently than most mortals, consider this to be very old rock.

On top of this foundation sits a slightly younger group of rocks known as the Ocoee series – mostly lightly metamorphosed sandstones and siltstones. This is the rock you see exposed along **Newfound Gap Road**, the park's main thoroughfare, which cuts across the mountains between Tennessee and North Carolina. Their nondescript gray color is relieved by splashes of iridescent green moss and grayish-green lichens. Early mountaineers called the house-sized boulders graybacks; other kinds of rock were known in the vernacular as flintrock, dirtrock and slaterock.

One member of the Ocoee group, the Thunderhead Sandstone, resists the work of the countless streams that churn down the mountainsides. The rock tends to form ledges over which the streams

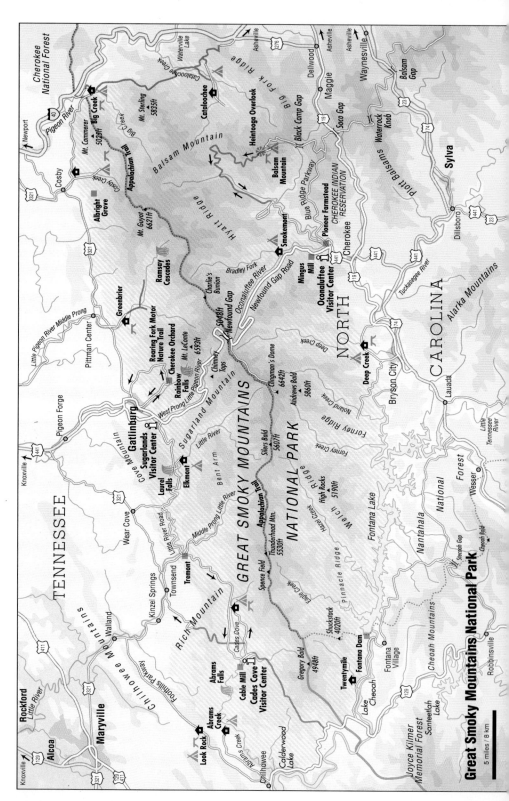

Great Smoky Mountains National Park

5 miles / 8 km

cascade. Many of these beautiful waterfalls are within reasonable walking distance, including Abrams, Rainbow, Grotto, Henwallow, Juneywhank and Laurel, just to name a few.

How these ancient rocks were uplifted to such great heights is something geologists are still trying to figure out. The classic theory is that two of Earth's major continental plates, the North American and African, crashed into each other about 270 million years ago. The immense compression of these two great masses literally buckled the crust up into mountains. This event may also have been responsible for the intense heat and pressure that changed sedimentary rocks into metamorphic rocks. Recent research has cast doubt on this textbook, continent-to-continent explanation, but key evidence remains to be found to support a revised view.

Cherokee homeland: When the first white settlers entered the region in the late 1700s, the Smokies were inhabited by the Cherokee Indians, who named the mountains *Shaconage*, "place of the blue smoke." The Cherokees built homes of logs and settled in villages along the **Oconaluftee River** and **Deep Creek**, on the southern edge of the present-day national park. Each of the seven clans chose its own "mother town" and chief. Their famous chief, Sequoyah, invented a written alphabet, and the Cherokees published their own newspaper.

The rocks, rivers and forests furnished the Cherokees with cane for their baskets, stone for their pipes, herbs for their medicines, and food for their stomachs. They held their annual celebrations beside the waters of the Oconaluftee. They believed that Long Man, the river, gathered together his Chattering Children, all the tributary streams. In caves in the mountains lived the Little People. Though mostly benevolent beings, at times the Little People could cause an outsider to lose his way.

The arrival of Europeans, mostly of Scotch-Irish heritage, in the 18th century spelled the demise of Cherokee society. Between 1783 and 1819, frontiersmen from Pennsylvania, Virginia and the Carolinas flooded through the gaps in the mountains. Revolutionary War veterans received land grants in the Smokies, and treaties were signed that left the Cherokees with only a remnant of their ancient homeland.

In 1838–39 most of the Cherokees were marched to Oklahoma on the infamous Trail of Tears. A few hid out in the fastness of the Great Smoky Mountains, in places like Deep Creek, but eventually the ones who remained were sequestered on the **Qualla Reservation** bordering the park in North Carolina.

A good place to learn more about Cherokee life and history is in **Cherokee**, North Carolina, just outside the park's south entrance. There you can visit **Oconaluftee Indian Village**, a replica of an 18th-century Cherokee settlement; the **Qualla Arts and Crafts Mutual Center**; and just across the street, the **Museum of the Cherokee Indian**. An outdoor drama, *Unto These Hills*, is performed in summer.

The flat valley of the Oconaluftee River was also one of the first choices for the homes and farms of the new

Crescent moon over Newfound Gap.

pioneers. Adjacent to the park's **Ocona-luftee Visitor Center**, about 2 miles (3 km) from Cherokee, you can get a sense of what life was like on a small, self-sufficient 19th-century farmstead. The **Mountain Farm Museum** is a collection of historic buildings moved from various locations throughout the park. During the **Mountain Life Festival** (held on the third weekend in September), the museum comes alive with a variety of living-history demonstrations. Activities vary from year to year, but you may be able to learn how to make molasses or apple butter, enjoy some mountain music, help a pioneer woman weave a coverlet, watch a farmer plow his field with draft horses, hear the clank of a blacksmith's hammer on hot iron, and inhale the sweet aroma of hickory smoke twining from a chimney. On a walk through the museum, you can also see a house, barn, corn crib and other original, finely crafted buildings.

A half-mile (1 km) away is **Mingus Mill**, where you can observe a working gristmill and talk to a miller. In 1886 Dr John Mingus, son of a pioneer Ocona-luftee settler, had Sion T. Early build a mill for him on **Mingus Creek**. The long wooden millrace delivers water from the creek to a penstock, then to a turbine beneath the three-story gray building. Inside, corn is fed into the maws of huge granite millstones.

A miller uses his senses of touch and hearing, more than sight, to tell whether his mill is operating properly. The pitch and hum of the stones as they grind, and the warm, soft feel of the meal between his thumb and forefinger, are the signs he observes. Some old-timers used to say a miller's thumb was worn smooth by feeling the texture of the meal; others of a more cynical bent said it was smooth because he held it on the scale when he weighed the meal!

On mill day, farmers loaded wheat and corn into their wagons and made the journey to the mill. While they waited for a "turn" of corn to be ground, they would swap news, catch up on family business and do a little trading with other farmers.

Interior of church...

Peak experience: From Mingus Mill, it's a slow, curving drive up Newfound Gap Road toward the highest peak in the Smokies – **Clingmans Dome**, at 6,642 feet (2,025 meters). At Newfound Gap, a mile (1.5 km) above sea level, take a 7-mile (11-km) spur road west to the Clingmans Dome parking lot, where a half-mile (1.5-km) trail leads to a concrete observation tower. Be prepared; at these heights, fog is common, and long vistas may be obscured. On a clear day, however, the great ramparts of the Smokies spread before you, blue ridge after blue ridge, separated by deep ravines. Lest you be deceived by their apparent softness, this is rough country.

Up here, the air is crisp (you'll no doubt notice the chill wind and sudden drop in temperature). The forest of red spruce and Fraser fir has the look of Canada. To tell these two evergreens apart, examine the cones and needles. The cones of Fraser fir stand upright on the branches, while the cones of red spruce hang like pendants. Fir needles are flat and blunt-tipped; spruce needles

are spiny and four-cornered. People of the southern mountains called Fraser fir "she balsam" for the white, resinous blisters on the bark that they thought looked like milk.

At Clingmans Dome, the spruce-fir forest reaches its farthest southern limits on the continent. This unique forest fascinates botanists and ecologists because this community is a relict of the ice ages. Once upon a time, glaciers encased a good deal of the southern Appalachians, and the spruce-fir forest enjoyed a wider range. But about 10,000 years ago, the glaciers receded. The boreal forest retreated with them, surviving now only as isolated "islands" in the highest parts of the mountains.

During World War I, red spruce was heavily logged because the wood was desirable for airplanes. And Fraser fir throughout the southern Appalachians are now dying at a swift rate owing to infestation of balsam woolly adelgids. These aphid-like insects attach to the bark and suck sap from the trees. In only a few years, an infested tree dies. So far,

..and mountaineer abin at ades Cove.

park managers have not found a way to stop the onslaught of this wind-borne, non-native insect. An insecticidal soap has been sprayed on some stands, but the extent of the devastation is sadly evident in the ghostly, denuded trees.

What will be the fate of the delicate wood sorrel, the rare northern flying squirrel and the other plants and animals of the spruce-fir forest as their habitat undergoes drastic change? The effects of losing one of the two major species of the spruce-fir forest are still unknown, but scientists agree that they are likely to be far-reaching.

Balds and gaps: Although the Smoky Mountains are not high enough to have a tree line, there are treeless places in these mountains that have drawn people for many, many years. They are called balds, openings covered with grasses or shrubs rather than trees. Pioneers grazed livestock on the balds, and hikers now trek to them for the views they afford. **Andrews Bald**, only 2 miles (3 km) from Clingmans Dome, is within closest walking distance. **Gregory Bald** is accessible along trails out of **Cades Cove**. Even though it is a 10-mile (16-km) round-trip hike, it is popular in late June for its world-class wild azaleas.

How balds originated, and how some have remained open, has raised lively speculation among botanists and others. The grassy balds, like Andrews and Gregory, are covered with mountain oat grass. They probably originated as natural openings, but they may have been maintained by burning, grazing or clearing. The heath balds are different. Here, a tangle of shrubs like sand myrtle, blueberry and laurel grows. Known to mountain people as "hells" or "slicks," heath balds are probably self-maintaining because of periodic fire.

A forest of American beech and yellow birch abuts the spruce-fir forest. These cold-loving northern hardwoods reach their prime in the southern part of the park. The shiny-barked birch are found atop "prop" roots, like Alice-in-Wonderland creatures standing on stilts. To see a pure stand of beech, continue along Newfound Gap Road to Newfound Gap, where you can pick up the Appalachian Trail for a 1-mile (1.5-km) walk to **Indian Gap**. Such beech "gaps" or "orchards" in the swales of the high mountain ridges are one of the mysteries of the Smokies' plant life. They may have been caused by wind.

Forest primeval: The forest of all forests in the southern Appalachians is the cove hardwood type. Used in this sense, "cove" refers to sheltered ravines with moist soils below 4,500 feet (1,372 meters) elevation. The rich conditions favor startling botanical diversity. You may notice as you round a bend on a trail that the woods become shadier, cooler, greener. You crane your neck to see the tops of the trees, 150 to 200 feet (46–61 meters) overhead. In your immediate surroundings there may be 30 different species of deciduous trees – basswood, yellow buckeye, tulip tree, silverbell, sugar maple, hickory and oak among them. Stately eastern hemlocks drape soft branches over dark rhododendrons.

Looking at these dense stands of trees today, it's amazing to think that nearly two-thirds of the Smokies' forests had

A former resident returns to Cades Cove.

been cut down for timber. Logging began on a small scale with the first wave of settlers but accelerated dramatically in the early 20th century as larger companies came into the region with railroads, laborers and steam-powered equipment. Entire mountainsides were denuded, and fires swept through the debris in the wake of logging. Such abuses led to an outcry to save what was left of this last great eastern forest.

But time cures many ills. When people return to their beloved Smoky Mountains these days, they see trees regrowing in the forest, and tangles of moss and vines taking over the old rock walls and home places – a land of infinite natural variety reclaiming itself.

In springtime, the forest will be painted with a breathtaking display of wildflowers – serviceberry, redbud, flowering dogwood, bellwort, bloodroot, fringed phacelia, trilliums, trout lilies, violets, miterwort. You can be certain you are in a cove hardwood forest, one of the most diverse, productive plant communities in the world. The **Cove**

Hardwood Nature Trail at the **Chimneys Picnic Area** (about 5 miles/8 km from Newfound Gap on Newfound Gap Road) is an excellent introduction. This ¾-mile (1 km) walk winds through a cathedral-like cove forest. In spring, the ground is covered in a white cloud of fringed phacelia.

The cove hardwoods were logged heavily during the early part of the century, but some steeper, higher forests were spared because of the difficulty of getting out the logs. You can explore a portion of this virgin, high-country forest farther along Newfound Gap Road at the **Chimney Tops Trail**, a steep 4-mile (6-km) round-trip scramble to the top of dramatic cliffs with glorious views of the surrounding peaks. About a mile away, the **Alum Cave Trail** makes a strenuous 5½-mile (9-km) climb to the 6,593-foot (2,010-meter) summit of **Mount LeConte**. Along the way you'll pass interesting geologic formations such as tunnel-like **Arch Rock** and the towering **Alum Cave Bluffs.** The trail eventually leads to rustic **LeConte**

Mountain farmstead.

Lodge (no electricity; reservations required), the only overnight accommodations in the park.

Cades Cove: From the Smokies' windswept crest, Newfound Gap Road winds down the north face of the mountains, following the tumbling water of the West Prong of the **Little Pigeon River** as it flows into **Sugarlands Valley**. Here you can take in the exhibits at **Sugarlands Visitor Center** and then follow **Little River Road** for a half- or full-day excursion to **Cades Cove**, where you'll find one of the country's best collections of pioneer homes and farmsteads in an "open-air museum."

White farmers began settling Cades Cove in the 1820s, clearing trees, planting crops and raising families. By 1850, nearly 685 people lived in the pastoral valley. Settlers built their homes near good "bold" springs that would reliably pour forth pure sparkling water. Every farm had a springhouse, a small structure built over the natural spring to keep out varmints and debris; it also served as a kind of refrigerator. A meat house, corn crib, hog pen, molasses mill, a few bee gums and an outhouse completed the layout of a typical southern Appalachian farm.

To clear the dense forest, pioneers girdled the bark on trees and left them standing in groves called "deadenings." They used fertile, flat land for their crops of corn, wheat, oats and rye. But as the ground gave out they were forced to move onto the steep-sided hills.

Corn, a gift from the Indians to white settlers, was the staff of life. "You couldn't live on money; you had to have corn," declared a Smokies farmer. Corn was ground into meal and baked into bread, and it was fed to pigs, chickens and horses. Corn in fermented liquid form – better known as "moonshine" – was also a well-known product.

Most farmers in Cades Cove took their wheat and corn to the **John Cable Mill**, powered by a large wooden water wheel near the **Cades Cove Visitor Center**. John Cable's daughter, known as "Aunt" Becky, lived most of her life in the nearby two-story frame house

Great Smoky Mountains is one of the largest parks in the East.

built in 1879. A big barn of cantilever construction is also located nearby. The tree the pioneers chose to make their cabins was the straight-grained yellow poplar, or tulip tree, hewn with a broad axe into logs. Chestnut was favored for split-rail fences. Hard hickory or oak was the best for fuel.

You can enter several other houses on or near the 11-mile (18-km) Cades Cove loop, including the **John Oliver Place**, **Elijah Oliver Place**, **Tipton Place** and **Carter Shields Cabin**. Stroll through a few of them and imagine what life was like a century ago. Notice how cabin corners are carefully joined by hand-hewn dovetail notches. Doors swing on wooden hinges, floors bow and creak, slate hearthstones are swept clean. The walls still give back a strong smell of kerosene and a faint odor of apples.

As soon as a house was finished and the fields were planted, the pioneers set about constructing places of worship. As you tour Cades Cove, you'll come upon the **Primitive Baptist**, **Missionary Baptist** and **Methodist churches**.

D.B. Lawson gave a half-acre (quarter-hectare) of land to the Methodist Church and deeded it to "God Almighty." Behind the immaculate white churches are the cemeteries. Gravestones bear the names of many early Cades Cove settlers – Tipton, Oliver, Gregory, Shields and others. The high number of infant burials bespeak the scarcity of medical care in the mountains in the old days.

People's lives matched the rhythms of the passing seasons. Without grocery stores, they relied on what the land provided. After a winter of eating dried foods, wild greens like watercress, "bear" lettuce and ramps were eagerly harvested in the spring. Summer meant blackberries, blueberries and gooseberries, along with onions, cabbages, peas and potatoes from the garden. In fall, chestnuts were gathered by the bushel, and corn, beans and apples were dried and stored.

Cades Cove is so popular that bumper-to-bumper traffic is a perpetual problem on the loop road. The best solution is to detour onto gravel country roads, like

Early-morning light over the Great Smoky Mountains.

Sparks Lane, park the car and take a picnic basket into the green pastures. Early morning is a magical time to see the cove, when the sun burns swirling mist off the surrounding mountains and spider webs sparkle with dew among the grass. Bluebirds perch on fence-posts, and the horses, cattle and deer go on grazing, oblivious to your presence.

If you're feeling more ambitious, you can pick up the trail to beautiful **Abrams Falls** at the Abrams Falls Parking Area at the west end of the loop road. This moderate, 5-mile (8-km) round-trip follows **Abrams Creek** through drier oak-pine forest. Along the way, watch for trailing arbutus in early spring as well as signs of river otters, graceful aquatic mammals successfully reintroduced here.

Entrance to Eden: If time allows, consider exploring some of the many other roads and trails the park has to offer. On the way back from Cades Cove, for example, you can stop at the **Laurel Falls Parking Area** for a relatively easy 2½-mile (4-km) round-trip to lovely **Laurel Falls**.

From the **Cherokee Orchard Road** in **Gatlinburg**, you can take a scenic drive on the self-guiding **Roaring Fork Motor Nature Trail**, which offers a fine introduction to the park's natural and cultural history as well as excellent views of the surrounding mountains. Hikers may want to stop along the way for a rather strenuous, 7-mile (11-km) round-trip to **Rainbow Falls**.

If you are feeling more ambitious, consider making a side trip out to **Greenbrier Cove**, where you can pick up the rugged 8-mile (13-km) round-trip trail to **Ramsay Cascades**, one of the park's most stunning waterfalls.

Farther east, near **Cosby**, Tennessee, the **Maddron Bald Trail** is a 7-mile (11-km) round-trip to **Albright Grove**, one of the finest stands of virgin forest in the Smokies. Like the park's other patches of old-growth forest, Albright Grove is turning out to be a critical place for certain vireos, warblers and orioles, which migrate to the southern hemisphere in winter and back to the Smokies in summer to breed.

Other good day hikes may include a jaunt on the Appalachian Trail – perhaps an 8-mile (13-km) round-trip from Newfound Gap to a rocky perch at **Charlies Bunion**, or a challenging 7-mile (11-km) round-trip from **Fontana Dam** to 4,020-foot (1,225-meter) **Shuckstack** in the solitary southwestern corner of the park. Longer treks on the Appalachian Trail offer glorious views, fairly moderate hiking and an intimate look at the spruce-fir forest.

For a remote, backroad experience, try **Cataloochee** on the eastern side of the park. "Catalooch," as it is fondly known, is a special place. One former resident recalled his boyhood there: "It was more like livin' in the Garden of Eden than anything I can think of." One of Cataloochee's most famous residents was "Turkey George" Palmer, a famed bear hunter who walked through the woods leading his horse, Old Sank. Turkey George got his name when, as a young boy, he caught some turkeys in a pen and went in to try to nab one. The turkeys, he said, "mighty nigh" killed him. Turkey George's old home place can still be visited, up **Pretty Hollow**.

In Cataloochee you'll find a small, quiet campground, miles of hiking trails (try the 7-mile/11-km round-trip on the **Boogerman Trail** near the campground, which winds through a mature hardwood forest), fine footbridges, plentiful trout in the streams, and another collection of early buildings, including the **Caldwell** and **Woody houses**, **Palmer Chapel** and **Beech Grove School**.

There are 10 established campgrounds within the park; some require advance reservations in summer. Backcountry campers should first obtain a free permit at the Sugarlands or Oconaluftee visitor centers or at any ranger station or campground. Camping along the Appalachian Trail requires registration several weeks in advance with the **Backcountry Reservation Office**.

There are no restaurants or gas stations within the park. Facilities and services are available in nearby towns, including several outfitters that specialize in rafting, fishing, cross-country skiing and horseback riding.

The Smoky Mountains support a large population of black bears.

236

SOUTHERN SEASHORES

Sky and water. Water and sky. Between these vast expanses, where their mighty forces meet, lies a necklace of wave-lapped beaches. From **Assateague Island National Seashore** on Maryland's east coast to **Cape Hatteras** and **Cape Lookout** on North Carolina's Outer Banks, south to **Cumberland Island**, **Canaveral**, and finally to the **Gulf Islands** that stretch from western Florida to Mississippi, these sandy seacoasts are elemental places where visitors are embraced by nature.

Many people come to these seashores to shed the cares of everyday life. "Rollers on the beach, wind in the pines, the slow flapping of herons across sand dunes drown out the hectic rhythms of city and suburb, time tables and schedules," wrote Anne Morrow Lindbergh in *Gift from the Sea*. "One falls under their spell, relaxes, stretches out prone. One becomes, in fact, like the element on which one lies, flattened by the sea; bare, open, empty as the beach, erased by today's tides of all yesterday's scribblings."

Although each seashore differs slightly in its native flora and fauna, all share a dynamic geologic history. During the past million years, glaciers periodically covered portions of North America. As they melted, swift rivers carried the sandy remains of ice-crushed boulders to the sea. There, longshore currents heaped the sediments into narrow islands that parallel the shore but rest several miles seaward.

These islands overwash during hurricanes and winter gales, serving as an important line of defense for the mainland behind them. The islands break the energy of huge storm waves, reforming them into smaller, weaker wavelets. The constant rearranging of sand dictates that the plants and animals of barrier islands withstand frequent assaults from the elements.

Assateague Island: Among the most famous inhabitants of the barrier islands are the ponies of Assateague. Legend claims that a Spanish ship en route from Peru ventured too close to shore in the late 18th century and broke up on shoals off the Maryland–Virginia coast. A few of their small ponies, bred especially to pull ore carts through mine tunnels, made it safely to shore.

American colonists also allowed their horses to graze freely in the salt marsh meadows here. Some escaped capture and interbred with the Spanish ponies. Today they form a band that numbers about 200 shaggy brown and pinto-marked animals. A quarter of the herd lives on the Maryland portion of 30-mile-long (48-km) Assateague Island. The remainder are owned by the Chincoteague Volunteer Fire Department, which rounds up the Virginia ponies and herds them across the inlet for its yearly auction of excess foals. The rest of the herd swims back to the island for another year of peaceful grazing. Among the best places to see the ponies are **Black Duck Marsh** (accessible via **Woodland Loop**) on the Virginia end of Assateague Island and near

the campgrounds on the Maryland side.

Among other types of wildlife easily seen on Assateague are beach-loving terns and sandpipers and long-legged egrets in tidal pools. Several short, self-guiding trails radiate from the campground to these habitats.

Beach and **Inner Dune trails** (each 10 miles/ 16 km, one-way) parallel the shore to the state line. Off-road vehicles are allowed on the beach (permits are required). The inner dunes are accessible only to hikers.

Migrant species of waterfowl – including huge flocks of snow geese, mallards, pintails and black ducks – gather in **Tom's Cove** and the adjacent marshes of **Chincoteague National Wildlife Refuge** from fall through early spring. The 3-mile (5-km) **Wildlife Loop** circles **Snow Goose Pool** and passes **Swan Pool**, both excellent for birding. Where the trail bisects pine forest, keep an eye out for the endangered Delmarva fox squirrel and Sika deer, a small elk imported from Asia in the 1920s.

Wildlife Loop is reserved for early-rising hikers and bikers. After 3pm, it opens to motor vehicles. Bicyclists are also welcome on Woodland Loop and a paved bikeway that connects the town of Chincoteague with refuge and park visitor centers. Surf-fishing, clamming and crabbing are legendary on Assateague. Park naturalists give demonstrations in summer. If you decide to try a do-it-yourself dinner, clam rakes and crab nets are available at local bait and hardware stores.

During the summer season, campgrounds at the seashore and adjacent **Assateague State Park** fill quickly. There are no campsites on the Virginia portion of the island, but the towns of Chincoteague, Berlin and Snow Hill offer a variety of campgrounds and motels. Brisk winds often romp with tents at seaside campsites, so bring long stakes and extra tie-downs. Sunglasses, wide-brimmed hats, light cover-up clothing, sunscreen and insect repellent are essential at any seashore park.

Cape Hatteras and Cape Lookout: Off the North Carolina coast, the **Outer**

Spiral stairway inside Bodie Island Lighthouse, Cape Hatteras.

Banks emerge like the head of a whale breaching into the Atlantic. Two national seashores, Cape Hatteras and Cape Lookout, preserve 120 miles (190 km) of these beaches on **Bodie**, **Hatteras** and **Ocracoke islands** and **Core** and **Shackleford banks**. While most coastal islands lie within 10 miles (16 km) of shore, the Outer Banks belong to the realm of the sea. In places, 30 miles (48 km) of water separate Hatteras Island from the mainland.

Outer Banks islands have wide, water-thrashed beaches. Scattered patches of sea oats and beach grasses bind low dunes behind them. Here and there, clumps of shrubby marsh elder and bayberry dot the swales. The mainland side of each island hosts extensive tidal marshes of swaying cordgrass.

Near **Buxton** on Hatteras Island and at the western end of Shackleford Banks are maritime forests. Waxy-leafed live oak and holly, plus a few hearty pines, form dense thickets. Most of the trees lean away from the sea, a concession to the salt spray that stunts tender branches on the windward sides of the trees.

Wind and waves refine beach profiles minute by minute. Infrequent hurricanes and winter gales redefine them entirely. Oncoming storms push extra water into the shallow sounds between the islands and the mainland. As storms pass, water surges back toward the ocean, often slicing through sandy spits that lie in its path. **Hatteras** and **Oregon inlets** were carved by a hurricane in 1848. **Old Drum** and **Chacandepeco** are among the inlets temporarily opened but later refilled with sand from longshore waves.

Two strong navigational currents pass off the Outer Banks. The Gulf Stream flows north from Florida at a speed of about 4 knots. It swings east near Cape Hatteras, providing a perfect send-off for ships bound for Europe. The cooler Virginia Coastal Drift flows closer to shore. It is an efficient southbound marine highway. Near the crook in Hatteras Island, navigational hazards in the form of shifting submerged sandbars reach 8 to 10 miles (13–16 km) out to sea. Early ship captains dreaded this passage; the

Wild horse grazing near Dungeness ruins on Cumberland Island.

islands are so low that to read natural landmarks, they had to remain close to shore. But they dared not venture too near **Diamond Shoals**, the "graveyard of the Atlantic." Over the centuries, more than 600 ships have ended their journeys here.

Construction of lighthouses to warn ships of hazardous waters was a high priority during colonial times. Cape Hatteras got its first lighthouse, a 90-foot (27-meter) sandstone tower, in 1803. The present one was completed in 1870. Containing 1.25 million bricks, it towers 208 feet (63 meters) above the beach and is the tallest lighthouse in the United States.

When completed, the **Cape Hatteras Light** stood 1,500 feet (450 meters) from shore. Decades of erosion have brought waves within 200 feet (61 meters) of its base. The Park Service is studying a proposal to move the spiral-striped structure 2,500 feet (760 meters) to the southwest, using a rail system similar to NASA'S to move the space shuttle to its launching pad.

Lighthouses mark other portions of the Outer Banks. All have distinctive exterior patterns and flash for different time periods at night to help navigators recognize them. The squatty, white-washed tower on Ocracoke was built in 1823. It is the oldest operating lighthouse in North Carolina. Diamond-patterned **Cape Lookout Light**, completed in 1859, warns sailors of the low-lying Core Banks. Horizontally-striped **Bodie Island Light**, placed in service in 1872, guards Oregon Inlet. From 1824 through 1967, a series of lightships were anchored on Diamond Shoals. They have been replaced by a light mounted on metal rigging.

During the late 19th century, the US Life-Saving Service established guard stations at 8-mile (13-km) intervals along the Outer Banks. Patrolmen paced the beaches, scouting for ships in distress. When a vessel grounded, they rushed to its aid with a lifeboat and rescue equipment. Two of the original lifesaving stations, **Chicamacomico** (at Rodanthe) and **Little Kinnakeet** (near Avon) remain. At Chicamacomico, park interpreters reenact lifesaving drills on Thursday afternoons in summer.

Cape Hatteras's islands are linked by Route 12. The Bodie Island and Hatteras Island sections of the seashore surround **Pea Island National Wildlife Refuge**. Observation platforms and several short trails lead from the highway to excellent viewpoints for watching the Canada and snow geese, whistling swans and migratory ducks that overwinter at the refuge. Pulloffs along Route 12 also offer access to the beach, where flocks of gulls, willets, sanderlings and turnstones feed. Long piers at **Rodanthe**, **Avon** and **Frisco** allow anglers to cast for deep-water species, such as cobia, king and Spanish mackerel, which aren't normally caught in the surf.

Fort Raleigh Historic Site, where the ill-fated "Lost Colony" settled, and **Wright Brothers National Memorial**, the site of the first powered airplane flight, are located near the northern entrance to Cape Hatteras. At **Nags Head**, many visitors stop to walk on **Jockeys Ridge**, a 100-foot (30-meter) medano, **Ghost crab...**

or unstabilized sand dune, that migrates with the prevailing winds. Access to Ocracoke, at the southern end of Cape Hatteras, is via a 2½-hour toll ferry ride from **Swanquarter** or **Cedar Island**.

Ocracoke is also the departure point for a 5-mile (8-km) ferry ride to the historic village of **Portsmouth**, at the north end of Cape Lookout. Early residents of Portsmouth made their living "lightering" (transferring) cargo from oceangoing vessels to shallow-draft boats that served **Core** and **Pamlico sounds**. The town is quiet now. A self-guiding trail winds among remaining structures, providing a glimpse into Portsmouth's former life.

Except for the visitor center on **Harkers Island**, Cape Lookout is waterbound. Most visitors ride excursion boats from Harkers Island to the lighthouse on **Core Banks** or from **Beaufort** to the west end of Shackleford Banks. Ferries that operate from April through November shuttle four-wheel-drive vehicles from Atlantic and Davis to the northern section of Core Banks.

Off-road vehicles may be used only on designated sections of beach. Otherwise, Cape Lookout's islands beckon backcountry hikers and campers. Take all necessary supplies and plenty of water. Arrange a return pickup time with the ferry operator before parting company, since you will be on your own in uninhabited areas where the sun, sea and wind prevail.

Cumberland Island: Although less than a mile from mainland Georgia, **Cumberland Island** retains isolated wilderness areas and beaches where you may feel as though you are the only person left on the planet. Cumberland's formation differs slightly from Assateague and the Outer Banks. It is a wider island with more varied habitats. Interdune meadows and shrubby thickets are broader and more diverse, and shelter a thick corridor of gnarled live oak trees with fan-leaf palmettos growing beneath them. Pine woods and mixed hardwood trees grow behind the oaks on central and northern portions of the island.

The island's forest provides enough

...and black skimmer chicks on the beach.

food and protection for white-tailed deer and wild turkeys. The oaks, festooned with pendant strands of Spanish moss, are host to a wide variety of avian species – from stoic great horned owls and pileated woodpeckers to showy painted buntings and summer tanagers. Sulphur butterflies flit among a rainbow of jessamine, scarlet sage and marsh pink blossoms.

The half-land, half-water world of the salt marsh dominates the mainland side of the island. Twice a day, tides flood these marshes with a nutrient-rich broth. Juvenile fish and shrimp hide among the submerged cordgrass stems, gobbling microscopic zooplankton. As the tide ebbs, fiddler crabs begin their hunt, sidestepping across the muck. Male fiddlers possess an enlarged claw, used in ritual displays. Gulls wheel overhead and raccoons patter along muddy trails. Both feast on the wealth of shellfish spawned in Cumberland's marshes.

The island is reached by ferry from **St Marys**, Georgia. Boats depart twice daily except during the period from October to March when there is no service on one or two days a week. Fresh water is available at several locations, but you must bring all your supplies. Day trips and overnight camping are equally popular.

Sea Camp has 16 campsites nestled near the beach, with restrooms and cold-water showers nearby. An easy half-mile walk from the dock, Sea Camp is often booked months in advance.

Visitors willing to travel a bit farther can usually find a site at one of the four backcountry campgrounds. **Stafford** is situated on the Atlantic shore, **Hickory Hill** and **Yankee Paradise** are in the maritime forest, and **Brickhill Bluff** overlooks marshes on the **Cumberland River**. They vary from 4 to 10.6 miles (6–17 km) from the dock along well-marked trails. All campers need permits, available at the **Sea Camp Visitor Center**. As you roam the island, you will glimpse several parcels of private land and historic structures once owned by wealthy families. But the days of harvesting oak timber for sailing ves-

Aerial view of Petit Bois, Horn and Ship Islands off the Mississippi coast.

sels and of slaves toiling in fields of sea cotton are just a memory. Cumberland Island has, for the most part, reverted to a place of peaceful beauty, in tune with nature's rhythms.

Canaveral: Among the most remarkable of these natural cycles is the instinctive return of female sea turtles to lay eggs on the beaches where they were born decades before. Although their nests are found on the Outer Banks and Cumberland Island, nowhere is their return more conspicuous than on **Canaveral National Seashore**.

More than 30 years ago, **Cape Canaveral Space Center** was constructed on a then-remote section of the Florida coast east of Orlando. Land buffering the launch area was offered to the National Park Service and US Fish and Wildlife Service. Since then, the area has seen a boom in development and construction. But Canaveral National Seashore, a pristine, 24-mile (39-km) stretch of beach, looks much the same as the shoreline Spanish explorers discovered five centuries ago. Female sea turtles gather offshore in late spring and wait until the pull of the full moon creates higher-than-normal tides. They lumber ashore at night, drag their heavy shells through the soft sand and dig a foot-deep hole with their flippers. Nearly exhausted, they finally begin releasing golf-ball-sized eggs into the cavity. After depositing four or five dozen, they tamp the sand back into place to discourage raccoons and crabs from feasting on the cache. Two months later, turtle hatchlings claw their way to the surface and scurry back to the sea.

Mosquito Lagoon (appropriately named for an abundant natural feature) and the backwaters of **Indian River** are home to alligators, occasional manatees and an array of crabs, fish and shellfish. Rangers often invite sneaker-clad visitors to join them in pulling a seine through the warm, shallow water and identifying some of the curious creatures the net brings to the surface. **Merritt Island National Wildlife Refuge**, which adjoins Canaveral, preserves coastal wetlands where more than 300

Water patterns in the sand.

species of birds have been seen. During the winter, the refuge is home to some 50,000 wintering ducks.

Two driving or biking trails offer superb views of waterfowl, wading birds, alligators and basking turtles. **Max Hoeck Creek Wildlife Drive** begins at **Playalinda Beach** and skirts the southern end of Mosquito Lagoon. **Black Point Wildlife Drive** traverses pinelands and marshes near Indian River. Both are one-way roads requiring a minimum of 30 minutes to drive.

Short walking trails at **Eldora** and **Castle Windy** sample the human history of the seashore. Turtle Mound trail combines a walk across an Indian shell midden with expansive views of Mosquito Lagoon or the Atlantic beach, depending on which direction you face. Two backcountry campsites are located along a canoe trail at the north end of Mosquito Lagoon. Canaveral has no other facilities for camping, but the nearby towns of **Titusville** and **New Smyrna Beach** offer a variety of accommodations to suit most budgets.

Gulf Islands: At the opposite end of Florida's coastline, barrier beaches known as the Gulf Islands span 140 miles (225 km), from east of Pensacola to Biloxi, Mississippi. Their legacy is diverse, preserving both human and natural history. Spanish explorers entered Pensacola Bay in 1559 and later built a fort overlooking the water. The harbor changed hands numerous times, with French, British and finally American flags flying over a succession of settlements. The War of 1812 convinced the US Congress to fund a full system of defensive forts along the Atlantic and Gulf coasts. Since Pensacola housed a strategic navy yard, the harbor was ringed by a trio of brick forts.

Fort Barrancas is the centerpiece of visitor facilities located off Route 295 at the **Naval Air Station**. The adjoining **Naval Air Museum** reminds all comers of advances in military aviation during the past century. It is also possible to tour the aircraft carrier *USS Lexington* when the vessel is in port.

Massive **Fort Pickens**, completed in

Seaside sketch.

1834, rests across the harbor on **Santa Rosa Island**. It saw action in the Civil War and was later used as a prison for the Apache warrior Geronimo. Refinements in coastal defenses were added around Fort Pickens during the Spanish–American War and both World Wars. A driving or biking tour circles the concrete bunkers, "disappearing" gun carriages and shield guns that were each, for a short time, state-of-the-art improvements in warfare.

Linear stretches of sugar-white sand on Santa Rosa Island beckon beachcombers to find colorful whelks, moons, cockles, scallops, sea pens, angel wings and arc shells. The eastern end of Santa Rosa (off Route 399) features an expansive swimming beach in addition to picnic shelters, a small exhibit area, restrooms and showers. A 200-site campground shares the west end of the island with the fortifications and several nature trails.

Naval Live Oaks, east of Pensacola, was an experimental tree farm. Nearly two centuries ago, John Quincy Adams set aside a handsome tract of live oak trees for renewable harvesting of ship timbers. Ancestors of these trees shaped colonial frigates. A visitor center on Highway 98 orients hikers and bikers to trails in the Live Oaks area.

The **Mississippi Gulf Islands** are a boater's paradise. Separated from the mainland by 10-mile-wide (16-km) **Mississippi Sound**, **Petit Bois**, **Horn** and **East Ship islands** are reached only by private or chartered vessels. An excursion boat from **Gulfport**, Mississippi, serves West Ship Island daily from March through October. Day trips connect Biloxi with the island in summer.

West Ship Island is the site of a D-shaped masonry fort completed in 1866. It houses one of the few remaining examples of a 15-inch (38-cm) Rodman cannon, a massive naval defense weapon that could hurl a 440-pound (200-kg) iron shot nearly 3 miles (5 km). Rangers provide frequent tours of the historic fort. West Ship's beach is popular with bathers during the hot, humid Mississippi summer.

Horn and Petit Bois are wilderness areas where backcountry camping is allowed. Petit Bois is 7 miles (11 km) long but contains only a small forested area in its midst. Horn is the site of experimental red-wolf reintroduction, and, thanks to a "hacking" program of transplanting chicks in the late 1980s, bald eagles are nesting again after a 50-year absence.

The only portion of the Mississippi Gulf Islands accessible by car is **Davis Bayou**, off Highway 90 in **Ocean Springs**. The tidal backwater shelters a 51-site campground, picnic pavilions, boat ramp and visitor center. Fishing and birding in the surrounding marshes are quite good.

As with the Atlantic seashores, the Gulf Islands are long on recreation and relaxation. The warmth of the sun, the refreshing coolness of the waves, the tangy taste of salt in the air and the wealth of life in the sea, marshes and beaches help to erode a visitor's sense of urgency. Travelers slacken their pace and open their senses to the soothing rhythms of the natural world.

Great blue heron at water's edge.

BIG SOUTH FORK

John Muir was awestruck. As a young man, the famed conservationist wandered through eastern Kentucky and Tennessee and was bowled over by the sheer density of green, growing things in this "ocean of wooded, waving, swelling mountain beauty."

Today, a small portion of this region is protected within the boundaries of **Big South Fork National River and Recreation Area**. The park lies within a remote pocket of the Cumberland Plateau, a densely forested shelf of high country furrowed by hundreds of streams and rivers that flow off the western flank of the Appalachian Mountains.

At the heart of the recreation area is the **Big South Fork of the Cumberland River**, which springs to life at the confluence of the **New** and **Clear Fork rivers** in northeastern Tennessee and flows into Kentucky's **Cumberland Lake**. Along its route, the Big South Fork courses beneath dramatic sandstone cliffs, over waterfalls, through treacherous boulder fields and into pools of placid green water.

River running is one of the big attractions here. Long stretches of calm water are perfect for greenhorns, who, with a little advance planning, can float for hours without encountering much more than a riffle. Experienced paddlers can ride thundering white water through rapids with menacing names like the **Washing Machine**, **Devils Jump**, and **Decapitation Rock**.

Beyond the river, Big South Fork is laced with more than 300 miles (480 km) of hiking, riding and mountain-biking trails, as well as several primitive roads for four-wheel-drive vehicles.

Although sparsely settled, the area has a long history of human occupation. Paleo-Indians hunted the Big South Fork as much as 14,000 years ago, using its huge natural rock shelters as campsites. White "long hunters" (named for the length of their rifles) made their first forays into the area in the late 1700s, followed by a hardy breed of pioneers who started trickling into the secluded bottomlands about 100 years later. Some families stayed on well into the 1950s or later. It's not uncommon for hikers to stumble upon the remains of an old log cabin or cemetery.

By the late 19th century, the Big South Fork was being heavily logged, and within about 50 years the area that John Muir hailed as the "forest gardens of our Father" was all but denuded. Most of the trees are now second- or third-growth, testimony to the recuperative powers of the eastern forest. There was a coal boom, too. Mining towns sprang up in remote hollows throughout the Cumberland Plateau and disappeared just as quickly, leaving behind little more than broken-down chimneys, rusted machinery and piles of refuse.

River walk: If this is your first visit to Big South Fork, the best place to start is the **Bandy Creek Visitor Center** in the mid-section of the park, about 15 miles (24 km) west of the little town of **Oneida**, Tennessee, on Route 297. Just inside the recreation area, a short spur road leads

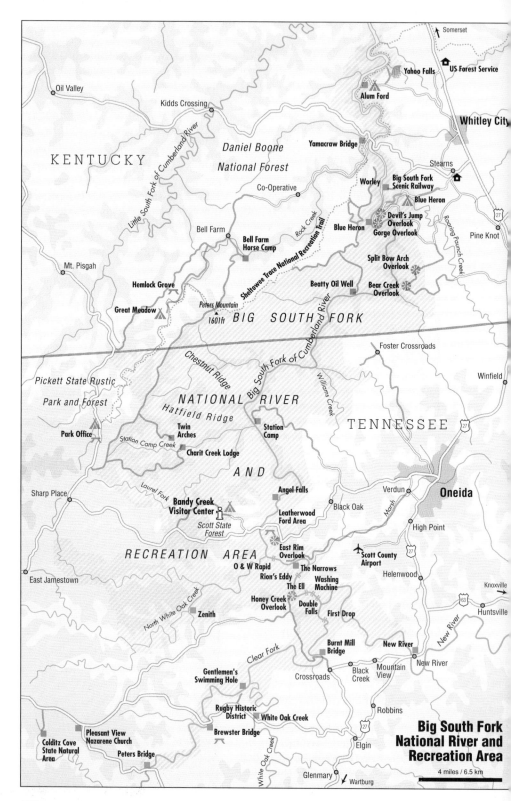

Somerset

Yahoo Falls
US Forest Service
Alum Ford

Oil Valley

Kidds Crossing

Whitley City

KENTUCKY

Daniel Boone
National Forest

Yamacraw Bridge

Co-Operative

Worley
Big South Fork
Scenic Railway

Stearns

Blue Heron

Bell Farm

Bell Farm
Horse Camp

Devil's Jump
Overlook
Gorge Overlook
Blue Heron

Pine Knot

Mt. Pisgah

Split Bow Arch
Overlook

Hemlock Grove

Beatty Oil Well

Bear Creek
Overlook

Great Meadow

Peters Mountain

1601ft   BIG   SOUTH   FORK

Foster Crossroads

Winfield

Pickett State Rustic
Park and Forest

Chestnut Ridge

NATIONAL   RIVER

Hatfield Ridge

TENNESSEE

Park Office

Twin
Arches

Station
Camp

Station Camp Creek

Charit Creek Lodge

AND

Angel Falls

Verdun

Oneida

Sharp Place

Laurel Fork

Bandy Creek
Visitor Center

Scott State
Forest

Leatherwood
Ford Area

Black Oak

High Point

RECREATION   AREA

East Rim
Overlook

O & W Rapid

Rion's Eddy

The Ell

The Narrows

Washing
Machine

Scott County
Airport

Helenwood

East Jamestown

North White Oak Creek

Zenith

Honey Creek
Overlook

Double
Falls

First Drop

Knoxville

Huntsville

Clear Fork

Burnt Mill
Bridge

New River

New River

Gentlemen's
Swimming Hole

Crossroads

Black
Creek

Mountain
View

Rugby Historic
District

White Oak Creek

Robbins

Pleasant View
Nazarene Church

Brewster Bridge

Colditz Cove
State Natural
Area

Peters Bridge

Elgin

Glenmary

Wartburg

**Big South Fork
National River and
Recreation Area**

4 miles / 6.5 km

to the **East Rim Overlook**, where a wooden platform perched on the edge of a cliff offers a breathtaking glimpse of the river as it winds through the wooded folds 500 feet (150 meters) below. Easy trails lead to less-visited viewpoints – **Sunset Overlook** and **Leatherwood Loop Overlook** – from the parking area on **East Rim Road**.

Route 297 gives drivers a hairpin descent to the river at **Leatherwood Ford** and then toils up the west rim to the Bandy Creek area, where you'll find campsites, picnic areas, a playground, pool, stable and gift shop. Gather maps, books and other information at the visitor center and then limber up with an easy 3.6-mile (6-km) walk on the self-guiding **Oscar Blevins Trail**, which loops past hardwood forests, rock shelters and old farmsteads.

The **John Litton/General Slaven Farm Loop** (6.3 miles/10 km round-trip) is more strenuous, but it offers a good look at another historic farmstead.

To get a closer look at the river, double back on Route 287 to Leatherwood Ford, where you can pick up **Angel Falls Trail**, a fairly level, 1.8-mile (3-km) hike along the east bank of the Big South Fork shaded by a canopy of towering hemlocks, white pine and a variety of hardwoods. This is an excellent wildflower trail, with shade-loving lady's slipper, trillium and Jack-in-the-pulpit in counterpoint with dainty dogwood blooms and softball-sized clusters of rhododendron blossoms. The trail reaches a wooden platform that overlooks **Angel Falls** – no longer a true waterfall but a series of rocky chutes created by a dynamite blast in the 1950s. The trail veers to the river's edge just beyond, where you can go boulder-hopping around a peaceful green pool or stretch out on a rock, watch a turkey vulture or red-shouldered hawk wheel over the bluffs, and let the murmur of the rapids lull you into an afternoon nap.

You can pick up several other trails from Leatherwood Ford, including a relaxing 4.6-mile (7-km) round-trip along the river to the old **O & W Bridge**, which once carried rail cars filled with coal and timber. A more challenging 3-

mile (5-km) route to **Angel Falls Overlook** leads across the river on the old **Leatherwood Ford Bridge** and then up a steep grade over stairs, boulders and a ladder to an unprotected bluff. It's a rough climb but worth it. The view of the river and watershed is spectacular.

The wild side: You'll get a different perspective on the park from its rugged western flank. Back roads here are tricky, so pick up a map and ask about road conditions at the visitor center. From Bandy Creek, it's a short drive on Route 297 to Route 154, then about 1.8 miles (3 km) north to **Divide Road**, a narrow, unpaved road that quickly gets swallowed up by the woods. The main attraction in this area is **Twin Arches**, a pair of natural bridges cut side-by-side into a sandstone ridge. The larger, the **South Arch**, is some 70 feet (21 meters) high and 135 feet (41 meters) across. The quickest route to Twin Arches is from the Twin Arches Trailhead, about 2½ miles (4 km) off Divide Road on Twin Arches Road. The trail is less than a mile (2 km) long but extremely steep,

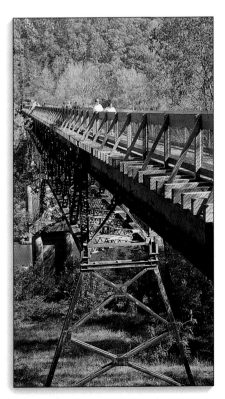

Cantilevered Blue Heron Bridge above the Big South Fork of the Cumberland River.

although stairs installed on the edge of the bluff make the climb a bit easier.

For a longer and more ambitious hike, consider tackling the entire **Twin Arches Loop**. The daylong, 6-mile (10-km) trek continues along the base of the bluff west of Twin Arches, passing a series of dramatic, scallop-shaped rock shelters eroded into the sheer walls of the bluff.

The trail eventually winds down to a clearing known as **Jakes Place**, where a broken-down chimney is all that remains of a farmstead established in the 1880s by Jake Blevins. He and his wife and their nine children scratched a living in this secluded valley.

Farther on, the trail passes the rustic **Charit Creek Lodge** (no electricity; reservations required), built around a log cabin dating back to the early 1800s. Other trails in the area lead to **Slave Falls**, one of several "hanging" waterfalls in the park that spill over a jutting ledge, and the slender 30-foot (9-meter) span of **Needle Arch**.

There are scores of other trails at Big South Fork, including long-distance hikes on the **John Muir Trail**, the **Sheltowee Trace Trail**, or the **Kentucky Trail**, all of which require several days of backcountry camping. A few other outstanding day hikes might include, in the southern portion of the park, a moderate 4-mile (6 km) jaunt along the scenic Clear Fork River on the **Burnt Mill Bridge Loop**, an extremely rugged 5.6-mile (9-km) outing on the **Honey Creek Loop** or, in the park's northern tip, a steep quarter-mile hike to **Yahoo Falls**, which sends a silver plume over the top of a cavernous rock shelter.

For those who would rather ride than walk, horseback riding and mountain biking are allowed on designated trails and some unused dirt roads; obtain a map at the visitor center. Stables at Bandy Creek offer boarding and guided pack trips. Mountain bikes can be rented outside the park.

"River rats" can run the Big South Fork into some of the park's wildest areas. Boat landings at several points allow paddlers to design trips of varying lengths and difficulties. In some areas,

Employees of the Stearns Coal and Lumber Company at Blue Heron Mine.

white water lunges over car-sized boulders, swirling off into powerful eddies and black holes. Rapids can be treacherous, especially during periods of high water, so be sure to consult park rangers before setting off on any river expedition. Outfitters in the area offer canoe rentals and guided raft trips.

Voice of the past: Big South Fork is rich in human history, too. Just south of the recreation area, for example, is the historic village of **Rugby**, founded in 1880 by Thomas Hughes, a British social reformer and author of *Tom Brown's School Days*, the popular 19th-century novel. Hughes's goal was to create a farming community for England's "second sons," the landless nobility who were denied their family's fortunes by the laws of primogeniture. The experiment flourished for about 30 years, but disease, fire and poor soil took a heavy toll on the colonists, many of whom weren't used to the backbreaking labor required to hack a living from the wilderness. Many of the town's handsome Victorian buildings, including the schoolhouse, Episcopal church, library and several homes, have been lovingly restored or reconstructed.

Guided tours start at the **Schoolhouse Visitor Center**, which houses a fine exhibit on Rugby's history. Visitors may also pick up a map at the visitor center and tour the village on their own. Ask a guide to direct you to **Canyon Road**, where you can pick up a short trail to the **Gentlemen's Swimming Hole**, a lovely little pool on the Clear Fork River set aside by Hughes and still popular with local residents.

In the northern tip of the recreation area about 12 miles (19 km) from **Whitley City**, Kentucky, is the former site of the **Blue Heron Mining Community**, operated by the Stearns Coal and Lumber Company between 1938 and 1962. Located in a narrow hollow along the Big South Fork, Blue Heron can be reached by car on Mine 18 Road or on the **Big South Fork Scenic Railroad**, which runs along the old K & T line from **Stearns**, Kentucky, from mid-April through October. The 12-mile (19-km) round-trip takes about 3 hours. The only building that still stands at Blue Heron is the tipple, a monstrous contraption that funnels coal into railroad cars waiting below. Visitors can walk along the top of the tipple and across the narrow cantilevered bridge that was used to transport coal across the river.

Although no other buildings remain, the Park Service has erected a large interpretation center with photographs and exhibits chronicling the town's history. There are also a dozen steel-frame "ghost structures" which serve as outlines for many of the last remaining buildings. Each structure is equipped with a recording of the people who once lived and worked at Blue Heron. At a touch of a button, their voices come alive, describing the details of everyday existence – the deafening rattle of the tipple, the endless dustings of coal, the pleasures of living close to nature.

As always, beauty is in the eyes of the beholder. One old-timer remembers Blue Heron as "the worst hell hole I ever saw", another as one of the most beautiful places in the world.

Big South Fork Scenic Railroad runs from Stearns, Kentucky, to Blue Heron.

MAMMOTH CAVE

The richest, most extensive region of caves in the United States is in south-central Kentucky. At the center of this region, between Elizabethtown and Bowling Green, is **Mammoth Cave National Park**. It's a place of enticing contrast. On the surface, sunshine fills a forest brimming with wildlife. Three hundred feet below, enormous caverns are engulfed in darkness.

At first glance, the rolling farms and woodlands in this region look like much of the mid-South. But something is missing. Geologists call the topography "karst," and if you were viewing the landscape from above, you would notice the difference quickly. There are no creeks, no streams, no babbling brooks. Instead, the land is pocked with thousands of funnel-shaped depressions. The largest are 100 feet (30 meters) deep and three times as wide. Like bathtubs without plugs, these sinkholes swallow up

Preceding pages: rainbow dome on the Travertine walk. Left, park ranger at River Styx spring. Right, problem passage for the plump.

the surface water. When it rains, runoff flushes down the slopes and quickly disappears, hinting at the mysteries waiting beneath the surface of the earth.

The geologic story of Mammoth Cave starts about 350 million years ago when what is now Kentucky was submerged under a shallow sea that gradually laid down a thick bed of limestone. Later, a river rivaling the Mississippi flowed south from the Great Lakes region. It deposited sediments on top of the limestone, which formed a cap of sandstone as much as 50 feet (15 m) thick.

When the ancient sea drained from North America about 280 million years ago, the earth's crust folded and twisted, buckling the overlying layers of rock. Rain, made slightly acidic by carbon dioxide in the air and soil, percolated through cracks in the limestone, eroding and widening the crevices. Some of these passages, including many in Mammoth Cave itself, grew to the size of subway tunnels.

The **Green River** now meanders across central Kentucky, slicing through the sandstone caprock and scoring the limestone. As the river cuts downward, water that was once trapped in limestone pockets drains into the Green River gorge. The empty caverns can't support the overlying rocks and collapse under the pressure, resulting in the sinkholes that signal your entry into Kentucky's cave country.

The human element: For thousands of years, Native Americans used rock outcrops at the mouths of caves in this area as shelters for their camps. Using torches of bundled reeds, some crept into the maze of passages in search of mineral deposits, including chalky gypsum, epsomite and mirabilite (both natural laxatives), and decorative aragonite crystals. Traces of soot and charred reeds have been discovered 2½ miles (4 km) into Mammoth Cave.

At least one Indian explorer lost his life in Mammoth Cave. Guides found the well-preserved body of a barefoot man, about 45 years old, entombed under a 6-ton slab of limestone. The good condition of the man's hair, teeth and bones, fragments of his woven clothing

Fat Man's Misery

and the small fiber bag he used to carry food and crystals gave archaeologists unusually detailed insight into his life, which ended about 2,000 years ago.

By the late 18th century, colonial explorers were seeking caves for saltpeter, which was used to preserve meats and make gunpowder. Cave soil, enriched by river nitrates, was a key ingredient in its manufacture. When European sources of gunpowder were cut off during the War of 1812, entrepreneurs turned Mammoth Cave into a saltpeter refinery, utilizing slave labor and an elaborate system of hollowed-out logs to extract and process nitrate found in sedimentary deposits deep inside the cavern.

Demand for saltpeter waned after the war, but promoters placed the curious crypt now called Mammoth Cave among the great wonders of the world. It began to attract a steady stream of tourists. "Mammoth" referred to the size of the cave's rooms. The gaping **Historic Entrance**, at 30 feet high and 60 feet wide (9 by 18 meters), is larger than most train tunnels. A hundred paces into the cool darkness, the passage broadens into the **Rotunda**, where three vast avenues converge. The ceiling towers 40 feet (12 meters) overhead; the walls are at least 140 feet (43 meters) apart. Lard-oil lamps used by early explorers could barely illuminate such expanses. No wonder visitors left wide-eyed, full of excited talk about this strange and awesome cavern.

In 1838 a lawyer, Franklin Gorin, purchased Mammoth Cave and assigned three of his slaves to guide tourists. For 17-year-old Stephen Bishop – curious, lithe and daring – caving became an obsession. He led party after party to cave sites such as **Giants Coffin**, **Gothic Avenue** and an extraordinary echo chamber known as the **Methodist Church** where preachers addressed worshippers from the lofty **Pulpit Rock**.

When there were no tourists to entertain, Bishop crawled into some of the smaller passages that branched off the main route. Among his discoveries were **Gorins Dome**, **Bottomless Pit** and **Mammoth Dome** – all smooth-walled vertical shafts that dropped from the

cave's upper level into a maze of lower passageways. One room on a lower level, decorated with delicate white crystals, was dubbed the **Snowball Room**. Bishop also stumbled across two streams – **River Styx** and **Echo River** – flowing inside the cave.

Tours eventually included skiff rides, which allowed visitors to float through the vaulted underground waterways. By 1850, Mammoth Cave rivaled Niagara Falls as one of the nation's most popular natural attractions.

The big connection: As more people realized just how priceless and fragile this underground treasure was, support grew for making Mammoth Cave a national park. When the park was dedicated in 1941, around 40 miles (64 km) of passages were known. But the curiosity of Indian explorers and Stephen Bishop also fired the imaginations of contemporary cavers who believed that there was more to discover.

"Beneath the cathedral ceiling you are dwarfed by time and by earth," wrote park ranger Joy Medley Lyons. "There,

A fallen log along the Green River near River Styx Spring.

262

in the cool grey solitude of the limestone walls, you hear it – the mighty ancient waters of a river carving rock, creating the cave."

Among Mammoth's most dedicated visitors are members of the Cave Research Foundation (CRF), volunteers who spend countless hours mapping and studying the cave. For years, these spelunkers – as cave explorers are called – speculated that Mammoth's passages were somehow tied to a system of caves on **Flint Ridge**, located several miles northeast of **Houchins Valley**.

CRF cavers squeezed through muddy leads on trip after trip, but the "Big Connection" eluded them. Then, in 1972, a young woman wriggled through a tight crevice and found an underground stream flowing from Flint Ridge toward Mammoth Cave. Joined by several others, she sloshed into the cold, neck-deep water. Twelve hours and six grueling miles after dropping into the ground on Flint Ridge, the explorers emerged in a large room. On the far wall they glimpsed a metal bar. One of them realized it was a hand rail in **Cascade Hall**, where the Echo River intersects the lower level of Mammoth Cave.

Tired but elated, they trekked along this tourist route to the Snowball Room and took the elevator to the surface. No one thought to ask for the tickets of these mud-caked human moles, for they were instant celebrities. Their odyssey proved that Mammoth was the longest cave in the world. With additional discoveries made in the past two decades, Mammoth Cave now encompasses 345 miles (555 km) of mapped passages. Some believe that another 100 miles (160 km) or so await discovery.

Although many people enjoy crawling through the cave on knees and elbows, there are easier ways to sample its vastness and beauty. Park rangers lead tours into various parts of the cave, based on the season, participants' interests and physical abilities. All tours meet at the visitor center. Cave tours frequently sell out, so be sure to make reservations by phone or mail well in advance (see Travel Tips section at the

South-central Kentucky is the most extensive cave region in the United States.

back of this book for details). Wear sturdy shoes and bring a jacket; the temperature averages 54°F (12°C). Inquire in advance about distances and staircases. Tours from one level of the cave to another may be strenuous.

To relive the history of Mammoth Cave, choose the 2-mile (3-km) **Historic Tour** or the 3-mile (5-km) **Violet City Lantern Tour**. The former winds from the natural entrance past the saltpeter mine and Methodist Church to displays of Indian artifacts. Peer into the blackness of **Bottomless Pit** and learn how deep it really is. Then climb the towering steel staircase that ascends from the bottom of Mammoth Dome to an upper level of the cave.

The Violet City Lantern Tour follows the first half-mile of the historic route, then veers past stone huts built in 1842 for experimental treatment of tuberculosis sufferers. The route passes some of the largest rooms in the cave. Some sections have no electric lights, so visitors carry nostalgic kerosene lanterns.

Unlike most "show" caves, many of the rooms in Mammoth lack fairyland formations. As water containing dissolved calcium carbonate drips through the rocks, the calcium may build up where it emerges into an air-filled cavity. Most of Mammoth's upper level is dry, but lower levels echo with the sounds of dripping water. A few places – notably the **Drapery Room** and the **Frozen Niagara** section – are decorated with pendant stalactites and conical stalagmites. Where the two meet and thicken, columns grow. When calcium precipitates on a wall, it forms rippled flowstone draperies. Tinted by the rusty hues of iron compounds, these resemble huge slabs of bacon. Delicate rimstone dams layer up at the edges of water-filled pools.

The ¾-mile (1.2-km) **Frozen Niagara Tour** and its shorter, easier version, the **Travertine Tour**, are extremely popular with visitors who want to see dripstone formations. To sample a greater variety of underground jewels, join the 1-mile **Great Onyx Tour**, which includes a bus ride to the cave's Flint

A dozen bat species inhabit the cave, including this eastern pipistrel.

Ridge entrance. Visitors carry lanterns to illuminate the delicate soda straws, knotted helictites and crystalline gypsum flowers that dangle from the walls of **Great Onyx Cave**. A tour for the handicapped is offered daily. These tours enter Mammoth Cave by elevator and are suitable for wheelchair passage.

Trogs: Children aged 8 to 12 are encouraged to join a ranger on a "**Trog**" (the Greek word for cave). Decked out in knee pads and helmets with lights, kids can ramble through pint-sized passages where they may spot salamanders, crickets or bats that live near the entrance. Farther along, they learn how the erosive force of water shaped the cave. Parents can join similar family caving tours.

For amateur spelunkers, there's wild caving. This 6-hour summer specialty is limited to those 16 and older who are in excellent physical condition. Wear old clothes and kneepads, because for 5 miles (8 km) you will slither through mole holes, pressing your cheeks and toes into the cool, moist earth to reach Mammoth Cave's off-trail wonders. The reward: viewing portions of the cave seen by few others and traveling at a pace that allows total absorption.

If you're lucky, you'll catch a glimpse of some of Mammoth's unusual wildlife. Cave, or camelback, crickets are abundant trogloxenes (cave guests), frequently seen near natural entrances. They are pale brown and have functioning eyes that are useful on regular migrations outside the cave for food gathering. Twelve species of bats also find refuge in Mammoth Cave in various seasons. Eastern pipistrels roost deep in the cave, where the air is saturated with humidity. Big brown bats roost singly, usually nearer entrances. Like crickets, they feed outside but bring nutrients into the cave in their droppings.

Among the oddest animals are ghostly troglobites (cave dwellers) that have adapted to life in darkness. They include slightly-larger-than-microscopic isopods and amphipods, skinny millipedes, thumbnail-sized shrimp and small fish and crayfish. All are unpigmented

A raccoon relaxes in the forest.

and eyeless. Instead of sight, they rely on smell and touch to find food and avoid danger. Their lifestyles are slow-paced, yet they live longer than topside relatives. Adept at evading predators, most troglobites retreat under rocks or into deeper water as visitors draw near. Although seldom seen, they survive and reproduce successfully in the recesses of the cave.

If possible, allow enough time to explore the park's surface, too. The mature oak-hickory forest supports a multitude of watchable wildlife, from white-tailed deer that graze at dawn and dusk to sassy squirrels, chipmunks, woodchucks, raccoons, skunks and ambling box turtles. Spring and summer mornings erupt in a cacophonous chorus of warblers, orioles and vireos. Woodpeckers drum a metronome accompaniment from hollow trees. One of the most delightful spots for a walk is the **Big Woods**, a 300-acre (120-hectare) section of old-growth beech-maple forest. Spring wildflowers, including trillium, jack-in-the-pulpit, dwarf iris and moun-tain laurel, grace surrounding bluffs and hollows. A 1½-mile (2.5-km) round-trip on **Cedar Sink Trail** is a wonderful way to sample the flavor of the Kentucky karst region.

The park offers three campgrounds and 70 miles (113 km) of wooded hiking trails. A popular outing follows the 2-mile (3-km) **Joppa Ridge Motor Nature Trail**, a one-way gravel road that wanders through former farmlands that are now reverting to forest.

The Green and **Nolin** rivers, which form deep gorges through sheer limestone and sandstone cliffs, are perfect for canoeing or fishing. During the summer, a concessionaire offers a scenic 8-mile (13-km) cruise on the *Miss Green River II*, which plies her namesake.

For those who take time to absorb the worlds above and below, the complexities of this extraordinary environment will become clearer. Clues in the rocks, the strange sinkholes, even the time-worn passages, are the outward signs of a process that continues to create the world's largest cavern.

Prehistoric artifacts are displayed in the cave.

ROUGHING IT

If you're smart, you won't venture into the wilderness with the idea of "roughing it." Instead, you'll take the advice of George W. Sears, an old-time mountain guide who scorned such a notion.

"I dislike the phrase," he wrote. "We do not go to the green woods and crystal waters to rough it. We go to smooth it. We get it rough enough at home; in towns and cities; in shops, offices, stores, banks... Don't rough it; make it as smooth, as restful and pleasurable as you can."

The best way to smooth out the rough spots in your outdoor travels is to acquire a reliable set of skills and the tools you need to draw on them. This combination will give you the edge in your outdoor travels, letting you move through the countryside easily and with little impact. With the proper preparation, you'll have a lot more fun, too.

For a day hike, bring along the essentials. Appropriate clothing might include shorts, a T-shirt, a synthetic undershirt, and a sweater or pile pullover. Footwear should include liner socks, wool socks, and a pair of sturdy lightweight hiking shoes.

Bring along a small first-aid kit, and don't neglect to carry food and water. A set of rainwear will keep you warm and dry if you're caught in a downpour. Make sure you have a compass and a map or guidebook of the area you plan to explore. Matches kept in a waterproof container could come in handy in an emergency, as will a flashlight if you are still out after dark. Pack these items in a small rucksack or daypack, and hit the trail.

Overnight trips are a bit more complicated and require a little more planning. Besides the items in the daypack, overnight hikers should bring along a small backpacking stove and fuel; a sleeping bag and sleeping pad; a spoon, bowl and cooking utensils; and a small plastic bag for garbage. Plan to sleep under a tarp or, especially during bug season, in a tent with mosquito netting. A careful selection of extra clothes will add to your comfort, especially at night at higher elevations, where temperatures can plummet.

To accommodate these additional items, you will need a true backpack. These can be either internal or external frame packs – just be sure the pack has a well-padded waist belt and shoulder pads. Generally, make sure all your gear is of high quality and is in good repair. The trail is no place for equipment failure. If you are inexperienced, or do not own your own equipment, begin your trip at an established outdoor equipment store with knowledgeable salespeople. Such stores are frequently found just outside the national parks or in nearby towns.

In truth, the most common problems you'll encounter will probably be quite banal. Lightning, bears and bandits make for the best storytelling, but blisters, sunburn and dehydration are by far the most frequent ailments. To avoid them, wear footwear that is comfortable and well broken in; cover up and use plenty of sunscreen; and drink lots of water throughout the day. If you are uncertain of the source, treat the water with iodine, or boil it for at least three minutes. Finally, don't bring along too much gear – traveling light is critical to a pleasant backcountry trip.

Wherever your rambles take you, remember the "low impact, no impact" ethic. Walk lightly on the land. Pack out your trash. Don't disturb rocks, plants, wildlife or other natural features, and don't build campfires where they don't belong. As the old saying goes, "take nothing but pictures, leave nothing but footprints." ∎

Winter camping.

HOT SPRINGS

Steam from the ground? It must have startled the Spanish explorers when they dropped by in 1541, after forging up the Arkansas River. They were presumably the first Europeans to see the place.

From a spot close to present-day Little Rock, Arkansas, they rode west into the rugged Ouachita Mountains and camped in a lush valley that contained, according to one of Hernando de Soto's people, "hot rivers and salt made from sand." It was probably **Hot Springs**.

The theory of how Hot Springs works goes like this. Rain falls somewhere north of the park and percolates very slowly through a porous layer of sedimentary rock. It penetrates a mile (1.5 km) or more beneath the surface, where it absorbs heat from the earth's inner core. Impurities are filtered out and a few minerals from the surrounding rocks are dissolved. The water eventually reaches a fault, where joints in a folded layer of sandstone allow the steaming solution to escape upward. It then surfaces at the base of **Hot Springs Mountain**, where the springs produce a huge flow, averaging 850,000 gallons (3.2 million liters) each day – enough water to fill 21,250 bathtubs to the rim.

As long as 10,000 years ago, Native Americans who lived in what is now Arkansas made pilgrimages to this sacred valley. One tribal legend has it that the Great Spirit banished a fearsome dragon to a cavern here. The enraged beast shook the earth, so the Spirit placed a mountain on top of the cavern. When steam from the dragon's breath rose through cracks in the rocks, the Spirit turned it into a stream of healing water. The valley became a place which all tribes could share in peace.

Quapaws, Caddos, even aggressive Osage warriors, laid aside their weapons upon entering the Valley of Vapors, as Hot Springs was known. Some built lodges of brush and skins. Tribal leaders took ritual sweat baths. The old and infirm soaked in warm pools and sipped the bubbling, mineral-laden waters.

From grandparent to grandchild, they passed on this tradition of healing.

French trappers used the springs, too. After the United States purchased the Louisiana Territory in 1803, President Thomas Jefferson sent two men, William Dunbar and George Hunter, to report on the area. Their expedition confirmed the existence of four dozen spring vents on a steaming terrace at the base of Hot Springs Mountain.

Healing waters: As settlers learned of the hot pools, a few traveled to the valley. Bathers hollowed portions of the steaming terrace, making depressions into which hot water flowed. Entrepreneurs erected huts with lattice floors above several springs. Increasing numbers of people claimed, or squatted on, land along **Hot Springs Creek**. At the urging of congressional delegate Ambrose Sevier, who wanted to preserve free access to the water, President Andrew Jackson reserved four sections of land surrounding the spring terrace in 1832. Hot Springs became the first government reservation to protect a natural

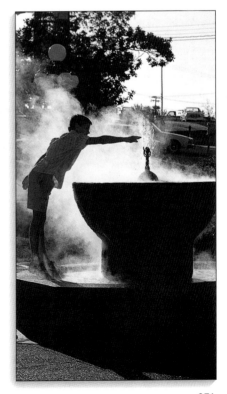

Preceding pages: acorns and autumn leaves. **Left**, azalea blooms at DeSoto Rock Spring. **Right**, mineral water fountain.

resource, predating the founding of Yellowstone by four decades. (Hot Springs Reservation became a national park in 1921.)

In the 1830s, Hot Springs was a bone-jarring, two-day stagecoach trip from **Little Rock**. At several places along the difficult 50-mile (80-km) route, passengers disembarked and walked while the coach and driver teetered precariously across steep cliffs.

But despite the harrowing trip, bathers arrived in record numbers. Each bathhouse proprietor boasted that his or her own spring had particular curative powers: **Mud Spring** yielded hot packs for arthritis. **Arsenic Spring** enhanced ladies' complexions. **Alum Spring** bathed sore eyes. **Liver Spring** and **Kidney Spring** (both cold water) were believed to cure internal ailments. **Corn Hole Spring**, surrounded by wooden benches, was the place to dangle one's corns and bunions.

Although a preserve on paper, Hot Springs suffered a 40-year lapse between establishment and the arrival of the first superintendent. During the hiatus, shoddy tents occupied by diseased indigents sprang up along Hot Springs Creek. It became a foul sewer frequented by free-ranging hogs. Finally, a board of commissioners plotted an orderly network of lots for improved bathhouses. Broad avenues radiated from them into the growing city. Federal inspectors compelled bathhouse proprietors to meet strict standards of cleanliness. Hot Springs Creek was walled up and covered with a masonry arch.

Central Avenue, along which **Bathhouse Row** is located, conceals the stream. It now flows beneath the 100-foot (30-meter)-wide street for a mile (1.5 km) through the middle of town.

The elegant bathhouses constructed from the 1880s through the early 1900s promoted hydropathy, the treatment of maladies by drinking and soaking in hot mineral water. The steaming water induced profuse perspiration, which was believed to expel disease. Popular in Europe, the practice was prescribed by many American physicians around the turn of the century.

During that period, a visitor to Hot Springs would have seen small groups of people gathered at open springs, filling tin cups and sipping hot water. Others, with blankets slung over their shoulders or wrapped around them, sauntered to Bathhouse Row for daily soaks.

Inside the mansions of stone, marble and tile were elaborate tubs and steam cabinets. Some offered gymnasiums, billiard rooms and beauty, barber and shoeshine shops. Many were decorated with stained glass and imported statuary. Men and women bathed in separate areas, with trained attendants to help each patient into a hot bath. A diminutive hourglass timed bathers for 3 minutes, until their skin glowed lobster-red. After leaving the bath, cure-seekers sat in a box filled with dense steam or on top of the vapor box, with a blanket wrapped around them. All the while, they sipped hot water. Bashful bathers of the Victorian era soaked while attired in flannel underwear and heavy socks.

Physicians prescribed a bath a day for three weeks, then a week's rest, some-

Historic bathhouses like the Maurice...

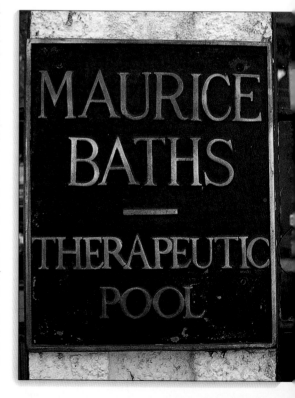

272

times followed by a second or third round of baths. The list of diseases thought to be cured by hydropathy was lengthy, but the curative power of Hot Springs water has been debated for years. Dr Howard Rusk, a specialist in rehabilitative medicine, concluded, "Most of the medicinal effects of spa therapy are indirect, resulting from relaxation of the patient as a result of environmental factors of the spa."

Indeed, Hot Springs did – and still does – provide a relaxing atmosphere. The city boasts fine restaurants, elegant hotels, refined entertainment, thoroughbred horse racing and carriage paths that meander across quiet mountain ridges. Whether or not the water has curative power, it is remarkably pure. In fact, it is so free of contaminants that it was used to store the first rocks brought back from the moon.

Touring the park: Hot Springs is unique among national parks since **Bathhouse Row** is located in a bustling city. Begin your tour at the **Fordyce Bathhouse**, which has been restored to its 1920s

opulence and serves as the park visitor center. Then head north on the **Grand Promenade**, a graceful brick walkway that parallels the spring terrace. You will pass display pools and thermal fountains, then arrive at a flowing spring. Watch the steamy vapors wafting across the tufa terrace and you may be able to visualize how the entire hillside appeared in the days of the pioneers.

Along the way, you may notice a profusion of what Dunbar and Hunter called "moss" growing around the spring vents. Botanists later identified this as green and blue-green algae. Seventeen species thrive in display springs and pools within the park. Most are so specialized they would not survive if water temperatures dropped as much as 10°F (5°C). One type of blue-green algae is found in only four places in the world: Hot Springs, Banff (Canada), Iceland and central Africa.

Complete the loop by walking out to Central Avenue and strolling in front of Bathhouse Row. The popularity of the water cure waned in the mid-20th cen-

...and Ozark still stand on Bathhouse Row.

tury, so several of these ostentatious buildings are no longer used for bathing. Their facades, however, are maintained in historical context. The **Buckstaff** (on Bathhouse Row), **Hot Springs Health Spa** (located within the Libbey Memorial Physical Medicine Center), and four nearby hotels continue to offer thermal bathing for those who wish to take "the cure."

Beyond the bath: Although the main focus of Hot Springs National Park is the healing water, the reservation contains 22 miles (35 km) of wooded trails suitable for hiking or horseback riding. Five miles (8 km) of winding carriage paths allow bicycle and vehicular access to the tops of **Hot Springs**, **North** and **West mountains**. Here, overlooks provide spectacular views of the nearby **Ouachita Mountains** rising within **Ouachita National Forest**.

Energetic hikers can sample a well-preserved forest of shortleaf pines, some more than 250 years old, on the **Sunset Trail**. It begins at the summit of **West Mountain Drive**. Following the ridgeline for 8½ miles (14 km), the trail passes within yards of the park's highest point, at 1,405 feet (428 meters).

Zigzagging east, it flirts with **Balanced Rock**, a chunk of novaculite perched precariously on **Sugarloaf Mountain**. If you don't want to hike the entire trail, check at the visitor center for directions to the 1-mile (1½-km) shortcut to Balanced Rock.

The park lies within a transition area between eastern forest, midwestern prairie and the lowland swamps of Louisiana and east Texas. While pines dominate the ridges, oaks and other hardwoods creep up the hollows. **Sleepy Valley** harbors the state champion black cherry tree. Squirrels, deer, foxes and wild turkeys feast on fruits and acorns in the remote western sections of the park. Quiet hikers can easily encounter them on early-morning or late-afternoon outings. A fortunate few catch glimpses of black bears. Road runners and armadillos, typical of the Southwest, are also quite common.

A profusion of wildflowers begins

Widow dragonfly covered with morning dew.

with spring blossoms of birdfoot violet, fawn lily and yellow star grass. March is especially beautiful, with blooms of wild plum, redbud and dogwood. Along sunny trails and roadsides, daisies and asters continue the colorful procession into late summer. Hardwood forests on the hills surrounding the spa burst into flaming gold, scarlet and crimson after October's first frost.

The **Goat Rock** and **Dogwood trails**, which radiate from **Gulpha Gorge Campground**, offer abundant spring wildflowers. **West Mountain Loop** is a pleasant forested walk for an autumn afternoon. Novaculite outcrops along Goat Rock Trail and near Balanced Rock reveal quarry marks where Native Americans chipped out stone blanks for knives, spears and arrow points.

Those seeking a more serious wilderness experience should consider exploring some of the 1.6 million acres (647,500 hectares) contained within Ouachita National Forest. Its thick forests, excellent trail network and abundant streams, lakes and waterfalls make it ideal for a few days of hiking, biking, boating, fishing or horseback riding. Backcountry camping is permitted throughout the national forest (unless otherwise posted); several campgrounds offer electrical hookups, bathrooms, showers and potable water.

As you roam Hot Springs National Park, you will see a loyal clientele of patrons filling jug after jug of water at the public fountains. For them, the magic of the springs is real. Take a sip. The water is pleasantly warm and refreshing. Thinking about taking a dip? It will be one of the most invigorating, yet relaxing, experiences of your stay here.

Calcium, silica, magnesium – none of the contents of the water is known to be curative, but for generations seekers have come to Hot Springs. Does the shimmering elixir help relieve afflictions? Or do the peaceful environs allow visitors to find inner solace? Sample the waters and decide for yourself. Perhaps you, too, will discover what continues to draw visitors to the Valley of Vapors.

White-tailed fawn.

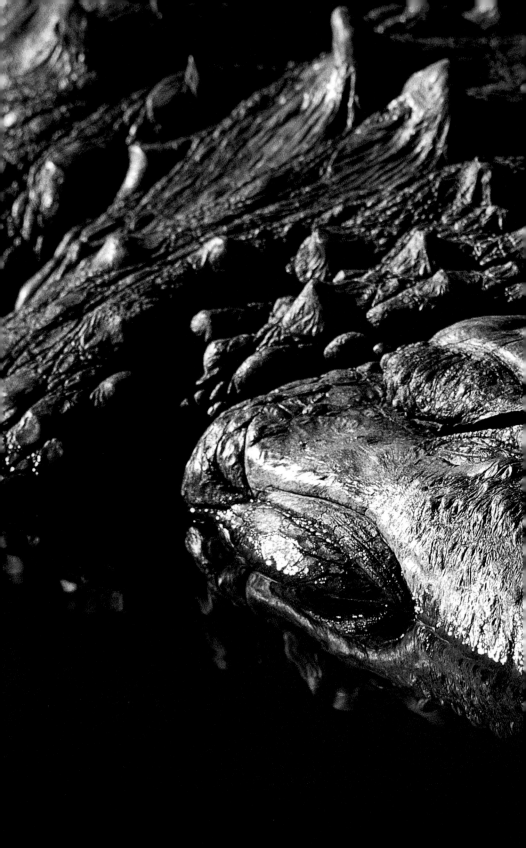

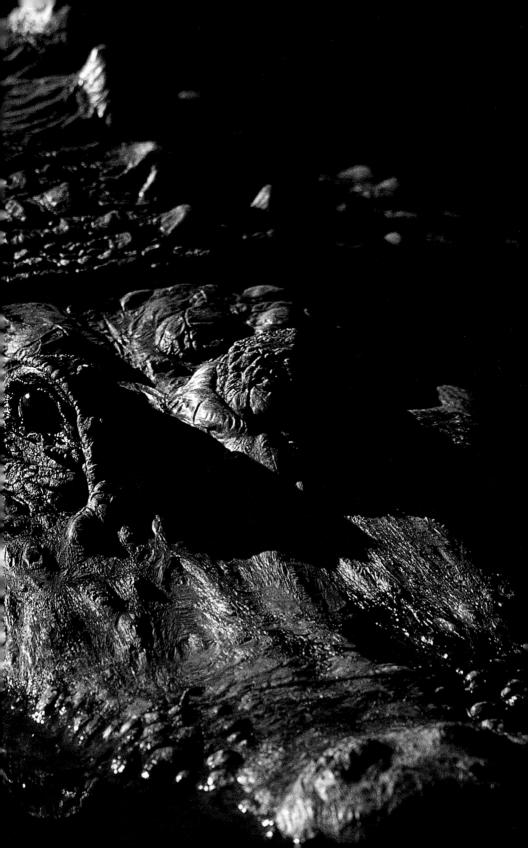

EVERGLADES

"There are no other Everglades in the world," wrote Marjory Stoneman Douglas in her classic book, *The Everglades: River of Grass.* Douglas moved to Miami in 1915, when this village of 3,000 inhabitants was still an outpost on the southern frontier.

No place in the nation has changed more during this century. Florida's first state legislature labeled the Everglades, which lay at Miami's back door, as "wholly valueless." In the early 1900s, Governor Napoleon Bonaparte Broward engineered a network of canals that sliced across southern Florida, carrying fresh water from interior marshes to the sea. Steam-powered dredges heaped spoil along canal banks, forming dry corridors suitable for travel by new-fangled horseless carriages. By the 1920s, all roads led to Miami, which boomed as realty agents sold tract after tract of swampland.

Fortunately, southern Florida's populace has always included a few conservationists. Among the earliest were members of the Florida Federation of Women's Clubs and a landscape architect, Ernest Coe. Together they lobbied and cajoled until 2,200 sq. miles (5,698 sq. km) at the southern tip of the peninsula were preserved in 1947 as Everglades National Park. Within its boundaries lived Florida panthers, tropical orchids and tree snails, alligators, manatees and a veritable rainbow of bird life.

As southern Florida grew and prospered, human neighbors pressed perilously close to the park. Some 5 million people now live on the lower east and west coasts of Florida. An estimated 1,000 per week are still moving into the state. Drive the Gold Coast today, and for nearly 100 unbroken miles (160 km), from Palm Beach south to Homestead, you pass from one development of stucco houses to the next. Fly into Miami or Fort Lauderdale and you will gaze down on acre after acre of red tile roofs and swimming pools, stretching from the lapping waves of the Atlantic Ocean into former Everglades marshes.

Over the years, valuable nature reserves have been acquired: coral reefs near Key Largo, portions of Biscayne Bay, much of the Big Cypress Swamp, and, most recently, an important watershed on the eastern boundary of Everglades National Park. Combined, they rival Yellowstone in size, but they protect only a fifth of the original Everglades ecosystem.

Threatened wilderness: Unfortunately, Everglades National Park is no longer a pristine place. Pollution creeps in from all sides. Burgeoning population and agriculture demand more and more water. Their byproducts degrade the quality of the flow that continues downstream into this huge wetland. Clean water, the lifeblood of the Everglades, is in short supply.

Signs are posted at several park ponds to alert fishermen that mercury contamination has rendered fish unsafe to eat, but no one has figured out how to warn the wildlife. As the numbers of

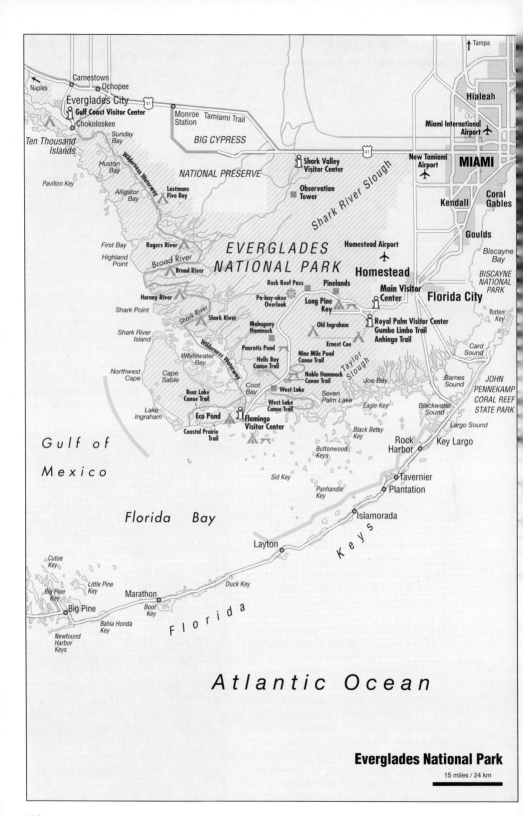

Everglades National Park

15 miles / 24 km

endangered Florida panthers in the park dropped to dangerously low levels, the remaining animals were radio-collared and their movements traced by aerial and ground monitoring. Several died despite no outward signs of injury or ill health. Tissue studies revealed that at least two of these panthers succumbed to mercury poisoning.

Despite its troubles, Everglades National Park has no peer. It is home to 14 species of endangered wildlife. It is an International Biosphere Reserve, a World Heritage Site, and a Wetland of International Significance. Yet first-time visitors are frequently disappointed. With elevations ranging from sea level to 8 feet (2.5 meters), the landscape seems to lack dimension. No cliffs. No waterfalls. At certain seasons, there are enough mosquitoes to send all but the most dedicated explorers racing back to air-conditioned cars. The Everglades is not always an easy place to love.

But Everglades National Park can provide moments of sheer magic. Witness an otter sharing food with her offspring. Like a pair of children eating the same hot dog, they gnaw at opposite ends of a hapless water snake. When it is gone, they bound up the trail, oblivious to the fact that you have been standing motionless nearby, mesmerized in wonder. The playful youngster nearly trips over your feet. Its mother sniffs your shoes, then snorts. Both scamper back to the water.

On another morning, you may be the first to arrive at the **Anhinga Trail**, which loops past the watery homes of fish, turtles and alligators. Grackles squawk and a red-shouldered hawk banks overhead. Suddenly a sharp crack echoes across the water. It sounds like a hammer hitting concrete. Through binoculars you find a huge alligator, half submerged in the dark water, a mossy-backed, football-sized turtle caught in its toothy grip. Once more you hear the tumultuous cracking and crushing. This time you see powerful jaws close around the alligator's breakfast.

Everglades magic is synonymous with birds. More than 300 species frequent the park. They range from diminutive

black-whiskered vireos and secretive white-crowned pigeons, both at northern extremes of their Caribbean ranges, to the ubiquitous crows that greet you at every picnic and parking area. The birds most people associate with the Everglades, however, are long-legged waders – egrets, ibises, herons, storks.

At one time they numbered beyond measure – thousands upon thousands trailing across the skies at dawn or streaming into nighttime roosts. "[We] saw immense flocks of cranes, pink spoonbills, curlew, and wild turkeys in plenty," wrote George Preble, who sloshed through the Everglades in 1842 during the Seminole Indian campaign.

Roughly 2 million wading birds lived at that time in what is now Everglades National Park. Their populations declined about a century ago because aigrette feathers, the lacy courtship plumage of herons and egrets, came into fashion to decorate ladies' hats and clothing. Market hunters invaded rookeries, gunning down adult birds and leaving the chicks to starve. The newly-organ-

The Shark Valley Tower shows visitors some of the Everglades' 14 species of endangered wildlife.

ized Audubon Society hired wardens to guard the rookeries and publicized the birds' plight. With protection, wading bird colonies increased again. Lately, poor water quality and quantity have caused the population of the park's wading birds to decline significantly.

Shark Valley: One of the best places to observe birds is **Shark Valley**, on the **Tamiami Trail** (US 41) 30 miles (48 km) west of Miami. The name is misleading, however – no sharks lurk here. They live miles downstream where the fresh waters from this slough meet the **Gulf of Mexico**. At Shark Valley, a narrow ribbon of pavement loops 15 miles (24 km) into the heart of the Everglades. You can explore on foot, on bicycle, or by joining a naturalist on a two-hour tram ride.

The Indians called this "pa-hay-okee," grassy waters. That's exactly what you will find – an ocean of saw grass growing in fresh water deep enough to slosh over your shoes. Travel down the road a mile or two and you will experience a horizon-to-horizon view of grassy waters dotted with hammocks. Glades extending forever. Ever-glades.

The water forms a shallow river, 50 miles (80 km) wide, only inches deep. Summer is a time of rejuvenation, when thunderstorms drench southern Florida. By November, the air cools a few degrees and drying breezes begin to evaporate water from the marsh. Although the land appears flat, the limestone beneath the saw grass is pocked with depressions. By mid-winter, the sheet flow of surface water may be gone, but solution holes in the limestone are wellsprings of life. Each hole is inhabited by at least one alligator. As winter water levels drop, the alligator thrashes around, slinging mud on the bank and deepening the hole. Turtles bask, fish wriggle, frogs croak, wading birds stalk, raccoons prowl, and snakes slither stealthily around the 'gator hole. All the energy of the ecosystem seems distilled into one storybook setting. Every week or two, the 'gator gets hungry and dines on one of these guests. That is only fair, since these water-dependent creatures owe

Cloudless sulphur butterfly.

their existence to the keeper of the pool.

By late spring, when it seems that gator holes will hold no more critters and the marly mud on the dry saw-grass plain can crack no more, thunderheads brew on the horizon. With rain, the river rises among the saw-grass stalks and returns to its southwesterly, inches-per-day flow. Fish swim back into the marsh and wading birds fan out to stalk them.

Homestead to Flamingo: The park encompasses more than saw grass. To sample its cornucopia of pinelands, tropical hammocks, mangroves and brackish bays, head for **Homestead**. Then drive southwest for 12 miles (19 km) past fields of tomatoes, green beans, squash and "U-pick" strawberries to the park's main entrance. Here you will encounter "high" pinelands, typical of those settled by early Miamians. A swath of limestone, the Atlantic Coastal Ridge, extends along Florida's east coast from Fort Lauderdale to Homestead, then swings southwest into the park. This limestone is a foot or two higher than the substrate under the marshes, thus it supports dry forest dominated by pines and palmettos. Much of the countryside between Miami and Homestead looked like this a century ago. But pinelands offered dry home sites. With trees cut and the jagged rock pulverized by bulldozers, valuable winter vegetables could be grown. Most of southern Florida's slash pines are gone now. Everglades National Park protects the last sizable tract of the trees, plus the myriad endemic shrubs and wildflowers that survive with them in this specialized habitat.

Stop at the **visitor center** near the park entrance for a schedule of ranger-guided activities and an overview of the wildlife you will see as you continue through the park. Then drive along the 38-mile (61-km) road that leads to **Flamingo**, where the mainland slips into **Florida Bay**. Along the way are a half-dozen pullouts with natural history exhibits and self-guiding boardwalks or short trails. Spend a few moments at each to sample the variety of life.

One of the most rewarding ventures is a walk along the **Anhinga Trail**, which

Many backcountry campsites may only be reached by water.

begins at **Royal Palm**, 4 miles (6 km) from the main entrance. This half-mile (1-km) loop is named for the long-necked, duck-footed birds that hang out like teenagers around a swimming pool. Anhingas plunge into the water when they are hungry and skewer fish on dagger-like beaks as they swim. Then they dry off by draping their broad black wings and tails in the sun. Various herons – from the amazingly camouflaged green-backed herons to the stately great blue herons – also hunt near the trail. It is a rare day when visitors fail to spot alligators and red-bellied turtles.

In contrast to the sunny openness of the Anhinga Trail, the **Gumbo-Limbo Trail** (also at Royal Palm) leads into a hammock. Hammocks, or tree islands, grow on limestone outcrops surrounded by glades. A moat eroded in the limestone around each hammock protects it from fires that periodically sweep the marshes and pinelands. Hammocks contain a rich variety of old-growth hardwood trees. This one is named for its abundant gumbo-limbos, which, with

their red, peeling bark, are sometimes dubbed "Florida tourist trees."

Hammocks normally have a dense canopy of branches overhead, shading orchids, ferns and mosses in the understory. In August 1992, Hurricane Andrew blasted across southern Florida with winds of 145 miles (233 km) per hour and some gusts exceeding 175 miles (281 km) per hour. Its path paralleled the park road from the visitor center to **Pa-hay-okee**. Many of the large trees in hammocks were toppled and crowns of pine trees snapped like matchsticks. Events such as fires and hurricanes traditionally shape the Everglades, but scars from Hurricane Andrew will be visible for years to come.

Short trails at **Long Pine Key Campground** and **Pinelands** (2 miles/3 km beyond the campground turnoff) are excellent places to learn about the role fire plays in maintaining the ecosystem. You may be lucky enough to visit while park rangers are conducting a "prescribed" burn. Like doctors ministering to an ailing patient, they select part of the pine forest that has not burned in several years. When temperature, wind and soil moisture conditions are perfect, they administer doses of burning fuel from hand-held drip torches, or drop small incendiary devices from a hovering helicopter.

Flames crackle through the thicket, consuming hardwoods that threaten to choke out the fire-dependent pines. Deer and birds skitter away from the smoke. Snakes and turtles drop into holes in the limestone and emerge unscathed after the blaze dies down. Within a week or two, new green vegetation bursts forth from the blackened plot, fertilized by the ash left in the fire's wake.

Sharp-eyed visitors may spot *Liguus* tree snails here. These thumb-sized creatures of Caribbean ancestry were collected in bygone days for their varicolored shells. Finding them is a bit like an Easter-egg hunt, since their pink, yellow and chestnut-brown bands blend with sunlight-dappled tree branches.

When you do locate a snail, admire it without picking it up. "Ligs" endure the dry winter by cementing themselves

Only 10 percent of the birds once found in the Everglades remain.

securely to tree bark to conserve water. Plucking the shell breaks the seal and will probably kill the snail. One of the treats of visiting during the summer rainy season is the chance to see snails emerge from their shells to graze on algae and lichens attached to tree bark.

A subtle change: Driving to Pa-hay-okee, you will cross **Rock Reef Pass**, elevation 3 feet (1 meter). At first glance, the roadside sign may seem like a prank. But if you take a moment to look, you will see hardwood shrubs growing on a linear limestone outcrop that intersects the road. Away from this ridge, where the substrate is a foot lower, saw grass grows. A subtle change in elevation, a big change in vegetation.

The short **Pa-hay-okee Trail** is on the eastern edge of **Shark River Slough**. As the ibis flies, you are only 15 miles (24 km) from the Shark Valley observation tower. Standing at either place, the view before you takes in much of the broad, shallow river that supplies life-giving water to the center of the park.

Back in the car, the road rises a final time to cross the end of the pineland ridge, then drops into glades sprinkled with tree islands. Among the largest is **Mahogany Hammock**, which houses several storm-battered but stately West Indian mahogany trees. Listen for the hoots of barred owls as you saunter along the boardwalk, breathing in the rich, earthy odors, a byproduct of fallen leaves and branches that are being transformed into the thin layer of life-giving soil that covers the gnarled limestone.

Your next roadside discovery – near **Paurotis Pond** – are portly little trees tiptoeing across the marsh. They are red mangroves. As you approach the salty water of Florida Bay, you will notice that they prosper – held up in the slick, shallow substrate by their arching prop roots. Along with black mangrove, white mangrove and buttonwood, they comprise a tangled forest from Key Largo to Everglades City and beyond.

Sample the mangrove landscape on the **Noble Hammock** or **Hells Bay** canoe trails. Navigating the twisting, prop-root-lined channels is like entering a

The "River of Grass."

hall of mirrors in a jungle. If you enjoy a challenge, try the 99-mile (159-km) **Wilderness Waterway** that provides backcountry boat access between Flamingo and **Everglades City**. If the sulfur-smelling, tannin-stained waters are not your cup of tea, a quick walk around the **Mangrove Trail** boardwalk at **West Lake** will suffice.

Flamingo and Everglades City are both laid-back, end-of-the- road fishing villages. Everglades City, 35 miles (56 km) from Naples, is a small town with a ranger station that serves as a gateway to the northwest corner of the park. One of the main industries here is seafood, and in season, local restaurants serve up some of the finest stone crabs and mullet on Florida's west coast. Sightseeing boats depart on numerous cruises into a mangrove estuary known as the **Ten Thousand Islands**. Although commercial airboats are not permitted in the park, several tour operators offer rides nearby along the **Tamiami Trail**.

Flamingo was a fishing and charcoal-making enclave until the creation of the park. Now it is the jumping-off point for water-based explorations such as sightseeing cruises, canoe and houseboat rentals, and sailing tours. A busy marina caters to local and vacationing sport fishermen. You can stay at a comfortable motel and the adjoining restaurant will cook your catch-of-the day for you. The Park Service provides a pleasant campground on **Florida Bay**, and naturalists lead a variety of hiking, biking, canoeing and birding activities. Be sure to bring your sunscreen, and don't forget to check the "mosquito barometer."

On the wall of the visitor center hangs a cartoon mosquito with a movable proboscis. On any particular day it may point to "enjoyable"… "bearable"… "unpleasant"… "horrible"… "hysterical." Forty-three mosquito species inhabit the park. In most areas they are a problem during the summer, especially from dusk to dawn. At Flamingo, where old-timers swear that they can swing a pint jar and catch a quart of mosquitoes, biting bugs can be a nuisance any time of the year. As a matter of fact, if the gauge reads "hysterical," you will know before you ever reach the visitor center.

Indeed, there are days when this is not an easy park to love. But given a chance, its subtle beauty begins to grow on you. The warm air shimmers. Billowing clouds surf across the horizon. Gentle breezes rustle the saw grass. Turtles blink. Alligators yawn. Manatees loll beneath the mangroves.

Spend a night. Listen to the insects humming softly in the marsh. Now and then comes a deep grunt from a pig frog or the otherworldly wail of a limpkin, the seldom-seen bird whose nickname is "night-crier." The same expanse of saw grass that appeared so lifeless by day erupts in a frenzy of splashes and clucks under the star-studded sky.

As foggy dawn gives way to full sunlight, the birds arrive. Long Vs of ibises head for drying pools beneath stunted cypress trees. Herons spear fish with stiletto bills, and storks hunch in the shallow water. For once, the often misused word "unique" is justified. As Marjory Stoneman Douglas said: "There are no other Everglades in the world."

Moonrise over royal palms.

THE FLORIDA PANTHER

In defense of the Everglades, Florida Senator Bob Graham wrote: "Victories for the environment are temporary. Losses are forever."

Despite valiant efforts, wildlife biologists are losing Florida panthers. The last matriarch in the clan that roamed Everglades National Park died in 1991. Only 30 to 50 adults remain statewide. Their last-stand refuge is the Big Cypress Swamp east of Naples, Florida, where they crisscross wet prairies, cypress stands and scattered hardwood forests in search of deer, feral hogs, rabbit and raccoons.

Historically, panthers were numerous throughout the Western Hemisphere. Also called cougars, pumas, mountain lions and painters, these tawny felines adapted to life in deserts, mountains, dense forests and steamy swamps. Geographical separation has created distinct subspecies. Among the rarest is the Florida panther (*Felis concolor coryi*), usually distinguished by a swirling cowlick on the neck, tan fur flecked with white at the shoulders and a crook at the tip of the tail. Once found across terrain extending from Florida and South Carolina to Louisiana, these panthers gradually fell prey to hunters and urbanization of their wilderness habitat.

A leading cause of death for Florida panthers is collisions with vehicles on the busy highway that bisects their once-pristine homeland. Chain-link fences along Interstate 75 usher Big Cypress panthers to underpasses away from traffic. Highway 41 near Ochopee and Highway 29 south of Immokalee have reduced-speed zones and eye-catching signs that caution motorists to be wary as they approach known panther crossings.

Necropsies of several panthers found dead in the Everglades have revealed high levels of mercury in their livers. These animals must have eaten many raccoons and some alligators that had dined on mercury-tainted fish from Shark Slough. After the last female in Everglades National Park died, the remaining male made his lonely way across the saw-grass prairies to join panthers in the Big Cypress.

Worries about pollution, poaching and highway collisions are well-founded, but US Fish and Wildlife Service Panther Recovery Coordinator Dennis Jordan warns of an even more troubling situation. "Because of the isolation of the Florida panther for probably a century or longer," Jordan explains, "the small population in South Florida is very inbred. That creates a number of physiological problems that will, in all likelihood, lead to extinction if they can't be corrected."

In 1991 state and federal officials agreed to capture wild panther kittens for a captive breeding program. So far, 10 young panthers representative of various wild gene pools have joined the program. Once mature, they will be mated to produce the most genetically diverse animals possible for future generations.

In the meantime, about a dozen radio-collared Texas cougars (*Felis concolor stanleyana*) have been released into the swamps and pine forests along the Florida–Georgia border to test whether that area can support a panther population. According to Jordan, the transplants are doing well. Eventually they will be recaptured. By that time, offspring from the captive breeders should be ready for release in northern Florida as well as to bolster the Big Cypress population.

"The real question is overcoming some of the genetic deficiencies," Jordan concludes. "If we can, I think the prospects for Florida panthers are really good." ∎

The endangered Florida panther.

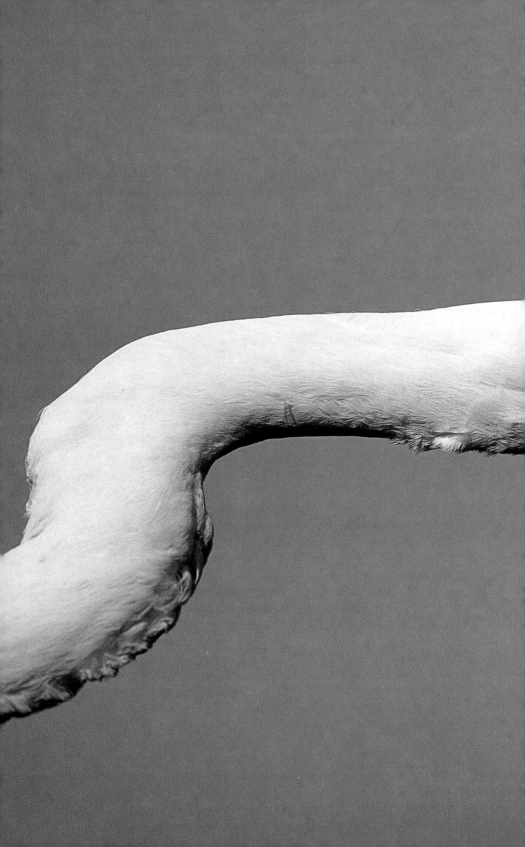

BISCAYNE AND DRY TORTUGAS

It is a still morning. The little waves of **Biscayne Bay** lap placidly against the jetty at **Convoy Point**. On the horizon, brown pelicans glide in single file, skimming low over the water. Periodically one wheels and dives headlong into the bay. Bobbing back to the surface, the bird squeezes excess water from its bulging throat pouch, tosses its beak skyward, and swallows a fishy prize. Then it flaps laboriously to rejoin the flight line.

For visitors first glimpsing this park at the end of the paved road from **Homestead**, Florida, Biscayne offers a view of vast water and a distant horizon. If they could rise with the pelicans, however, visitors would be treated to a different perspective. From the air, the park is a visual smorgasbord in painterly shades of green and blue. Beneath the shimmering aqua surface of Biscayne Bay rests a patchwork of sea-grass beds and sandy shoals. Several miles seaward stretches a breakwater of narrow islands draped in the emerald hues of tropical vegetation. Beyond them lie the cobalt depths of the **Gulf Stream**.

Before Spanish explorers came in the 1500s, Tequesta Indians plied Biscayne Bay in dugout canoes. Paddling to the islands from camps along the coast, they gathered sea grape and cocoplum fruits from the forest and harvested conchs, spiny lobsters, turtles and manatees from the sea.

By the 1700s, Spanish treasure ships sailed past Biscayne on their homeward journeys from Latin America. Unmarked reefs and unpredictable hurricanes sometimes grounded them, and pirates lurked about. One of the most notorious pirates, Black Caesar, hid his sloops in the narrow cut that winds between **Adams** and **Old Rhodes keys**. When Spanish vessels lumbered by, he darted out to relieve them of their riches. The passage still carries Caesar's name.

About a century ago, hearty "conch" settlers farmed Elliott and Old Rhodes keys. They supplied pineapples, limes and tomatoes to Key West and Miami until, as happens periodically, a hurricane blew through and salted the soil.

Geologically, Florida is young. Only 100,000 years ago ocean waters engulfed the peninsula, with coral thriving in the shallow sea. Later, when water levels dropped, reefs emerged. Along Florida's lower east coast they embody a chain of limestone keys (from the Spanish *cayo*, or small island), extending 150 miles (241 km) from **Key Biscayne** to **Key West**, then skipping intermittently west another 70 miles (113 km) to the **Dry Tortugas**.

Jungle islands: Biscayne National Park includes about three dozen keys, ranging from 2 to 8 feet (0.5–2.5 meters) above sea level. Most are small, their combined mass accounting for a twentieth of Biscayne's surface area. **Elliott**, Old Rhodes, **Totten** and **Sands** keys are home to diverse hardwood forests with Caribbean species, including West Indian mahogany, Jamaica dogwood, wild coffee, cinnamon bark, strangler fig, gumbo-limbo, lignum vitae, torchwood and lancewood. They are

knit into near impenetrability by spike-stemmed vines and twisted lianas, among them cat's claw, hold-back vine and spiny nickerbean. Foot travel in the forest is further hindered by mosquitoes, which are always present and usually ravenous. But hikers, who should be protectively cocooned in long sleeves, long pants and a liberal slathering of insect repellent, will find the nearly 7-mile (11-km) trail on **Elliott Key** a fascinating window into this jungle.

Only months before the park was set aside, those who favored commercial development of the area bulldozed a swath for a six-lane highway down the length of Elliott Key. In the past 25 years, **Spite Highway** has revegetated into a hiking trail. Along its edges orb spiders weave golden webs, and endangered indigos – large but exceedingly gentle snakes – prowl for rodents, ground-nesting birds, even other snakes. Schaus swallowtail butterflies, also endangered, flutter on dark wings decorated with pale-yellow chevrons. Females deposit eggs on the leaves of torchwood and wild lime, the sole food for their finicky maroon caterpillars.

Some 175 species of birds frequent Biscayne. Forest-feeding white-crowned pigeons and diminutive black-whiskered vireos are tropicals attracted to this northernmost range of Caribbean hardwoods. Many of Biscayne's avian residents, including pelicans, cormorants, ibises, spoonbills and a plethora of lanky herons and egrets, haunt shoals and tidal flats near the islands.

The cooling ponds of **Turkey Point** power plant, on the southwestern park boundary, attract nesting crocodiles, one of the park's endangered species. Although alligators are more numerous in southern Florida, they dwell in fresh rather than salt water. A few alligators do occasionally swim into Biscayne Bay. They are dark-skinned, with blunt snouts. Crocodiles have olive skins and long, narrow snouts.

The tide-washed edges of the keys are vegetated by four varieties of mangroves, trees that require a frost-free climate. Red mangroves creep farthest

The endangered manatee, a sea mammal, often passes through Biscayne Bay.

from shore on emergent, prop-like roots. Their seeds develop to cigar size before dropping into the sea. They bob upright until they encounter a shoal, then spawn new mats of stabilizing roots. Black mangroves employ pencil-thin breathing tubes that extend above the water. They shed excess salt by "sweating" through their leaves. White mangroves occupy slightly higher ground, and buttonwood, from which settlers made charcoal, occupies sites flooded only during spring tides or tropical storms.

While arching roots of red mangrove colonize shoal waters, they are simultaneously colonized by such tidal dwellers as barnacles, tubeworms and snails. Beneath the surface, colorful sponges and clusters of algae attach. Immature shrimp, lobsters, snook, snappers and sea trout seek food and shelter here. As fleshy mangrove leaves fall into the water and decay, they produce a nutrient-rich detritus broth, making the tidal mangrove zone a vital nursery for sport and commercial fish. This is also a wonderful place to snorkel. Pinfish and silvery mullet dart about beneath the roots, an occasional mangrove snapper or toothy barracuda in pursuit.

Biscayne Bay, which averages 5 feet (1½ meters) deep, hosts large turtle grass beds. Protective cover offered by the ribbony leaves lures grass shrimp, sea horses, pipefish, small crabs, myriad minnow-sized fishes and oddities such as boxfish and puffers. These latter imbibe a belly full of sea water when threatened, pumping themselves into spine-covered spheres undesirable to predators. While inflated, they bob like submerged soccer balls. Once danger passes, they deflate, returning to their normal boxy-looking profile.

Whether viewed through snorkel mask or glass-bottomed boat, the buzz of aquatic life in the grass beds is an invitation to learn more about Biscayne's underwater world, which makes up 95 percent of the park. Begin your exploration at the **Convoy Point Visitor Center**, which features exhibits and a half-mile boardwalk that stretches seaward on a long jetty. Here you can fish, bird watch or look for tidal marine life.

A concessionaire operates boat tours and snorkel or dive trips from Convoy Point. Private boaters launch from the county marina next door or set sail from Miami. Check fuel and supplies before leaving the mainland, since there are no provisions at the small harbor on Elliott Key. The concessionaire provides a water taxi service for those who wish to hike, camp or use the small swimming beach on Elliott.

Beneath the surface: Biscayne is home to the northernmost coral reefs in this hemisphere. In order for corals to flourish, sea water must be clear, rich in nutrients, and remain above 68°F (20°C). The proximity of the Gulf Stream, awash with tropical currents, and the mild climate of southern Florida, often combine to raise water temperature into the 80s Fahrenheit (around 27°C).

There are some 50 types of corals in the park. Most easily recognized are elkhorn, staghorn, star and large "heads" of convoluted brain coral. These are "hard" corals, with tentacles in multiples of six. The polyps feed at night,

Playing on the beach.

withdrawing by day into limy protective cups. "Soft" corals, including branched sea whips, colorful sea fans, plumes and feathers, sway with the passing waves. Their tentacles are arranged in eights, and they feed during the day.

Some of Biscayne's most interesting patch reefs lie 2 to 3 miles (3–5 km) east of Elliott Key. They are marked with blue-and-white mooring buoys, which allow boaters to tie up without setting anchor in the fragile corals below. **Elkhorn** and **Star Coral reefs** feature many varieties of coral, including lettuce and finger corals in calmer areas. Swimmers should watch for fire coral on the seaward edges of these reefs. Contact with the white-tipped formations causes a sharp stinging sensation.

Dome Reef is host to an array of soft corals, including beautiful purple sea fans. Various sponges decorate this reef, their urn-shaped bodies appearing in hues of red, green, purple and brown. During the mid- to late 1800s, sponges were harvested commercially in southern Florida, but overharvesting took a toll. Within the park, reef creatures are now protected.

Another mooring buoy marks **Schooner Wreck Reef**, where one of the approximately 40 known shipwrecks in the park slowly decays. The most obvious remaining features here are two large piles of ballast rock. At other wrecks, divers may encounter barnacle-encrusted timbers or rusting hardware.

The most remarkable residents of Biscayne's reefs are the fish. Whether snorkeling or diving, exploring a reef means entering a weightless, seemingly carefree realm in which fish of all sizes and shapes and every color of the rainbow surround you. The sensation is much like being in the midst of a three-dimensional Jacques Cousteau film.

You may see broken corals around some reefs, evidence of Hurricane Andrew, which blasted Biscayne with winds in excess of 150 miles (241 km) per hour in August 1992. New growth is gradually covering the underwater scars, as are toppled mangroves and forest hardwoods sprouting anew on the is-

Reeling in a toothy barracuda.

lands. Facilities at Convoy Point and Elliott Key have been repaired. Picnic sites, short trails and other facilities on Adams and **Boca Chita** keys are scheduled to reopen in 1996.

Whether you gaze toward the low-lying keys from the mainland or slip underwater for an up-close and personal view of a reef, Biscayne is a park with a sea-oriented perspective. It preserves an amazingly pristine section of Florida's coast, where creatures such as dolphins, sea turtles and eagles thrive within sight of Miami's skyline.

Dry Tortugas National Park: At the opposite end of the keys, occupying a lonely outpost that is a gateway to the Gulf of Mexico, lies **Dry Tortugas National Park**, one of the most remote and least-visited national parks in the lower 48 states. Spanish explorer Ponce de Leon named the seven tiny coral keys *Las Tortugas* for the abundance of sea turtles he found on his voyage of discovery in 1513. But the islands offered no fresh water. Other than temporarily harboring pirate ships and providing a home for wildlife, they remained unused for another three centuries.

As coastal defense became a growing concern, military planners realized the strategic importance of the island cluster. In 1846 the War Department began construction of the nation's largest brick fort on **Garden Key**. **Fort Jefferson** is a half-mile in perimeter, with walls 50 feet (15 meters) high and 8 feet (2½ meters) thick. During the 1860s, it guarded military prisoners, including Dr Samuel Mudd, who set the broken leg of John Wilkes Booth, the assassin of President Abraham Lincoln.

After the Civil War, outbreaks of yellow fever and a hurricane caused abandonment of this "Gibraltar of the Gulf." Sooty terns, which fly over the Atlantic Ocean and Caribbean Sea during most of the year, nest on the sands of **Bush Key** each spring. President Theodore Roosevelt designated the Tortugas a wildlife refuge in 1908 to protect the islands from egg collection. Two decades later, the ruins of the fort and the nearby keys were upgraded to a national monument. In 1992 the surrounding 100-sq. mile (259-sq. km) coral reef was deemed significant enough to be designated a national park.

Geographic isolation is part of the fascination of the Tortugas. About 40,000 visitors annually charter boats and seaplanes from the Florida Keys or pilot their own craft to reach Garden Key. The fort is open for self-guided tours during daylight hours. Camping and picnicking are permitted on the grassy area outside the moat. Some 99.9 percent of the park is submerged. Snorkelers can explore coral jungles only a few yards from the swimming beach, while divers seek deeper reefs and relics from the 250 shipwrecks lying offshore in the warm, clear water.

If you are planning a trip, remember that the nearest food, fresh water and supplies are located 68 miles (110 km) away in **Key West**. Provide for anticipated needs, then kick back and relax. Lulled by lapping waves and the chatter of sea birds, it's easy to forget that there is a real world beyond the endless blue sea that surrounds the Dry Tortugas.

A feather-duster brightens up the reef.

VIRGIN ISLANDS

"Today a little more land may belong to the sea, tomorrow a little less," Rachel Carson wrote. "Always the edge of the sea remains an elusive and indefinable boundary." At **Virgin Islands National Park** located on the little island of **St John** in the US Virgin Islands, this mingling of sea and sand creates a rich and scenic tapestry.

About 100 million years ago, formation of the Virgin Islands began off the northern shoulder of South America. Lava flowed from cracks in the earth's crust deep beneath the sea, building a broad volcanic base. Some 30 million years later, the ocean floor was thrust toward the surface. Volcanic eruptions continued, pushing jagged, conical profiles above the sea.

Rain, wind and waves softened these rugged features, covering the islands with a thin coating of soil. Air and water delivered the elements of life: floating seeds, flying insects, migrant birds and bats, and lizards clinging to seagoing logs. As eons passed, the islands flowered under a nurturing tropical sun.

The Virgin Islands are located in the **Lesser Antilles**, the archipelago that separates the Atlantic and Caribbean. The first humans arrived on the islands more than 5,000 years ago by sailing north from South America. Centuries later, Christopher Columbus claimed the region for Spain and named them *Las Once Mille Virgines*, The Eleven Thousand Virgins.

A series of Spanish, Dutch, English and French colonists followed Columbus. Denmark occupied the Virgin Islands early in the 1700s. During that era, plantation owners imported slave labor to clear tropical forests and plant cotton, indigo, tobacco and sugar cane. Sugar was the most profitable of these crops, with excess cane converted to molasses and rum. After the abolition of slavery in 1848, the great estates were abandoned and fell into disrepair. **Annaberg Plantation** in Virgin Islands National Park is one of only a few well-

preserved sites from the colonial period.

In 1917 Denmark sold St Croix, St Thomas, St John and about 50 smaller islands to the United States. The Navy managed the Virgin Islands until 1931, when they became self-governing US territories. Tourism now provides the islands' major source of revenue.

From forest to sea: Tourists arrive on **St Thomas** either by plane or on the cruise ships that dock in the deep natural harbor of the capital, **Charlotte Amalie**. Historic buildings in the old town were constructed of thick masonry walls so that they could withstand hurricanes, fires and the cannons of passing pirates. Following narrow streets, the city rises from the harbor in a picturesque array of historic red-roofed stucco homes and shops, now interspersed with modern condominiums.

More than a million visitors find their way every year to the small island of St John. Many of these trips begin with an unforgettable taxi ride from St Thomas's airport or harbor along winding roads to **Red Hook**, at the eastern end of the

Preceding pages: the beach at Trunk Bay, with Trunk and Whistling Cays in the distance. Left, ruins of Annaberg Sugar Mill. Right, bluestriped grunt.

island. Here visitors board public ferries for the 20-minute crossing of **Pillsbury Sound**. The 3-mile (5-km) passage ends at **Cruz Bay**, a mellow village that serves as the gateway to the park and home to the visitor center, where you'll find free maps, brochures and a few books. Jitneys provide shuttle service from Cruz Bay to destinations throughout the island. If you decide instead to rent a vehicle, remember that residents drive on the left, pass on the right, and converse with their horns.

About two-thirds of St John and its adjacent waters are preserved within Virgin Islands National Park. From tropical forest atop 1,277-foot (389-meter) **Bordeaux Mountain** to cactus-studded scrub on the eastern shore, to the coral canyons of outlying reefs, the park offers amazing diversity within an area just 5 by 9 miles (8 by 14½ km) at the widest points.

For a short foray on St John, sample the tropical beauty with a circular tour that follows serpentine **Centerline Road** across the backbone of the island. Thick

stands of mahogany, gumbo-limbo, kapok, fragrant bay rum and ironwood shade much of the drive.

As you approach the eastern shore, you'll see the turquoise waters of **Coral Bay**, where schooners carrying slaves and sugar once anchored. Continue to historic **Annaberg**, on the north shore, where locals weave baskets and cook native foods much as their ancestors did on the many plantations that once dotted this island. You may sample kalaloo, a spicy meat and seafood stew, or soursops, which are indigenous sweet-tart fruits. Pause to marvel at the clever combination of ballast brick, coral and native rock that masons crafted into the thick walls of the sugar factory and windmill.

Rainbow world: On the return, take **North Shore Road** to **Cinnamon Bay** or **Trunk Bay**, which is blessed with one of the most beautiful beaches in the Caribbean. Here you can don snorkel mask and fins (available for rent at both beaches) and dip into the fascinating coral gardens located a few yards beyond the beach. Join a ranger-led swim or consult a lifeguard for a quick lesson if you have not snorkeled before. Although passing storms create occasional ground swells, on most days the water is so calm that even timid swimmers float fearlessly over this rainbow realm.

Corals are colonies of tiny animals called polyps, simple creatures with cavernous mouths surrounded by tentacles that paralyze plankton prey. As polyps grow, they secrete the limey calcium carbonate that builds reefs. Easily recognized are large heads of convoluted brain coral, which form on the seaward sides of reefs. Elk and staghorn corals may be found reaching for the surface at mid-reef. Star corals look like asterisk-studded mounds and are usually found in the lee of the waves. Leathery gorgonians and gaudy purple sea fans sway in the current.

At first you may think your ears have not cleared properly because of the static background noise in the water. This is actually the crunching of parrotfish as they graze on algae that grows on dead coral. Parrotfish bite chunks of coral

The thick trunk and roots of a strangler fig hold it firmly in place.

with their hooked "beaks," crushing it with plate-like teeth. They can quickly change color to blend with various backgrounds. The largest and brightest are stoplight parrotfish which, as they mature, actually change in both color and, remarkably, sex; they start out as red females and turn into blue-green "supermales." Schools of yellow-and-blue French grunts also swim through these submerged canyons, grunting as they go.

Several varieties of angelfish, resembling jewel-studded pancakes on edge, graze daintily on sponges. While watching them, you may be suddenly surrounded by a school of indigo-colored blue tangs. They are named for the hinged spine at the base of the tail that flicks out like a switch-blade to warn away intruders. The unusual trumpet fish, which actually resembles a clarinet as it floats head-down, vacuums smaller fish into its bell-shaped mouth. Green and hawksbill sea turtles occasionally paddle by. Watch, too, for bright-red cleaner shrimp that set up stations among the coral where larger fish come to be groomed of their parasites.

If you have more time, join a night dive. After dark, the reef is amazingly different. Parrotfish excrete a mucous cocoon around themselves each evening and pass the night in this snug sleeping bag. Tight groups of porkfish and grunts that school on the reef by day disperse to feed over fringing grass beds at night. They are replaced by reddish squirrel fish and bigeyes that emerge from coral crevices to hunt marine worms and smaller fish. Moray eels leave their dens. These snake-shaped fish constantly open and close their toothy jaws to pump water across their gills. While this imparts a sinister appearance, eels hunt by smell. They are normally quite gentle around divers.

Please, protect reefs by refraining from touching these delicate formations. Many corals grow only a few inches per year or less, and individual polyps can be killed by a visitor's unconscious grasp. If you cruise to more distant reefs in a rental boat, tie up to a mooring buoy

Arrow crab feeding.

or anchor downwind over a patch of sand. When diving to view fish or formations, float over the reef rather than standing on it. Try not to disturb bottom sediments with your flippers.

Several topside trails can transport you into equally varied tropical habitats. A fascinating trail rises from the cobbles of **Salt Pond Beach**, switchbacking for about a mile up **Ram Head**. The arid surroundings support agave, branching cereus cactus and barrel-shaped, pink-flowered Turk's cap. From the windswept precipice, birders may spot brown pelicans, brown boobies and red-tailed and white-tailed tropicbirds.

Reef Bay Trail begins in the moist mountain forest off Centerline Road. It descends for 2½ miles (4 km), passing into dry forest at lower elevations. Halfway down the mountain, a spur trail leads to boulders decorated with petroglyphs. The humanlike faces may have been carved by early Indians or Africans. Near the trail's terminus stand ruins of the **Reef Bay Sugar Factory**. If you join a ranger or make prior arrangements, you can board a boat here to return to Cruz Bay without hiking back up the steep mountainside.

Accommodations include basic campsites or fully-outfitted tents. Nearby **Maho Bay**, a private camp, offers tent-cottages built on platforms in the forest. For the ultimate luxury, you might try the resort at **Caneel Bay**. Here you can relax with a frothy pina colada while listening to the strains of a steel band.

No matter where you roam on St John, there is beauty and serenity. Waves lap alluringly on the sugary beaches, and the warm, clear water invites leisurely exploration. The Virgin Islands are an exotic, exciting playground. One visit may not be enough.

Buck Island Reef National Monument: If you're looking for additional diving spots, consider visiting the coral reef at **Buck Island**, generally regarded as one of the most pristine underwater habitats in the world. Its isolated location, 6 miles (4 km) from **Christiansted** off the northeast coast of **St Croix**, is washed by the plankton-laden waters of the Atlantic. A typical section of reef here supports about 40 types of coral and more than 300 varieties of fish.

Numerous charter boats depart daily from Christiansted harbor. A typical trip includes a morning of snorkeling along an underwater trail where curious fish often follow swimmers. At lunchtime, your skipper may dock near the shimmering white beach. Buck Island was named for the *bocken* (goats) pastured here in centuries past. Energetic hikers can follow a wandering trail to the summit for a grand panorama. You can't stay overnight on the small island, so charter operators return to Christiansted in the afternoon.

For an unforgettable evening, rent your own boat and anchor offshore. Watch the red sun silhouette the rolling hills of distant St Croix as it dips below the horizon. One by one the stars appear, filling the night sky with millions of twinkling jewels. Warm breezes and gentle swells will rock you to sleep, although here in the Virgin Islands you may already have discovered the place of your dreams.

Left, the feathery polychaete is a species of marine worm. **Right**, a horse of a different color.

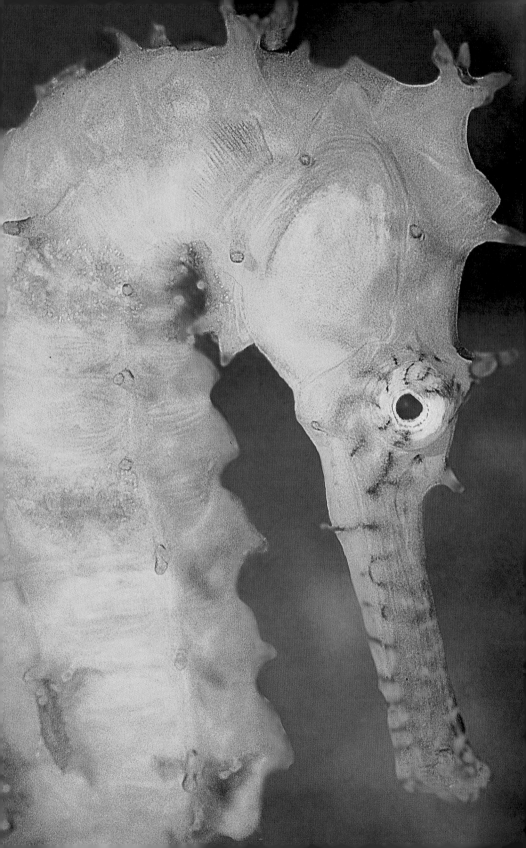

INSIGHT GUIDES
Travel Tips

FOR THOSE
WITH MORE THAN
A PASSING INTEREST
IN TIME...

Before you put your name down for a Patek Philippe watch *fig. 1*, there are a few basic things you might like to know, without knowing exactly whom to ask. In addressing such issues as accuracy, reliability and value for money, we would like to demonstrate why the watch we will make for you will be quite unlike any other watch currently produced.

"Punctuality", Louis XVIII was fond of saying, "is the politeness of kings."

We believe that in the matter of punctuality, we can rise to the occasion by making you a mechanical timepiece that will keep its rendezvous with the Gregorian calendar at the end of every century, omitting the leap-years in 2100, 2200 and 2300 and recording them in 2000 and 2400 *fig. 2*. Nevertheless, such a watch does need the occasional adjustment. Every 3333 years and 122 days you should remember to set it forward one day to the true time of the celestial clock. We suspect, however, that you are simply content to observe the politeness of kings. Be assured, therefore, that when you order your watch, we will be exploring for you the physical—if not the metaphysical— limits of precision.

Does everything have to depend on how much?

Consider, if you will, the motives of collectors who set record prices at auction to acquire a Patek Philippe. They may be paying for rarity, for looks or for micromechanical ingenuity. But we believe that behind each $500,000-plus

bid is the conviction that a Patek Philippe, even if 50 years old or older, can be expected to work perfectly for future generations.

In case your ambitions to own a Patek Philippe are somewhat discouraged by the scale of the sacrifice involved, may we hasten to point out that the watch we will make for you today will certainly be a technical improvement on the Pateks bought at auction? In keeping with our tradition of inventing new mechanical solutions for greater reliability and better time-keeping, we will bring to your watch innovations *fig. 3* inconceivable to our watchmakers who created the supreme wristwatches of 50 years ago *fig. 4*. At the same time, we will of course do our utmost to avoid placing undue strain on your financial resources.

Can it really be mine?

May we turn your thoughts to the day you take delivery of your watch? Sealed within its case is your watchmaker's tribute to the mysterious process of time. He has decorated each wheel with a chamfer carved into its hub and polished into a shining circle. Delicate ribbing flows over the plates and bridges of gold and rare alloys. Millimetric surfaces are bevelled and burnished to exactitudes measured in microns. Rubies are transformed into jewels that triumph over friction. And after many months—or even years—of work, your watchmaker stamps a small badge into the mainbridge of your watch. The Geneva Seal—the highest possible attestation of fine watchmaking *fig. 5*.

Looks that speak of inner grace *fig. 6.*

When you order your watch, you will no doubt like its outward appearance to reflect the harmony and elegance of the movement within. You may therefore find it helpful to know that we are uniquely able to cater for any special decorative needs you might like to express. For example, our engravers will delight in conjuring a subtle play of light and shadow on the gold case-back of one of our rare pocket-watches *fig. 7*. If you bring us your favourite picture, our enamellers will reproduce it in a brilliant miniature of hair-breadth detail *fig. 8*. The perfect execution of a double hobnail pattern on the bezel of a wristwatch is the pride of our casemakers and the satisfaction of our designers, while our chainsmiths will weave for you a rich brocade in gold *figs. 9 & 10*. May we also recommend the artistry of our goldsmiths and the experience of our lapidaries in the selection and setting of the finest gemstones? *figs. 11 & 12*.

How to enjoy your watch before you own it.

As you will appreciate, the very nature of our watches imposes a limit on the number we can make available. (The four Calibre 89 time-pieces we are now making will take up to nine years to complete). We cannot therefore promise instant gratification, but while you look forward to the day on which you take delivery of your Patek Philippe *fig. 13*, you will have the pleasure of reflecting that time is a universal and everlasting commodity, freely available to be enjoyed by all.

Should you require information on any particular Patek Philippe watch, or even on watchmaking in general, we would be delighted to reply to your letter of enquiry. And if you send

fig. 1: *The classic face of Patek Philippe.*

fig. 4: *Complicated wristwatches circa 1930 (left) and 1990. The golden age of watchmaking will always be with us.*

fig. 6: *Your pleasure in owning a Patek Philippe is the purpose of those who made it for you.*

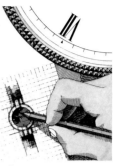

fig. 9: *Harmony of design is executed in a work of simplicity and perfection in a lady's Calatrava wristwatch.*

fig. 5: *The Geneva Seal is awarded only to watches which achieve the standards of horological purity laid down in the laws of Geneva. These rules define the supreme quality of watchmaking.*

fig. 10: *The chainsmith's hands impart strength and delicacy to a tracery of gold.*

fig. 7: *Arabesques come to life on a gold case-back.*

fig. 11: *Circles in gold: symbols of perfection in the making.*

fig. 2: *One of the 33 complications of the Calibre 89 astronomical clock-watch is a satellite wheel that completes one revolution every 400 years.*

fig. 3: *Recognized as the most advanced mechanical regulating device to date, Patek Philippe's Gyromax balance wheel demonstrates the equivalence of simplicity and precision.*

fig. 8: *An artist working six hours a day takes about four months to complete a miniature in enamel on the case of a pocket-watch.*

fig. 12: *The test of a master lapidary is his ability to express the splendour of precious gemstones.*

PATEK PHILIPPE
GENEVE
fig. 13: *The discreet sign of those who value their time.*

your card marked "book catalogue" we shall post you a catalogue of our publications. Patek Philippe, 41 rue du Rhône, 1204 Geneva, Switzerland, Tel. +41 22/310 03 66.

A Wise Man Never Thinks How Far He's Come. He Thinks How Far He Can Still Travel.

REMY XO BECAUSE LIFE IS WHAT YOU MAKE IT

Getting Acquainted

Time Zones

The continental US is divided into four time zones. From east to west, later to earlier, they are Eastern, Central, Mountain and Pacific, each separated by one hour. Thus, when it is 8pm Greenwich Mean Time, it is 3pm in New York City, 2pm in Chicago, 1pm in Denver and noon in Los Angeles. National parks covered in this book are located in two different time zones.

Eastern Time Zone: Acadia, Cape Cod, Independence, Delaware Water Gap, New River Gorge, Shenandoah, Big South Fork, Blue Ridge Parkway, Great Smoky Mountains, Sleeping Bear Dunes, Pictured Rocks, Assateague Island, Cape Hatteras, Cape Lookout, Cumberland Island, Everglades, Biscayne, Dry Tortugas,Virgin Islands.

Central Time Zone: Indiana Dunes, Apostle Islands, Mammoth Cave, Ozark Riverways, Buffalo River, Voyageurs, Hot Springs.

Climate

Climate in the national parks varies dramatically by region, season and elevation. Bad weather, including violent rain, snow or thunderstorms, can kick up unexpectedly. A change in elevation can cause temperatures to fall or rise by 10°–20°F (–12° to –7°C). It may be warm and sunny in low-lying areas but frigid in the mountains. In some parks, daytime temperatures can top 90°F (32°C) and then plummet below freezing during the night. Similarly, a day may start clear and sunny but end with cold, drenching rain. Snowfall may close roads in some mountain parks in winter. Heavy rain and floods can make river boating and hiking extremely dangerous.

It is imperative to call the parks in advance for up-to-date weather, road and trail conditions. For specific weather information, *see* park listings.

Best Time to Visit

The parks tend to be crowded in summer and (in the East Coast parks) autumn. Traffic jams, inadequate parking and crowded facilities are common at Great Smoky Mountains, Shenandoah, Acadia, Mammoth Cave and other parks during peak season. To beat the rush, consider visiting in late spring or very early fall. The weather may not be quite as balmy, but it's worthwhile to see the parks without the crowds. Weekends are the busiest times, so try to visit on weekdays. Some mountain roads and trails may be closed in winter, but snowshoeing, cross-country skiing and other winter activities are often permitted and give visitors a unique perspective on the parks.

In tropical and subtropical parks such as the Everglades, Biscayne, Gulf Islands, Dry Tortugas and Virgin Islands, fall, spring and winter are equally pleasant. But with summer temperatures in excess of 90°F (32°C), extreme humidity and an abundance of biting insects being able to enjoy these parks in June, July, and August can be a challenge.

Planning the Trip

Clothing

Weather can change unpredictably in any season, so be prepared for just about anything. The best plan is to dress in layers that can be pulled off or put on as conditions dictate. Bringing rain gear is always a good idea.

If you plan on hiking any distance, consider investing in a sturdy pair of hiking boots. Properly broken in, they will save painful blisters and protect your feet from bumpy trails, jagged rocks, thorns and other hazards. Two pairs of socks – a polypropylene inner and a heavy outer – will also help keep your feet dry and comfortable.

Day hikers should also consider bringing a small backpack (or, in American parlance, "fanny pack") to carry essentials. A checklist of necessary items includes a compass, map, guidebook, flashlight, sunglasses, pocket knife, lighter, candle, water bottle, high-energy food, water-purification tablets, first-aid kit, hat, sweater and rain gear. A high-SPF sunblock is a good idea, too, even if the day starts out cloudy. The sun can be merciless, especially in coastal areas where there is little shade.

Electrical Adapters

Standard American electric current is 110 volts. An adapter is necessary for European appliances, which run on 220–240 volts.

Film

A variety of 35mm, 110 and cartridge films are available in most grocery stores, pharmacies and convenience stores. Concessionaires in most of the larger parks carry film, although many smaller parks or parks without concessionaires do not. Call ahead to be sure. If you need professional-quality photographic equipment or film, consult the local telephone directory for the nearest camera shop. If you don't have a camera, consider the relatively inexpensive disposable cameras that are now available at many supermarkets, pharmacies and late-night convenience stores.

Maps

Free maps of the national parks are available from the National Park Service regional offices or directly from the parks themselves (*see following listing for telephone numbers and addresses*). Free city, state and regional maps as well as up-to-date road conditions and other valuable services are also available to members of the Automobile Association of America. If you plan on driving any distance, the service is well worth the price of a year's membership. Free maps may also be available from state tourism bureaux (*see listing*).

High-quality topographical maps of the national parks and other natural areas are available from **Trails Illustrated**, PO Box 3610, Evergreen, CO 80439, tel: 800-962-1643 or 303-670-3457. Topographical maps are also available from the **US Geological**

Excuse me, where is the nearest toilet please?

Per favore, dov'è la toilette?

Perdone, ¿dónde está e servicio más cercano?

请问最就近的洗手间在那里?

Простите, скажите, пожалуйста, где здесь туалет?

Unskyld, men hvor er det nærmeste toilet?

Με συγχωρείτε, ξέρετε αν υπάρχουν τουαλέτες εδώ κοντά;

Alternatively, we offer three ways to clear up diarrhoea.

Delhi belly. Montezuma's revenge. Spanish tummy. Call it what you will, for an acute attack of diarrhoea, you won't find a quicker remedy than Diocalm* Ultra with its loperamide formula.

Or you may prefer the dual action of Diocalm tablets. They help stop those nasty tummy pains, and things going from bad to worse.

Either way you'd be well advised to take Diocalm Replenish as well. It helps replace the essential fluids, minerals and salts you lose when you have diarrhoea. Diocalm Replenish is the only type of diarrhoea treatment recommended by the World Health Organisation, and by doctors for kids under six. Always read the label.

So if you want to send diarrhoea packing, pack Diocalm.

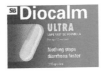  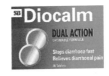

WHATEVER YOUR SYMPTOMS, WHAT A RELIEF.

He'll take you to paradise and back for just 50 pesos

Cash only, of course.

OYSTER GLX

Survey, PO Box 25286, Denver Federal Center, Denver, CO 80225, tel: 303-236-7477.

Entry Regulations
Passports & Visas

A passport, a visitor's visa and evidence of intent to leave the US after your visit are required for entry into the US by most foreign nationals. Visitors from the United Kingdom and several other countries (including but not limited to Japan, Germany, Italy, France, Switzerland, Sweden and the Netherlands) staying less than 90 days may not need a visa if they meet certain requirements. All other foreign nationals must obtain a visa from the US consulate or embassy in their country. An international vaccination certificate may also be required, depending on your country of origin.

Exceptions are Canadians entering from the western Hemisphere, Mexicans with border passes, and British residents of Bermuda and Canada. Normally, these travelers do not need a visa or passport, although it's best to confirm visa requirements before leaving your home country.

Once admitted to the US, you may visit Canada or Mexico for up to 30 days and re-enter the US without a new visa. If you lose your visa or passport, arrange to get a new one at your country's nearest consulate or embassy. For additional information, contact the US consulate or embassy in your country or the **US State Department**, tel: 202-663-1225.

Customs

All people entering the US must go through Customs. Be prepared to have your luggage inspected and keep the following guidelines in mind:

● There is no limit to the amount of money you can bring into the US. If, however, the amount exceeds $10,000 (in cash and other negotiable instruments), you must file a special report.

● Any objects brought for personal use may enter duty-free.

● Adults may enter with a maximum of 200 cigarettes or 50 cigars or 2 kilograms (4 lb) of tobacco and/or 1 liter (2 pints) of alcohol duty-free.

● Gifts valued at less than $400 may

be brought into the US free of duty.

● Agricultural products, meat and animals are subject to complex restrictions; to avoid delays, leave these items at home unless absolutely necessary.

● Illicit drugs and drug paraphernalia are strictly prohibited. If you must bring narcotic or habit-forming medicines for health reasons, be sure that all products are properly identified, carry only the quantity you will need while traveling, and have either a prescription or a letter from your doctor.

For additional information, contact **US Customs**, 1301 Constitution Avenue NW, Washington, DC 20229, tel: 202-927-6724.

Extensions of Stay

Visas are usually granted for 6 months. If you wish to remain in the country longer than 6 months, you must apply for an extension of stay at the **US Immigration and Naturalization Service**, 2401 E Street, Washington, DC 20520, tel: 202-514-4330.

Currency

Credit Cards and ATMs: Major credit cards are widely accepted at shops, restaurants, hotels and gas stations, although not all cards are accepted by every vendor. To be safe, try to carry at least two kinds. Major credit cards include American Express, Visa, MasterCard, Carte Blanche, Discover and Diners Club. Some credit cards may also be used to withdraw cash from automatic teller machines (ATMs) located in most larger towns and cities. Out-of-town ATM cards may also work. Check with your bank or credit-card company for the names of the systems your card will operate.

Money may be sent or received by wire at any **Western Union** office (tel: 800-325-6000) or **American Express Money Gram** office (tel: 800-543-4080).

American Currency & Exchange

American money is based on the decimal system. The basic unit, a dollar ($1), is equal to 100 cents. There are four basic coins, each worth less than a dollar. A penny is worth 1 cent (1¢). A nickel is worth 5 cents (5¢). A dime

is worth 10 cents (10¢). And a quarter is worth 25 cents (25¢).

In addition, there are several denominations of paper money. They are: $1, $5, $10, $20, $50, $100 and, very rarely, $2. Each bill is the same color, size and shape, so be sure to check on the face of the bill.

It's advisable to arrive with at least $100 in cash (in small bills) to pay for ground transportation and other incidentals. It's always a good and safe idea to carry internationally recognized traveler's checks rather than cash. Traveler's checks are usually accepted by retailers in lieu of cash. They can also be exchanged for cash at most banks. Bring your passport with you to the bank. Major credit cards are also a big help and are necessary if you want to rent a car.

Foreign currency is rarely accepted. You can exchange currency at major big-city banks, hotels, international airports and currency-exchange offices.

Public Holidays

Holiday closings vary from park to park, but in most cases, park facilities are open every day except Christmas. They may, however, be closed on Thanksgiving and New Year's Day. Usually, wild areas never close.

Outside the parks, all government offices, banks and post offices are closed on public holidays. Public transportation usually runs less frequently.

January 1
New Year's Day
January 15
Martin Luther King, Jr's Birthday
Third Monday in February
Presidents' Day
March/April
Easter Sunday
Last Monday in May
Memorial Day
July 4
Independence Day
First Monday in September
Labor Day
Second Monday in October
Columbus Day
November 11
Veterans Day
Fourth Thursday in November
Thanksgiving Day
December 25
Christmas Day

Generally speaking, there is very little public transportation to or within the national parks. In order to see them conveniently, you must either travel by car or join a private bus tour.

By Air

If driving directly to the parks is impractical because of distance, the next best way to get there is to fly to a nearby city and rent a car. The major hubs closest to the eastern and midwestern parks are:

Northeast: Airports in this region include Newark International (New Jersey), Kennedy International (New York), LaGuardia International (New York), Philadelphia International (Pennsylvania), Logan International (Massachusetts), Portland International (Maine).

Inquire about connections to smaller air terminals at Trenton (Maine), Barnstable and Provincetown (Massachusetts), Allentown (Pennsylvania).

Midwest: Chicago-O'Hare International (Illinois), Minneapolis-St Paul International (Minnesota), Duluth International (Minnesota), Lambert-St Louis International (Missouri).

Inquire about connections to smaller air terminals at Thunder Bay (Ontario), International Falls (Minnesota), Traverse City and Houghton (Michigan).

Southeast: Dulles International (Virginia), Norfolk International (Virginia), Jacksonville International (Florida), Miami International (Florida), Nashville International (Tennessee).

Inquire about connections to smaller air terminals at Charlottesville, (Virginia), Roanoke (Virginia) , Asheville (North Carolina), Knoxville (Tennessee), Pensacola and Key West (Florida) Biloxi/Gulfport (Mississippi), Little Rock (Arkansas), Charlotte Amalie (St Thomas, Virgin Islands).

By Train

Amtrak services more than 500 destinations across the US. Many are near national parks where you can rent a car or arrange another mode of transportation. Most trains are comfortable and reliable, with lounges, restaurants, snack bars and, in some cases, movies and live entertainment.

Amtrak's **Northeast Corridor** runs from Boston to Washington, DC, with stops near park areas at New York City and Philadelphia, Pennsylvania.

The **Old Dominion and Virginian** runs from New York to Washington, DC, with stops near park areas at Fredericksburg and Richmond, Virginia.

The **Silver Meteor and Silver Star** runs from New York to Miami, with stops near park areas at Washington, DC; Fredericksburg, Richmond and Petersburg, Virginia; and Jacksonville, Florida.

The **Cardinal** runs from New York to Chicago, with several stops near park areas at Philadelphia, Pennsylvania; Washington, DC; Manassas and Charlottesville, Virginia; and Hinton, Thurmond and Charleston, West Virginia.

The **Crescent** runs from New York to New Orleans, with stops near park areas at Philadelphia, Pennsylvania; Washington, DC; Manassas and Charlottesville, Virginia; and Charlotte, North Carolina.

The **Texas Eagle** runs from Chicago to Houston and San Antonio, with stops near park areas at St Louis and Poplar Bluff, Missouri; and Newport and Little Rock, Arkansas.

Be sure to ask about two- or three-day stopover discounts, senior citizens' and children's discounts, and Amtrak's motorcoach tours. Tel: 800-USA-RAIL for detailed information.

By Bus

One of the least expensive ways to travel in America is by bus. The biggest national bus company is Greyhound (tel: 800-231-2222). The company routinely offers discounts such as a $99 go-anywhere fare and a $1 ticket for moms on Mother's Day. Call the Greyhound office nearest you for information on special rates, discounts and package tours. A car rental or other mode of transportation to the national parks may be necessary from major cities and hubs. ·

By Car

Driving is by far the most flexible and convenient way of traveling to the national parks. Major roads are well-maintained, although backcountry roads in or near the parks may be unpaved. If you plan on driving into remote areas or will be encountering heavy snow, mud or severe weather, it's a good idea to use a four-wheel-drive vehicle with high chassis clearance.

Your greatest asset as a driver is a good road map. They can be obtained from state tourism offices, filling stations, supermarkets and convenience stores. Although roads are maintained even in remote areas, it is advisable to listen to local radio stations and to check with highway officials or park rangers for the latest information on weather and road conditions, especially if you plan on leaving paved roads. Driving conditions vary depending on elevation.

In winter, your car should be equipped with snow tires or chains, a small collapsible shovel, and an ice scraper. Also, be prepared for the extra time required to drive along winding, narrow mountain roads.

If you plan to drive in remote areas, carry extra water – at least 1 gallon (4 liters) per person per day. It's a good idea to take along some food, too.

Service stations can be few and far between in these areas. Not every town will have one, and many close early. Check your gas gauge often. It's always better to have more fuel than you think you will need.

A word of caution: If your car breaks down on a back road, do not attempt to strike out on foot. A car is easier to spot than a person and gives shelter from the elements. Sit tight and wait to be found.

Finally, if you intend to do a lot of driving, it's a good idea to join the **American Automobile Association**. The AAA offers emergency road service, maps, insurance, bail bond protection and other services (AAA, 1000 AAA Drive, Heathrow, FL 32746, tel: 407-444-4300).

Car Rental

National car rental agencies are located at all airports, cities and large towns. In most places, you must be at least 21 years old (25 in some states) to rent a car, and you must have a valid driver's license and at least one major credit card. Foreign drivers must have an international driver's license. Be sure that you are properly insured for both collision and personal liability. Insurance may not be included in the

Swatch. The others just watch.

seahorse/fall winter 94-95

shockproof
splashproof
priceproof
boreproof
swiss made

base rental fee. Additional cost varies depending on the car and the type of coverage, but usually ranges between $10 and $20 per day. You may already be covered by your own auto insurance or credit-card company, so be sure to check with them first.

It is also a good idea to inquire about an unlimited mileage package. If not, you may be charged an extra 10¢–25¢ or more per mile over a given limit. Rental fees vary depending on time of year, how far in advance you book your rental, and if you travel on weekdays or weekends. Be sure to inquire about discounts or benefits for which you may be eligible, including corporate, credit-card or frequent-flyer programs.

Alamo: 800-327-9633.
American International: 800-669-7312.
Avis: 800-331-1212.
Budget: 800-527-0700.
Dollar: 800-800-4000.
Enterprise: 800-325-8007.
Hertz: 800-654-3131.
National: 800-227-7368.
Thrifty: 800-331-4200.

RV RENTAL

No special license is necessary to operate a motor home (or recreational vehicle – RV for short), but they aren't cheap. When you add up the cost of rental fees, insurance, gas and campsites, you may find that renting a car and staying in motels or camping is less expensive.

Keep in mind, too, that RVs are large and slow and may be difficult to handle on narrow mountain roads. If parking space is tight, driving an RV may be extremely inconvenient and tiring. Access to some park roads may be limited; call the parks in advance for details. For additional information about RV rentals, call the **Recreational Vehicle Rental Association**, tel: 800-336-0355.

Hitchhiking

Hitchhiking is illegal in many places and ill-advised everywhere. It's an inefficient and dangerous method of travel. In a word, don't do it!

Special Facilities

Traveling with Children

Children love the parks, but it is important to take precautions. First, take everything you need. Some parks are quite remote and supplies may be limited. If you need baby formula, special foods, diapers or medication, carry them with you. It's also a good idea to bring a general first-aid kit for minor scrapes and bruises. Games, books and crayons help kids pass time in the car. Carrying snacks and drinks in a day pack will come in handy when kids (or adults) get hungry and there are no restaurants or campsites nearby.

Inquire about campfire talks, guided nature tours and special children's programs. Rangers do a fine job of interpreting the natural and cultural features of the parks and kids usually find these presentations fascinating.

The parks can be dangerous. Children need close supervision. Ask a ranger if a specific trail or region is suitable for children. Are there steep slopes, cliffs, river crossings, other hazards? Is the trail too strenuous for a child? Are there special precautions in regard to wildlife?

Avoid dehydration by having children drink plenty of water before and during a hike, even if they don't seem particularly thirsty. Put a wide-brimmed hat and high-SPF (at least 30 SPF) on children to protect them from the sun. Don't push children beyond their limits. Rest often, provide plenty of snacks, and allow for extra napping.

Give yourself plenty of time. Remember, kids don't travel at the same pace as adults. They're a lot less interested in traveling from point A to point B than in exploring their immediate surroundings. What you find fascinating (a rare species of bird), they may find boring. And what they think is "really cool" (a bunch of ants in the parking lot) you may find utterly uninteresting.

Disabled Travelers

The Park Service makes an effort to accommodate travelers with disabilities. Although accessibility varies from park to park, it's not unusual for visitor centers, exhibits, some campsites and short nature trails to be wheelchair-accessible. Braille and tape-recordings may also be available in some parks.

For information on handicapped accessibility, contact the parks directly (see listing to follow) and ask for the accessibility coordinator.

Visitors with a permanent handicap can obtain a Golden Access Passport at any park. The passport entitles the holder and his or her party (so long as they ride in the same car) to free entry as well as a 50 percent discount on park facilities, tours and other services, except those offered by independent concessionaires.

For general information on travel for the handicapped, contact the **Moss Rehabilitation Hospital Travel Information Service**, 1200 West Tabor Road, Philadelphia, PA 19141, tel: 215-456-9600 or **The Information Center for Individuals with Disabilities**, 27–43 Wormwood Street, Boston, MA 02210, tel: 617-727-5540.

Good resources for handicapped travelers include the *Access America Guides to the National Parks*, Northern Cartographic, Inc., PO Box 133, Burlington, VT 05402; *Access National Parks: A Guide for Handicapped Visitors*, Superintendent of Documents, US Government Printing Office, Washington, DC 20402.

Practical Tips

Weights & Measures

Despite efforts to convert to metric, the US still uses the Imperial System of weights and measures.

Imperial		Metric
1 inch	=	2.54 cm
1 foot	=	30.48 cm
1 yard	=	0.9144 meter
1 mile	=	1.609 km
1 pint	=	0.473 liter
1 quart	=	0.946 liter
1 ounce	=	28.4 gm
1 pound	=	0.453 kg
1 acre	=	0.405 ha
1 sq. mile	=	259 ha

Metric		Imperial
1 cm	=	0.394 inch
1 meter	=	39.37 ins

1 km	=	0.621 mile
1 liter	=	1.057 quarts
1 gram	=	0.035 oz
1 kg	=	2.205 pounds
1 ha	=	2.471 acres
1 sq. km	=	0.386 sq. mile

Security & Crime

Don't be lulled into complacency by the beautiful surroundings. Crime is on the rise in the national parks, but a few common-sense precautions will help keep you safe. For starters, don't carry large sums of cash or wear flashy or expensive jewelry. Keep them locked in your trunk or in a hotel safe. Lock unattended cars and keep your belongings in the trunk. If possible, travel with a companion.

If you are a witness to or victim of a crime, or need to report an emergency situation of any kind, immediately contact the nearest ranger or call park headquarters.

Firearms may not be carried into many national parks areas unless they are completely broken down, unloaded and encased. They must be kept in your car and out of sight. Unless hunting is explicitly allowed by the park superintendent, assume that it is forbidden. Poaching is a federal offense and is severely punished.

Fishing is allowed in some areas depending on the site and the season. Permits and state licenses may be required. Inquire in advance at park headquarters.

Backcountry permits are required in many parks. Speak with park rangers before heading into the backcountry.

A few parks have restrictions on carrying and/or drinking alcohol. Contact the park in advance if you intend to bring alcohol. State and local liquor laws apply.

Business Hours

Standard business hours are 9am–5pm, Monday–Friday. Many banks open a little earlier, usually 8–8.30am, and nearly all close by 3pm. Some open on Saturday morning, mainly in larger towns. Most stores keep weekend hours and may stay open late one or more nights a week.

Hours at park facilities vary from site to site and season to season. During peak months, park facilities tend to stay open from 8.30am–5pm, 7 days a week. Hours may be limited during the off-season. Holiday closings, if any, may include Thanksgiving, Christmas and New Year's Day.

Tipping

As elsewhere, service personnel who work in and around the parks depend on tips for a large part of their income. With few exceptions, tipping is left to your discretion; gratuities are not automatically added to the bill. In most cases, 15–20 percent is the going rate for tipping waiters, taxi drivers, bartenders, barbers and hairdressers. Porters and bellmen usually get about 75¢–$1 per bag, but never less than $1 total.

Media

Books & Magazines

The parks offer a variety of free flyers, brochures and maps. Additional books can be purchased at visitor centers or by contacting the parks' cooperating associations (*see list to follow*).

The following magazines often feature articles about the national parks, natural history, environmental issues and outdoor recreation:

Audubon, 700 Broadway, New York, NY 10003, tel. 800-274-4201.

Backpacker, Rodale Press, Inc., 33 E. Minor Street, Emmaus, PA 18098, tel: 800-666-3434.

National Geographic & National Geographic Traveler, 1145 17th Street NW, Washington, DC 20036, tel: 800-638-4077.

National Parks, 1776 Massachusetts Avenue NW, Suite 200, Washington, DC 20036, tel: 202-223-6722.

National Wildlife, 8925 Leesburg Pike, Vienna, VA 22184, tel: 800-432-6564.

Natural History, American Museum of Natural History, Central Park West at 79th Street, New York, NY 10024, tel: 800-234-5252.

Outdoor Traveler, WMS Publications, One Morton Drive, Suite 102, Charlottesville, VA 22903, tel: 804-984-0655.

Outside, 400 Market Street, Santa Fe, NM 87501, tel: 800-678-1131.

Sierra, 730 Polk Street, San Francisco, CA 94109, tel: 415-923-5653.

Postal Services

Even the most remote towns are served by the US Postal Service. Smaller post offices tend to be limited to business hours (9am–5pm, Monday–Friday), although central, big-city branches may have extended weekday and weekend hours.

Stamps are sold at post offices and some convenience stores, filling stations, hotels and transportation terminals, usually in vending machines.

For reasonably quick delivery at a modest price, ask for first-class or priority mail. Second- and third-class mail is cheaper and slower. For expedited deliveries, often overnight, try **US Express Mail** or one of several international courier services: **Fedex** (tel: 800-238-5355), DHL (tel: 800-345-2727), **United Parcel Service** (tel: 800-272-4877) or other local services listed in the telephone directory.

Telephone, Telegram, Telex & Fax

Public telephones are located at many highway rest areas, service stations, convenience stores, bars, motels and restaurants. The quickest way to get assistance is to dial 0 for the operator; or if you need to find a number, call information at 555-1212. Local calls can be dialed directly. Rates vary for long-distance calls, but they can also be dialed directly with the proper area and country code. If you don't know the codes, call information or dial 0 and ask for the international operator.

Make use of toll-free numbers whenever possible. For information on toll-free numbers, dial 800-555-1212. For personal calls, take advantage of lower long-distance rates on weekends and after 5pm on weekdays.

To dial other countries (Canada follows the US system), first dial the international access code 011, then the country code. If using a US phone credit card, dial the company's access number below, then 01, then the country code. Sprint, tel: 10333; AT&T, tel: 10288.

Western Union (tel: 800-325-6000) can arrange telegram, mailgram and telex transmissions. Check the local phone directory or call information for local offices. Most hotels and even some motels have fax machines. Printers, copy shops, stationers and office-supply shops may also have them, as well as some convenience stores.

Embassies

Australia: 1601 Massachusetts Avenue NW, Washington, DC 20036, tel: 202-797-3000.

Belgium: 3330 Garfield Street NW, Washington, DC 20008, tel: 202-333-6900.

Canada: 501 Pennsylvania Avenue NW, Washington, DC 20001, tel: 202-682-1740.

Denmark: 3200 Whitehaven Street NW, Washington, DC 20008, tel: 202-234-4300.

France: 4101 Reservoir Road NW, Washington, DC 20007, tel: 202-944-6000.

Germany: 4645 Reservoir Road NW, Washington, DC 20007, tel: 202-298-4000.

Great Britain: 3100 Massachusetts Avenue NW, Washington, DC 20008, tel: 202-462-1340.

Greece: 2221 Massachusetts Avenue NW, Washington, DC 20008, tel: 202-667-3168

Israel: 3514 International Drive NW, Washington, DC 20008, tel: 202-364-5500.

Italy: 1601 Fuller Street NW, Washington, DC 20009, tel: 202-328-5500.

Japan: 2520 Massachusetts Avenue NW, Washington, DC 20008, tel: 202-939-6700.

Mexico: 1911 Pennsylvania Avenue NW, Washington, DC 20006, tel: 202-728-1600.

Netherlands: 4200 Wisconsin Avenue NW, Washington, DC 20016, tel: 202-244-5300.

New Zealand: 37 Observatory Circle NW, Washington, DC 20008, tel: 202-328-4800.

Norway: 2720 34th Street NW, Washington, DC 20008, tel: 202-333-6000.

Portugal: 2125 Kalorama Road NW, Washington, DC 20008, tel: 202-328-8610.

Singapore: 3501 International Place NW, Washington, DC 20008, tel: 202-537-3100.

Spain: 2375 Pennsylvania Avenue NW, Washington, DC 20037, tel: 202-452-0100.

Taiwan: 4201 Wisconsin Avenue NW, Washington, DC 20016, tel: 202-895-1800.

Special Tours & Tour Guides

The following organizations offer park tours with special activities:

Earthwatch, 680 Mount Auburn Street, Watertown, MA 02272, tel: 617-926-8200.

Gray Line Worldwide Association, 13760 Noel Road, Dallas, TX 75240, tel: 214-934-8700 or 800-243-8353.

National Audubon Society, 613 Riversville Road, Greenwich, CT 06831, tel: 203-869-2017.

National Wildlife Federation, 8925 Leesburg Pike, Vienna, VA 22184, tel: 703-790-4000 or 800-432-6564.

Sierra Club, 730 Polk Street, San Francisco, CA 94109, tel: 415-776-2211.

Useful Addresses
State Tourism Offices

See listings under individual National Parks for regional tourism offices or chambers of commerce.

Alabama Tourism, 401 Adams Avenue, Montgomery, AL 36104, tel: 334-242-4169 or 800-252-2262.

Arkansas Tourism, 1 Capital Mall, Little Rock, AR 72201, tel: 501-682-1088.

Connecticut Tourism, 865 Brook Street, Rocky Hill, CT 06067, tel: 203-258-4355 or 800-282-6863.

Delaware Travel and Tourism, 99 Kings Highway, Dover, DE 19903, tel: 302-739-4271 or 800-441-8846.

Florida Tourism, 107 W Gaines Street, Collins Building, Suite 558, Tallahassee, FL 32399, tel: 904-488-5607.

Georgia Tourism, 285 Peachtree Center Avenue, Suite 1000, Atlanta, GA 30303, tel: 404-656-3590.

Illinois Tourism, James R. Thompson Center, 100 W Randolph, Suite 3-400, Chicago, IL 60601, tel: 217-782-7139 or 800-223-0121.

Indiana Tourism, 1 N Capital, Suite 100, Indianapolis, IN 46204, tel: 317-232-8800 or 800-382-6771.

Iowa Tourism, 200 E Grand Avenue, Des Moines, IA 50309, tel: 515-242-4705 or 800-345-4692.

Kentucky Tourism, 2200 Capitol Plaza Tower, Frankfort, KY 40601, tel: 502-564-4930 or 800-225-8747.

Louisiana Tourism, PO Box 94291, Baton Rouge, LA 70804-9291, tel: 504-342-8119 or 800-633-6970.

Maine Tourism, PO Box 2300, Hallowell, ME 04347, tel: 207-623-0363 or 800-533-9595.

Massachusetts Travel and Tourism, 100 Cambridge Street, 13th Floor, Boston, MA 02202, tel: 617-727-3201.

Michigan Travel, 333 S Capital Avenue, Suite F, Lansing, MI 48909, tel: 517-373-0670 or 800-543-2937.

Minnesota Tourism, 375 Jackson Street, St Paul, MN 55101-1848, tel: 612-296-5029.

Mississippi Tourism, PO Box 1705, Ocean Springs, MS 39566-1705, tel: 601-359-3297.

Missouri Tourism, PO Box 1055, Jefferson City, MO 65102, tel: 314-751-4133 or 800-877-1234.

New Hampshire Tourism, PO Box 1856, Concord, NH 03302-1856, tel: 603-271-2343/800-386-4664 (x145).

New Jersey Travel and Tourism, CN826, 20 W State Street, Trenton, NJ 08628, tel: 800-537-7397.

New York Tourism, 1 Commerce Plaza, Albany, NY 12245, tel: 518-474-4116/800-225-5697.

North Carolina Division of Travel and Tourism, 430 N Salisbury Street, Raleigh, NC 27611, tel: 919-733-4171.

Ohio Tourism, Vern Riffe Center, 77 S High Street, Columbus, OH 43215, tel: 614-466-8844/800-282-5393.

Pennsylvania Travel, Room 453, Forum Building, Harrisburg, PA 17120, tel: 717-787-5453/800-847-4872.

Rhode Island Tourism, 7 Jackson Walkway, Providence, RI 02903, tel: 401-277-2601.

South Carolina Tourism, 1205 Pendelton Street, Columbia, SC 29201, tel: 803-734-0101.

Tennessee Tourism, 320 6th Avenue North, 5th Floor, Nashville, TN 37219, tel: 615-741-2159 or 800-836-6200.

Vermont Tourism, PO Box 37, Montpelier, VT 05601, tel: 802-223-3443.

Virginia Tourism, 901 E Byrd, 19th floor, Richmond, VA 23219, tel: 804-786-4484.

Virgin Islands Tourism, PO Box 6400, St Thomas, VI 00804, tel: 809-774-8784 or 800-372-8784.

West Virginia Tourism, State Capitol Complex, 1900 Canawha Boulevard East, Charleston, WV 25305, tel: 304-558-2766/800-225-5982.

Wisconsin Tourism, PO Box 55, Dodgeville, WI 53533, tel: 608-266-2161/800-432-8747.

Hiking & Camping

Environmental Ethics

The old saw is good advice: "Take nothing but pictures, leave nothing but footprints." The goal of low-impact/no-impact backpacking is to leave the area in the same condition as you found it, if not better. If you're camping in the backcountry, don't break branches, level the ground or alter the landscape in any way. Make fires in designated places only. Otherwise, use a portable stove. When nature calls, dig a hole 6 inches (15 cm) deep and at least 100 ft (31 meters) from water, campsites and trails. Pack out all trash, including toilet paper.

Hiking Plan

Avoid solitary hiking. The best situation is to hike with at least two other partners. If one person is injured, one member of the party can seek help while the other two remain behind. If you must hike alone, be sure to tell someone your intended route and time of return. A permit may be required for backcountry hiking. Ask a ranger before setting out.

Camping Reservations

Most tent and RV sites in the national parks are available on a first-come, first-served basis. Arrive as early as possible to reserve a campsite. Campgrounds fill early during the busy summer season but a limited number of campsites in the most popular parks can be reserved in advance (*see park listings*). Fees are usually charged for campsites. Backcountry permits may be required for wilderness hiking and camping.

Wildlife

Never approach wild animals. Don't try to feed or touch them, not even the "cute" ones like chipmunks, squirrels and prairie dogs (they may carry diseases). Some animals, such as bison, may seem placid and slow-moving but will charge if irritated. People who have tried to creep up on bison in order to get a better photograph have been seriously injured by the animals. If you want a close-up, buy a telephoto lens.

Store your food in airtight bags or containers, especially in bear country. Hang food at least 15 ft (5 meters) above the ground and a couple of hundred yards from camp. If you've been fishing, change clothes before bedding down for the night. Be careful with deodorants, colognes, perfumes and anything else that a bear might think has an interesting odor.

Pets

Except for guide dogs, pets are generally prohibited from park facilities, trails, campgrounds and backcountry areas. Leashes are required elsewhere. Some parks offer kennels. Inquire in advance.

Entrance Fees & Park Passports

Many parks charge an entrance fee which entitles you to enter and exit as much as you like for one week. US citizens 62 years or older may obtain a **Golden Age Passport** at any park with appropriate identification; the passport entitles the holder to free admission and a 50 percent discount on camping fees and cave tours except those that are offered by independent concessionaires.

If you plan on visiting several parks, consider a **Golden Eagle Pass**. It can be obtained at any park that charges an entrance fee or by mail from park headquarters or regional offices. The price of the pass entitles the holder to free admission to any park for one year. Permanently disabled travelers may obtain a free **Golden Access Passport**. It entitles the holder to free admission to any park and a 50 percent discount on cave tours and camping fees except those that are offered by private concessionaires.

Health & Safety

Most accidents and injuries are caused by inattentive or incautious behavior. You may be on vacation but your brain shouldn't be. Pay attention to where you are and what you are doing. Keep your eyes on the road when driving. If you want to gaze at the scenery, use an overlook or pullout. Better yet, get out of the car and walk. Don't take unnecessary chances on the trail. You have nothing to prove to yourself or your companions. Heed all posted warnings. When in doubt, seek the advice of rangers.

Fitness & Altitude Sickness

Use common sense. Don't attempt trails that are too strenuous for you. Ask rangers how long and steep the trail is before beginning. You may want to "warm up" on a shorter, less strenuous trail before starting a long hike. Concentrate on what you're doing and where you're going. Even well-trod and well-marked trails can be dangerous. Be careful near cliffs, rocky slopes, ravines, rivers and other hazards. Don't attempt anything you're not comfortable with or anything that's beyond your level of skill.

Remember that the air is thinner at higher elevations. Unless properly acclimated, you may feel uncharacteristically winded. If you experience nausea, headache, vomiting, extreme fatigue, lightheadedness or shortness of breath, you may be suffering from altitude sickness. Although the symptoms may be mild at first, they can develop into a serious illness. Return to a lower elevation and try to acclimate gradually.

Water

It's always a good idea to carry a little more water than you think you'll need. The rule of thumb is a gallon (4 liters) a day per person, more in extreme conditions. Drink at least a quart (1 liter) at the start of a hike, and prevent dehydration by drinking at regular intervals while you're on the trail even if you don't feel particularly thirsty. Don't wait until you've become dehydrated before you start drinking.

All water taken from natural sources must be purified before drinking. *Giardia* is found in water (even crystal-clear water) and can cause severe cramps and diarrhea. The most popular methods of purifying water are using a water-purification tablet, a water-purification filter (both available from camping supply stores) or by boiling water for at least 15 minutes.

Foot Care

Even if you plan to do only short day hikes, it's worthwhile to invest in a sturdy pair of hiking shoes or boots. Consider buying them a half or full size larger then usual and be sure to break them in properly before arriving. A thin, inner polypropylene sock and a thick, outer sock will help keep your feet dry and comfortable. If blisters or sore spots develop, quickly cover them with moleskin, available at just about any pharmacy or camping supply store.

Sunburn

Protect yourself from the sun by using a high-SPF sunscreen and wearing a wide-brimmed hat and sunglasses, even if the day starts out cloudy. Avoid hiking during the midday hours.

Lyme Disease

Lyme disease is carried by tiny deer ticks no larger than a poppy seed. To protect yourself from ticks, wear long pants tucked into your socks and a long-sleeved shirt. Insect repellent will help, too. Check your body after hiking. If you find a deer tick, remove it carefully. If you develop a rash (look for the classic bull's-eye pattern), run a fever or suffer other flu-like symptoms within several weeks, consult a physician immediately.

Frostbite & Hypothermia

Hypothermia – the potentially fatal loss of core body temperature – is preventable. First, dress appropriately. It's best to dress in layers so that you can take clothes off or put them on as required. The first layer should be made of fabrics that wick moisture away from the skin such as silk, wool or synthetics. Avoid being both cold and wet. Bring along extra layers in case you get soaked. Keep your body well fueled and hydrated with food and water. Be prepared to turn back or seek shelter if weather turns bad. Keep in mind that it doesn't have to be freezing for you to get hypothermia.

The telltale signs of hypothermia are extreme shivering, loss of coordination and inability to reason (an outdoor writer calls these symptoms "the umbles": stumbling, fumbling, mumbling). If a member of your party is hypothermic, set up camp and establish a stable, warm environment as quickly as possible. Put up a tent, build a fire or light a portable stove. Remove the victim's wet clothes and put him or her into a prewarmed sleeping bag. Try to reduce all heat loss from wind or moisture. If conscious, have the victim drink sweet, warm fluids. Remember, if one person is hypothermic, others may be too. Check all members of your party for symptoms of hypothermia.

Frostbite occurs when living tissue freezes. Symptoms include numbness, pain, blistering and whitening of the skin. The most immediate remedy is to put frostbitten skin against warm skin. Simply holding your hands for several minutes over another person's frostbitten cheeks or nose, for example, may be sufficient. Otherwise, immerse frostbitten skin in warm (not hot) water. Refreezing will cause even more damage, so get the victim into a warm environment as quickly as possible. Again, if one person is frostbitten, others may be too. Check all members of your party for frostbite.

Swimming

Even the strongest swimmers can drown. Check with park rangers before swimming in any body of water. Strong currents and cold water can quickly overcome even an experienced swimmer. Wear a life vest when boating, and avoid hypothermia by staying out of frigid water.

National Parks

The National Park Service is administered by the Department of the Interior. For general information about the parks, contact the **Office of Public Inquiries, National Park Service**, PO Box 37127, Washington, DC 20013, tel: 202-208-4747.

Information is also available from the appropriate regional offices:

Midwest Region, National Park Service, 1709 Jackson Street, Omaha, NE 68102-2571. Tel: 402-221-3471.
Mid-Atlantic Region, National Park Service, US Custom House, 200 Chestnut Street, Philadelphia, PA 19106. Tel: 215-597-7013.
National Capital Region, National Park Service, 900 Ohio Drive SW, Washington, DC 20242. Tel: 202-485-9880.
North Atlantic Region, National Parks Service, 15 State Street, Boston, MA 02109. Tel: 617-223-5001.
Southeast Region, National Park Service, 75 Spring Street SW, Atlanta, GA 30303. Tel: 404-331-5185.
National Trails System Branch, National Park Service, 1800 N Capitol Street, Suite 490, Washington, DC 20013-7127. Tel: 202-343-3780.

Other wilderness areas are administered by:
Bureau of Land Management, US Department of the Interior, 1849 C Street NW, Washington, DC 20240. Tel: 202-208-5717.
Fish and Wildlife Service, US Department of the Interior, 1849 C Street NW, Washington, DC 20240. Tel: 202-208-5634.
Forest Service, US Department of Agriculture, 14th and Independence Avenue SW, S Agriculture Building, Washington, DC 20250. Tel: 202-205-8333.

National Rivers & Recreation Areas

In addition to the parks and monuments covered in the main section of this book, the National Park Service administers a system of protected, free-flowing streams and rivers. Contact these units directly for information on hours, seasons, access, recreational opportunities, weather and road conditions.
Bluestone National Scenic River, c/o New River Gorge National River, PO Box 246, Glen Jean, WV 25846. Tel: 304-465-0508.
Cuyahoga Valley National Recreation Area, 15610 Vaughn Road, Brecksville, OH 44141. Tel: 216-650-4636.
Delaware National Scenic River, c/o Delaware Water Gap National Recreation Area, River Road, Bushkill, PA 18324. Tel: 717-588-2435.
Gauley River National Recreation Area, c/o New River Gorge National

River, PO Box 246, Glen Jean, WV 25846. Tel: 304-465-0508.

Lower Saint Croix National Scenic Riverway, c/o Saint Croix National Scenic Riverway, PO Box 708, St Croix Falls, WI 54024. Tel: 715-483-3284.

Mississippi National River and Recreation Area, 175 E 5th Street, Suite 418, Box 41, St Paul, MN 55101-2901. Tel: 612-290-4160.

Obed Wild and Scenic River, PO Box 429, Wartburg, TN 37887.
Tel: 615-346-6294.

Saint Croix National Scenic Riverway, PO Box 708, St Croix Falls, WI 54024. Tel: 715-483-3284.

Upper Delaware Scenic and Recreational River, PO Box C, Narrowsburg, NY 12764. Tel: 717-729-8251.

National Trails System

The National Park Service, in association with other state and federal agencies, manages a system of scenic, historic and recreational trails, many of which pass through or between national parks and monuments. Contact these regional offices for maps and information on access, recreational activities and weather conditions.

Appalachian National Scenic Trail, Appalachian Trail Conference, PO Box 807, Harpers Ferry, WV 25425.
Tel: 304-535-6331.

Florida National Scenic Trail, US Forest Service, 325 John Knox Road, Suite F-100, Tallahassee, FL 32303. Tel: 904-942-9300.

Ice Age National Scenic Trail, National Park Service, 700 Rayovac Drive, Suite 100, Madison, WI 53711. Tel: 608-264-5610.

Lewis and Clark National Historic Trail, National Park Service, 700 Rayovac Drive, Suite 100, Madison, WI 53711. Tel: 608-264-5610.

Natchez Trace National Scenic Trail, c/o Natchez Trace Parkway, RR 1, NT-143, Tupelo, MS 38801.
Tel: 601-842-1572.

North Country National Scenic Trail, National Park Service, 700 Rayovac Drive, Suite 100, Madison, WI 53711. Tel: 608-264-5610.

Overmountain Victory National Historic Trail, Southeast Region, National Park Service, 75 Spring Street, SW, Atlanta, GA 30303. Tel: 404-331-5465.

Potomac Heritage National Scenic Trail, National Capital Region, 900

Ohio Drive, SW, Washington, DC 20242. Tel: 202-485-9880.

Trail of Tears National Historic Trail, Long Distance Trails Group Office-Santa Fe, National Park Service, PO Box 728, Santa Fe, NM 87504-0728. Tel: 505-988-6888.

Cooperating Associations

Books, maps, special seminars, tours and other services are available from the following organizations:

Blue Ridge Parkway Association, PO Box 453, Asheville, NC 28802.
Tel: 704-298-0398.

Eastern National Parks and Monuments, 446 N. Lane, Conshohocken, PA 19428. Tel: 610-832-0555.

Florida National Parks and Monuments Association, PO Box 279, Homestead, FL 33030. Tel: 305-247-1216.

Great Smoky Mountains Natural History Association, 115 Park Headquarters Road, Gatlinburg, TN 37728.
Tel: 615-436-7318.

Isle Royale Natural History Association, 800 E Lakeshore Drive, Houghton, MI 49931. Tel: 800-678-6925.

Lake States Interpretive Association, 3131 Highway 53, International Falls, MN 56649-8904. Tel: 218-283-2103.

Ozark National Riverways Historical Association, PO Box 490, Van Buren, MO 63965. Tel: 314-323-4236.

Shenandoah Natural History Association, Route 4, Box 348, Luray, VA 22835. Tel: 703-999-3581.

Park Accommodation

The price guide indicates an approximate room/cabin rate for accommodation within the following list of National Parks.

    ☆ $50 or less
    ☆☆ $50–$100
    ☆☆☆ $100–$150
    ☆☆☆☆ $150 plus

The Northeast
Maine

ACADIA NATIONAL PARK

PO Box 177, Bar Harbor, ME 04609, tel: 207-288-3338.

Access: The visitor center is about 3 miles (5 km) northwest of Bar Harbor via Route 3.

Seasons & Hours: The park is open year-round, but snow in winter limits access. The visitor center is open daily May–October, 8am–4.30pm, extended hours in summer.

Entrance Fee: Yes.

Handicapped Access: Nature center and Abbe Museum, carriage roads and campsites; limited at visitor center.

Activities: Scenic drive, hiking, camping, boating, swimming, fishing, wildlife-watching, carriage rides, horseback riding, biking, nature cruises, cross-country skiing, snowshoeing, interpretive programs.

Visitor Facilities: Visitor center, museum, nature center.

Camping: Reservations recommended in summer. Contact:

    Mistix, PO Box 85705, San Diego, CA 92186-5705, tel: 800-365-2267.

    Otherwise, campsites are first-come, first-served.

Permits & Licenses: Maine fishing license for inland waters.

Accommodations: None in the park. Lodging is available in Bar Harbor, Northeast Harbor, Southwest Harbor and surrounding towns. Contact:

    Bar Harbor Chamber of Commerce, PO Box 158, Bar Harbor, ME 04609, tel: 207-288-5103.

    Mount Desert Chamber of Commerce, Sea Street, Northeast Harbor, ME 04662, tel: 207-276-5040.

Food & Supplies: The restaurant and gift shop at Jordan Pond House are open seasonally. Additional services are available in Bar Harbor, Northeast Harbor, Southwest Harbor and surrounding towns.

Weather: Summer is pleasant, with temperatures usually 55°–80°F (13°–27°C). Winters are cold and snowy, 10°–35°F (–12°–2°C). The coast is often shrouded in fog.

General Information: Rocks along the shore may be slippery. Keep an eye on incoming tides and unusually high waves. These can trap hikers or sweep them out to sea.

Maryland

ASSATEAGUE ISLAND NATIONAL SEASHORE

7206 National Seashore Lane, Berlin, MD 21811, tel: 410-641-3030.

Access: The national seashore is about 16 miles (26 km) south of Ocean City, Maryland, via Highway 50 and Route 611.

Seasons & Hours: The visitor center is open daily 9am–5pm. Closed Thanksgiving, Christmas and New Year's Day.

Entrance Fee: Yes.

Handicapped Access: Visitor center, bathhouses, some trails and campsites.

Activities: Hiking, camping, boating, swimming, fishing, wildlife-watching, interpretive programs.

Visitor Facilities: Visitor center, museum, nature center.

Camping: Reservations recommended in summer. Contact:

    Mistix, PO Box 85705, San Diego, CA 92186-5705, tel: 800-365-2267.

    Otherwise, campsites are first-come, first-served.

Permits & Licenses: Backcountry camping permits required.

Accommodations: None in the park. Lodging is available in Ocean City, Maryland, and Chincoteague, VA. Contact:

    Ocean City Chamber of Commerce, 12320 Ocean Gateway, Ocean City, MD 21842, tel: 410-213-0552.

    Chincoteague Chamber of Commerce, PO Box 258, Chincoteague, VA 23336, tel: 804-336-6161.

Food & Supplies: Services are available in Ocean City, Maryland, and Chincoteague, Virginia.

Weather: Summer is hot and humid, with temperatures usually 75°–90°F (24°–32°C). Winters are cold, with occasional snow, 25°–50°F(–4°–10°C).

General Information: Never swim

alone. Mosquitoes are abundant; insect repellent recommended. Use a high-SPF sunscreen and wear a hat to avoid sunburn. Do not approach or attempt to feed ponies.

For information and details about the adjacent wildlife refuge, contact the Chncoteague National Wildlife Refuge, PO Box 62, Chincoteague, VA 23336, tel: 804-336-6122.

Massachusetts

CAPE COD NATIONAL SEASHORE

Po Box 250, South Wellfleet, MA 02663, tel: 508-349-3785.

Access: The national seashore is about 100 miles (161 km) southeast of Boston via Highways 93, 3 and 6.

Seasons & Hours: The park is open daily year-round. Beach parking lots are closed in summer midnight–6am. The Salt Pond Visitor Center in Eastham is open daily March–December, 9am–4.30pm. Province Lands Visitor Center is open daily April 15–November 30, 9am–4.30pm.

Entrance Fee: No, but there is a beach-use fee.

Handicapped Access: Visitor centers and some trails.

Activities: Hiking, camping, boating, swimming, fishing, wildlife-watching, interpretive programs.

Seasonal Events:

    June: Blessing of the Fleet in Provincetown.

    July: Provincetown Carnival is a week-long street fair: musicians, parades, special performances.

    July: The Barnstable County Fair features livestock shows, rides, arts and crafts, musicians, special performances and food.

Visitor Facilities: Visitor center, museum, nature center.

Camping: No.

Permits & Licenses: Massachusetts fishing license for inland waters.

Accommodations: Lodging is available in Provincetown, Eastham, Hyannis and surrounding towns. Contact:

    Cape Cod Chamber of Commerce, Junction of Highways 6 and132, Hyannis, MA 02601, tel: 508-362-3225.

Food & Supplies: Services are available in Provincetown, Wellfleet, Eastham, Hyannis and surrounding towns.

Weather: Summer is pleasant, with temperatures usually 70°–80°F (21°–27°C). Ocean temperatures usually 50°–60°F (10°–16°C). Spring and fall are cool but damp and foggy. Winter is cold, with occasional snow.

General Information: Ocean currents may be dangerous. Lifeguards may not be available; never swim. Do not bring rafts, tubes, glass containers, surf boards or diving gear on guarded beach. Use a high-SPF sunscreen and wear a hat to avoid sunburn. Do not climb sand bluffs. Expect crowded conditions during summer weekends and holidays; consider visiting on weekdays or off-season.

New York

FIRE ISLAND NATIONAL SEASHORE

120 Laurel Street, Patchogue, NY 11772, tel: 516-289-4810.

Access: The island is on the southern shore of Long Island about 6 miles (10 km) from Bay Shore on the Robert Moses Causeway and 6 miles (10 km) from Shirley on the William Floyd Parkway. Public ferries depart from Patchogue, Sayville and Bayshore.

Seasons & Hours: The seashore is open daily, year-round. The visitor center is open seasonally, hours vary.

Entrance Fee: No.

Handicapped Access: Visitor center, island boardwalks.

Activities: Hiking, swimming, camping, fishing, wildlife-watching, historic buildings, interpretive programs.

Visitor Facilities: Visitor center, historic sites, marina.

Camping: Reservations required, contact headquarters.

Permits & Licenses: Backcountry camping permit required.

Accommodations: Lodging is available in Cherry Grove, Ocean Beach, Bay Shore, Sayville, Patchogue and surrounding area. Contact:

    Fire Island Tourism Bureau, 49 N Main Street, Sayville, NY 11782, tel: 516-563-8448.

Food & Supplies: Services are available in Watch Hill, Davis Park, Sailors Haven, Cherry Grove, Ocean Beach, Fire Island Pines, Fair Haven.

Weather: Summer temperatures are usually 75–90F. Spring and fall 55°–75°F (13°–24°C). Winter is cold, with occasional accumulations of snow.

General Information: Never swim alone. Use a high-SPF sunscreen and wear a hat to avoid sunburn. Dunes are easily damaged; do not walk or ride on them.

For ferry information, contact Fire Island Ferries, tel: 516-665-2115, or the Fire Island Tourism Bureau, tel: 516-563-8448.

Pennsylvania

DELAWARE WATER GAP NATIONAL RECREATION AREA

River Road, Bushkill, PA 18324, tel: 717-588-2435.

Access: The recreation area is on the New Jersey-Pennsylvania border about 5 miles (8 km) east of Stroudsburg via Interstate 80.

Seasons & Hours: The park is open daily, year-round. The Kittatinny Point Visitor Center is open daily 9am–4.30pm, extended hours in spring and summer. The Dingmans Falls Visitor Center is open daily 9am–5pm, closed during the winter.

Entrance Fee: No.

Handicapped Access: Visitor centers, historic village and recreation sites.

Activities: Hiking, swimming, canoeing, camping, fishing, wildlife-watching, historic village, craft demonstrations, interpretive programs.

Visitor Facilities: Visitor centers, boat ramps.

Camping: Reservations are required inside Worthington State Forest in New Jersey and at Dingman's Campground in Pennsylvania. Canoe camping at designated sites for overnight river trips only.

Permits & Licenses: New Jersey and/or Pennsylvania fishing and hunting licenses.

Accommodations:

Old Mine Road Youth Hostel, PO Box 172, Layton, NJ 07851, tel: 201-948-6750.

Additional lodging is available in Delaware Water Gap, Shawnee-on-the-Delaware and Stroudsburg. Contact:

Pocono Mountains Vacation Bureau, 1004 Main Street, Stroudsburg, PA 18360, tel: 717-421-5791.

Food & Supplies: Services are available in Columbia and Walpack Center, New Jersey, and in Delaware Water Gap, Shawnee-on-the-Delaware and Stroudsburg, Pennsylvania.

Weather: Summer is hot and humid, with temperatures usually 75°–85°F (24°–30°C). Spring and fall are moderate, 60°–75°F (16°–24°C). Winter is cold, with occasional heavy snow storms and ice.

General Information: The river is especially dangerous during periods of high water, but visitors should exercise caution at all times. Do not dive into the river. Always wear a life jacket when boating. Local concessionaires rent canoes, tubes and other equipment; contact park headquarters for an up-to-date list.

West Virginia

NEW RIVER GORGE NATIONAL RIVER

PO Box 246, Glen Jean, WV 25846, tel: 304-465-0508.

Access: Several routes lead into the national river from Beckley and Fayetteville, including Highway 19 and Interstate 64, and Route 20 from Hinton.

Seasons & Hours: The park is open daily, year-round. Canyon Rim Visitor Center is open daily, 9am–5pm. Closed Christmas and New Year's Day. Other visitor centers and facilities are open seasonally, hours vary.

Entrance Fee: No.

Handicapped Access: Visitor centers, Thurmond Depot, Glen Jean Bank.

Activities: Hiking, camping, boating, fishing, wildlife-watching, historic sites, interpretive programs.

Visitor Facilities: Visitor centers, historic sites, boat launches.

Camping: Primitive camping in designated areas only. Campgrounds are available in nearby state parks.

Permits & Licenses: West Virginia fishing license and state trout stamp. Backcountry camping permits needed.

Accommodations: None in the park. Lodging is available in Fayetteville, Beckley, Oak Hill, Hinton, Charleston. Contact:

Fayetteville Chamber of Commerce, 310 Oyler Avenue, Oak Hill, WV 25901, tel: 304-465-5617.

Charleston Chamber of Commerce, 106 Capitol Street, Charleston, WV 25301, tel: 304-345-0770.

Food & Supplies: Services are available in Fayetteville, Beckley, Oak Hill, Hinton, Charleston.

Weather: Summer is hot and humid, with temperatures usually 70°–90°F (21°–32°C). Spring and fall are moderate, 65°–80°F (18°–27°C). Winter is cold, 25°–55°F (–4°–13°C), with occasional snow.

General Information: The river is especially dangerous during periods of high water, but visitors should exercise caution at all times. Do not dive into the river. Never swim alone. Always wear a life jacket when boating. Local concessionaires rent canoes and other equipment; contact park headquarters for an up-to-date list.

The Midwest

Indiana

INDIANA DUNES NATIONAL LAKESHORE

1100 N Mineral Springs Road, Porter, IN 46304, tel: 219-926-7561.

Access: The national lakeshore is between Gary and Michigan City off Highway 12.

Seasons & Hours: The visitor center is open 8am–5pm, extended hours in summer. Closed Thanksgiving, Christmas and New Year's Day.

Entrance Fee: No.

Handicapped Access: Visitor center and nature trail. Visitor may request a "sand wheel chair" for beach access.

Activities: Hiking, biking, swimming, horseback riding, wildlife-watching, fishing, interpretive programs.

Visitor Facilities: Visitor center, boat launch.

Camping: First-come, first-served.

Permits & Licenses: Indiana fishing license.

Accommodations: Lodging is available throughout the region. Contact:

Chesterton Chamber of Commerce, 303 Broadway Chesterton, IN 46304; tel: 219-926-5513.

Michigan City Chamber of Commerce, 200 E Michigan Road, Michigan City, IN 46360, tel: 219-874-6221.

Food & Supplies: Food and supplies are available throughout the region.
Weather: Summer is hot and humid, with temperatures usually 75°–90°F (24°–32°C). Expect snow and bitter cold in winter, usually 0°F–35°F (–18°–2°C). Windy at all times of year.
General Information: Some beaches may not have lifeguards. Be careful of strong lake currents when swimming.

Michigan

ISLE ROYALE NATIONAL PARK

800 E. Lakeshore Drive, Houghton, MI 49931-1895, tel: 906-482-0984.

Access: The park may be reached only by boat or floatplane.
Seasons & Hours: The park is open April 16–October 31, but concession boats run mid-May–mid-October. Information centers on the island are open daily mid-June–September.
Entrance Fee: No.
Handicapped Access: Park headquarters, Rock Harbor Lodge and some campsites. Concessionaire boats to island are wheelchair-accessible with assistance.
Activities: Hiking, camping, boating, island cruises, scuba diving, fishing, wildlife-watching, interpretive programs.
Visitor Facilities: Information centers.
Camping: First-come, first-served.
Permits & Licenses: Backcountry camping permits required; Michigan fishing license is required for Lake Superior.
Accommodations:
  Rock Harbor Lodge★★–★★★, PO Box 405, Houghton, MI 49931, tel: 906-337-4993.
  Additional lodging is available in Copper Harbor, Houghton and Grand Portage. Contact:
  Upper Peninsula Travel and Recreation Association, PO Box 400, Iron Mountain, MI 49801, tel: 906-774-5480.
  Minnesota Office of Tourism, 375 Jackson Street, St Paul, MN 55101-1848, tel: 612-296-5029.
Food & Supplies: Limited food and supplies are available in Rock Harbor and Windigo. Additional services are available in Copper Harbor, Houghton and Grand Portage.
Weather: Summer temperatures are usually 75°F (24°C) and rarely exceed 80°F (27°C). Nights may be very cool; bring a warm sleeping bag and clothes. Spring and fall are cool and often cloudy or foggy, with nighttime temperatures occasionally dipping below freezing.
General Information: Facilities on the island are limited; bring all camping gear and adequate food. Foul weather may cause delays in the boat schedule. Sudden storms can make boating dangerous. Motorboats are permitted only on Lake Superior. Canoes, kayaks and other small boats may be brought to the island on island ferries.

Insect repellent is recommended. There are no public telephones on the island. The park is closed in winter.

For information and reservations on the Park Service boat from Houghton, Michigan, to Rock Harbor, contact park headquarters.

For boats from Copper Harbor, Michigan, to Rock Harbor, contact Isle Royale Ferry Service, PO Box 24, Copper Harbor, MI 49918, tel: 906-289-4437.

For boats from Grand Portage, Minnesota, to Windigo and Rock Harbor, contact Grand Portage-Isle Royale Transportation, 1507 N First Street, Superior, WI 54880, tel: 715-392-2100.

For seaplanes, contact Isle Royale Seaplane Service, PO Box 371, Houghton, MI 49931, tel: 906-482-8850.

Canoe and equipment rentals are available from National Park Concessions, PO Box 405, Houghton, MI 49931-0405, tel: 906-337-4993.

PICTURED ROCKS NATIONAL LAKESHORE

PO Box 40, Munising, MI 49862, tel: 906-387-3700.

Access: The lakeshore is on Lake Superior on Michigan's Upper Peninsula between Munising and Grand Marais.
Seasons & Hours: The park is open daily, year-round. Munising Visitor Center is open daily 9am–4.30pm, extended hours in summer. Closed Thanksgiving and Christmas. Grand Sable Visitor Center is open in summer only, hours vary.
Entrance Fee: No.
Handicapped Access: Visitor centers, some campsites, some nature trails.
Activities: Hiking, camping, boating, cruises, scuba diving, fishing, wildlife-watching, interpretive programs.
Visitor Facilities: Visitor, information and interpretive centers; Grand Marais Maritime Museum.
Camping: First-come, first-served.
Permits & Licenses: Backcountry camping permits required; Michigan fishing license.
Accommodations: None in the park. Lodging is available in Munising and Grand Marais. Contact:
  Upper Peninsula Travel and Recreation Association, PO Box 400, Iron Mountain, MI 49801, tel: 906-774-5480.
Food & Supplies: Food and supplies are available in Munising and Grand Marais.
Weather: Summer temperatures are usually 50°–75°F (10°–24°C) and rarely exceed 80°F (27°C). Nights may be very cool; bring a warm sleeping bag and clothes. Spring and fall are cool and often cloudy or foggy, with nighttime temperatures occasionally dipping below freezing. Winter is bitterly cold, with abundant snowfall. Expect windy conditions along the lakeshore in any season.
General Information: Sudden storms can make boating dangerous on Lake Superior. Insect repellent is recommended. Be careful at the edge of bluffs and cliffs. Contact the park for a list of companies that rent boats and equipment.

SLEEPING BEAR DUNES NATIONAL LAKESHORE

9922 Front Street, Empire, MI 49630, tel: 616-326-5134.

Access: The lakeshore is on Lake Michigan on Michigan's Lower Peninsula about 23 miles (37 km) west of Traverse City via Route 72.
Seasons & Hours: The park is open daily, year-round. The visitor center is open daily 9.30am–4pm, extended weekend and summer hours. Closed Thanksgiving and Christmas.
Entrance Fee: No.
Handicapped Access: Visitor center, maritime museum, some campsites and overlooks; island ferry is wheelchair-accessible with assistance.
Activities: Hiking, camping, boating, cruises, fishing, cross-country skiing, wildlife-watching, interpretive programs.

Visitor Facilities: Visitor center, maritime museum.

Camping: First-come, first-served.

Permits & Licenses: Backcountry camping permits required; Michigan fishing license.

Accommodations: None in the park. Lodging is available in Glen Arbor, Empire, Frankfort and Traverse City. For details contact:

Traverse City Chamber of Commerce, 202 E Grandview Parkway, Traverse City, MI 49684, tel: 616-947-5075.

Leelanau County Chamber of Commerce, 105 Philips, Lake Leelanau, MI 49653, tel: 616-256-9895.

Food & Supplies: Limited services are available in the park. Additional services are available in Glen Arbor, Empire, Frankfort and Traverse City.

Weather: Summer temperatures are usually 50°–75°F (10°–24°C) and rarely exceed 80°F (27°C). Nights may be very cool; bring a warm sleeping bag and clothes. Spring and fall are cool and often cloudy or foggy, with nighttime temperatures occasionally dipping below freezing. Winter is cold, with abundant snowfall. Expect windy conditions in any season.

General Information: Sudden storms can make boating dangerous on Lake Michigan. Insect repellent is recommended. Be careful at the edge of bluffs. Contact the park for a list of companies that rent boats and other equipment.

Minnesota

VOYAGEURS NATIONAL PARK

3131 Highway 53, International Falls, MN 56649-8904, tel: 218-283-9821.

Access: The Kabetogama Lake Visitor Center is about 140 miles (225 km) north of Duluth via Highway 53 and Route 122. There are no public roads in the interior of the park; travel is limited to boats and floatplanes.

Seasons & Hours: The park is open daily, year-round. Visitor centers are open seasonally. Days and hours vary, contact park headquarters for details.

Entrance Fee: No.

Handicapped Access: Kabetogama Lake and Rainy Lake visitor centers and portion of nature trail; boat trips are wheelchair-accessible with assistance.

Activities: Hiking, camping, boating, cruises, fishing, cross-country skiing, snowmobiling, wildlife-watching, interpretive programs.

Visitor Facilities: Visitor center, boat rentals.

Camping: First-come, first-served.

Permits & Licenses: Minnesota fishing license.

Accommodations in the park:

Kettle Falls Hotel✶✶, PO Box 1272, International Falls, MN 56649, tel: 218-374-3511.

Additional lodging is available in International Falls, Ray and at resorts adjacent to the park. Contact:

International Falls Chamber of Commerce, PO Box 169, International Falls, MN 56649, tel: 218-283-9400.

Crane Lake Visitor and Tourism Bureau, 7238 Handberg Road, Crane Lake, MN 55725, tel: 218-993-2901.

Food & Supplies: There is a restaurant at Kettle Falls Hotel.

Additional services are available in International Falls and Ray.

Weather: Summer temperatures are usually 60°–85°F (16°–29°C). Nights may be very cool; bring a warm sleeping bag and clothes. Spring is cool and rainy. Fall is moderate, with nighttime temperatures occasionally dipping below freezing. Winter is bitterly cold, with abundant snowfall.

General Information: Sudden storms can make boating hazardous. Wear life jackets; also insect repellent.

For information and reservations on Rainy Lake contact Voyageurs National Park Boat Tours, Route 8, Box 303, International Falls, MN 56649, tel: 218-286-5470.

For cruises on Kabetogama Lake, contact Sight-Sea-Er Boat Tours, 10502 Gamma Road, Ray, MN 56669, tel: 218-875-2111.

Resort communities on the edge of the park provide a variety of services, including houseboats and canoe rentals, cruises and fishing guides.

Missouri

OZARK NATIONAL SCENIC RIVERWAYS

PO Box 490, Van Buren, MO 63965, tel: 314-323-4236.

Access: The park is about 170 miles (274 km) southeast of St Louis via Interstate 44 and Highway 68.

Seasons & Hours: The park is open daily, year-round. The information center is open 8am–5pm, Monday–Friday. Closed on Bank holidays.

Entrance Fee: No.

Handicapped Access: Information center, some campsites, ground floor of Alley Spring Gristmill.

Activities: Hiking, camping, canoeing, fishing, swimming, caving, wildlife-watching, interpretive programs.

Visitor Facilities: Information center, historic buildings, boat ramps.

Camping: First-come, first-served.

Permits & Licenses: Missouri fishing license.

Accommodations:

Rustic cabins✶, Big Spring Concessioner, PO Box 602, Van Buren, MO 63965, tel: 314-323-4423.

Additional lodging is available in Eminence, Van Buren, Salem, Ellington, Mountain View and surrounding towns. Contact:

Ozark Area Chamber of Commerce, PO Box 450, Ozark, MO 65721, tel: 417-581-6139.

Van Buren Chamber of Commerce, PO Box 356, Van Buren, MO 63965, tel: 314-323-4782.

Food & Supplies: Limited services are available in the park. Additional services are available in Eminence, Van Buren, Salem, Ellington, Mountain View and surrounding towns.

Weather: Summer temperatures are usually 60°–90°F (16°–32°C). Spring and fall 45°–75°F (7°–24°C) and rainy. Winter is mild, with occasional dustings of snow.

General Information: The rivers are especially dangerous during periods of high water, but visitors should exercise caution at all times. Do not dive into the river. Always wear a life jacket when boating. Be careful along unprotected bluffs. Consult with rangers before entering caves. Local concessionaires rent canoes, tubes and other equipment; contact park headquarters for an up-to-date list.

Wisconsin

APOSTLE ISLANDS NATIONAL LAKESHORE

Route 1, Box 4, Bayfield, WI 54814, tel: 715-779-3397.

Access: The visitor center is about 84

miles (29 km) east of Duluth, Minnesota, via Highway 2 and Route 13.

Seasons & Hours: The visitor center is open 8am–4.30pm, extended hours in summer. Closed Thanksgiving, Christmas and New Year's Day. Island tours are offered mid-May–mid-October.

Entrance Fee: No.

Handicapped Access: Visitor center, Apostle Island Cruise Service boat with assistance, Stockton Island Visitor Center.

Activities: Hiking, camping, boating, fishing, scuba diving, sailing, wildlife-watching, historic sites, interpretive programs.

Visitor Facilities: Visitor centers, lighthouse, boat launches.

Camping: First-come, first-served.

Permits & Licenses: Wisconsin fishing license, backcountry camping and scuba diving permits required.

Accommodations: Lodging is available in Bayfield, Ashland, Washburn, Cornucopia. Contact:

> **Bayfield Chamber of Commerce**, 42 S Broad Street, Bayfield, WI 54814, tel: 715-779-3335.

Food & Supplies: Services are available in Bayfield, Ashland, Washburn, Cornucopia.

Weather: Summer temperatures are usually 55°–85°F (13°–29°C). Nights may be very cool; bring a warm sleeping bag and clothes. Spring and fall are cool and often cloudy or foggy, with nighttime temperatures occasionally dipping below freezing. Winter is very cold, with considerable snowfall. Expect windy conditions in any season.

General Information: Sudden storms can make boating dangerous. Lake Superior is frigid; swimming may be dangerous. Insect repellent is recommended. Always be careful at the edge of cliffs. Contact the park for a list of local companies that rent boats and sports equipment.

The South
Arkansas

BUFFALO NATIONAL RIVER

PO Box 1173, Harrison, AR 72602-1173, tel: 501-741-5443.

Access: The national river is about 13 miles (21 km) south of park headquarters in Harrison via Route 7, or 31 miles (50 km) southeast of Harrison via Highway 65.

Seasons & Hours: The park is open year-round; the visitor center is open daily 8am–4.30pm. Closed Christmas and Thanksgiving.

Entrance Fee: No.

Handicapped Access: Visitor center, some trails (with assistance) and campsites.

Activities: Canoeing, kayaking, swimming, fishing, backpacking, hiking, wildlife-watching, interpretive programs.

Visitor Facilities: Visitor center, exhibits, ranger stations.

Camping: First-come, first-served.

Permits & Licenses: Arkansas hunting and fishing permits required.

Accommodations: Rustic cabins are available in the park. Contact:

> **Buffalo Point Concessions**, HCR 66, Box 388, Yellville, AR 72687, tel: 501-449-6206.

> Additional lodging is available in nearby Yellville, Harrison, Jasper, Mountain Home and surrounding towns. Contact:

> **Harrison Chamber of Commerce**, 501-741-2659, PO Box 939, Harrison, AR 72601.

Food & Supplies: Available in Yellville, Harrison, Jasper, Mountain Home and surrounding towns.

Weather: Summers are hot and very humid, with temperatures often in excess of 90°F (32°C); thunderstorms are common in spring and summer. Winter tends to be mild, with occasional light snow.

General Information: The river is especially dangerous during periods of high water, but visitors should exercise caution at all times. Do not dive into the river. Be careful along unprotected bluffs. Always wear a life jacket when boating. About 25 concessionaires along the river rent canoes and other equipment; contact park headquarters for an up-to-date list.

HOT SPRINGS NATIONAL PARK

PO Box 1860, Hot Springs, AR 71902, tel: 501-624-3383.

Access: The visitor center is on Route 7 (Central Avenue) in the city of Hot Springs.

Seasons & Hours: The park is open year-round; the visitor center is open daily 9am–5pm. Closed Christmas and New Year's Day.

Entrance Fee: No.

Handicapped Access: Visitor center, Promenade Walkway, restrooms, some campsites.

Activities: Scenic drive, hiking, biking, wildlife-watching, interpretive programs.

Visitor Facilities: Visitor center, thermal baths.

Camping: First-come, first-served.

Permits & Licenses: No.

Accommodations: None in the park. Lodging is available in Hot Springs. Contact:

> **Hot Springs Convention and Visitors Bureau**, PO Box K, Hot Springs, AR 71902, tel: 800-543-2284.

Food & Supplies: Available in Hot Springs.

Weather: Summer is hot and humid, with temperatures often in excess of 90°F (32°C) in July and August; thunderstorms are common. Winter is generally mild, with lows in the 30°F (–2°C) and an occasional light snow.

General Information: Additional backpacking and camping are offered at nearby Ouachita National Forest, tel: 501-321-5202.

Florida

BIG CYPRESS NATIONAL PRESERVE

HCR 61, Box 110, Ochopee, FL 33943, tel: 813-695-4111.

Access: The visitor center is located 55 miles (88 km) east of Naples via Highway 41.

Seasons & Hours: The park is open daily, year-round. The visitor center is

open daily, 8.30am–4.30pm.
Entrance Fee: No.
Handicapped Access: Visitor center.
Activities: Hiking, camping, canoeing, wildlife-watching, fishing, interpretive programs.
Visitor Facilities: Visitor center.
Camping: First-come, first-served.
Permits & Licenses: Florida fishing license.
Accommodations: None in the park. Lodging available in Naples. Contact:
  Naples Chamber of Commerce, 3620 Highway 41 North, Naples, FL 33940, tel: 813-262-6141.
Food & Supplies: Available in Naples and Everglades City.
Weather: Summer is hot and humid, with temperatures often in excess of 90°F (32°C); thunderstorms are common. Winter is short and mild.
General Information: Insect repellent is recommended. Use a high-SPF sunscreen and wear a hat to avoid sun burn.

BISCAYNE NATIONAL PARK

PO Box 1369, Homestead, FL 33090-1369, tel: 305-230-7275.

Access: Convoy Point Visitor Center is 9 miles (15 km) east of Homestead on North Canal Drive.
Seasons & Hours: The park is open daily, year-round. The Convoy Point Visitor Center is open daily, 8.30am–4.30pm, extended weekend hours.
Entrance Fee: No.
Handicapped Access: Visitor center and concessionaire boat tours.
Activities: Hiking, wildlife-watching, swimming, snorkeling, scuba diving, glass-bottom boat excursions, fishing, boating, water skiing, interpretive programs.
Visitor Facilities: Visitor centers, docking facilities.
Camping: First-come, first-served.
Permits & Licenses: Free backcountry camping permits required. Florida saltwater fishing license.
Accommodations: None in the park. Lodging is available in Homestead, Florida City and surrounding area.
  Homestead/Florida City Chamber of Commerce, 160 Highway 1, Florida City, FL 33034, tel: 305-247-2332.
Food & Supplies: Available in Homestead, Florida City and surrounding area.

Weather: Summer is hot and humid, with temperatures often in excess of 90°F; thunderstorms are common. Winter is short and mild.
General Information: Currents can be strong; never swim alone. Insect repellent is recommended. Use a high-SPF sunscreen and wear a hat to avoid sun burn. Coral is easily damaged; never touch or anchor boats on coral reefs.

For information on glass-bottom boat cruises, snorkeling and scuba diving excursions, contact Biscayne National Underwater Park Company, PO Box 1270, Homestead, FL 33090, tel: 305-230-1100.

CANAVERAL NATIONAL SEASHORE

308 Julia Street, Titusville, FL 32796, tel: 407-267-1110.

Access: The Southern entrance is on Florida's east coast 5 miles (8 km) east of Titusville via Route 406.
Seasons & Hours: The park is open 6am–8pm in summer and 6am–6pm in winter. Visitor center is open daily 9am–4.30pm.
Entrance Fee: No.
Handicapped Access: Visitor center, boardwalks, some beach access, restrooms.
Activities: Hiking, wildlife-watching, swimming, fishing, boating, interpretive programs.
Visitor Facilities: Visitor center.
Camping: Primitive backcountry camping. Beach camping in some areas is restricted in spring and summer to protect sea turtle nesting sites.
Permits & Licenses: Free backcountry camping permits required. Florida saltwater fishing license.
Accommodations: None in the park. Lodging is available in Titusville and New Smyrna Beach. Contact:
  Titusville Chamber of Commerce, 2000 S Washington, Titusville, FL 32780, tel: 407-267-3036.
  New Smyrna Beach Chamber of Commerce, 115 Canal Street, New Smyrna Beach, FL 32168, tel: 904-428-2449.
Food & Supplies: Available in Titusville and New Smyrna Beach.
Weather: Summer is hot and humid, with temperatures often in excess of 90°F (32°C); thunderstorms are common. Winter is short and mild.
General Information: There are no lifeguards. Ocean currents can be strong;

swim at your own risk. Insect repellent is recommended. Be sure to use a high-SPF sunscreen.

DRY TORTUGAS NATIONAL PARK

c/o Everglades National Park, 40001 State Road 9336, Homestead, FL 33034, tel: 305-247-6211.

Access: The park is about 70 miles (113 km) west of Key West and may be reached by boat or seaplane only. Contact the Key West Chamber of Commerce for charter information, Old Mallory Square, Key West, FL tel: 305-294-2587.
Seasons & Hours: The park is open daily; Fort Jefferson is open during daylight hours only.
Entrance Fee: No.
Handicapped Access: Fort entrance.
Activities: Snorkeling, scuba diving, wildlife-watching, swimming, fishing, boating, self-guiding tour of fort.
Visitor Facilities: Docks, orientation program, salt-water toilets, grills, picnic tables.
Camping: Primitive camping only. First-come, first-served.
Permits & Licenses: Florida saltwater fishing license. Campers must register at the fort upon arrival.
Accommodations: None in the park. For lodging information, contact:
  Key West Chamber of Commerce, Old Mallory Square, Key West, FL tel: 305-294-2587.
Food & Supplies: None in the park.
Weather: Summer is hot and humid, with temperatures often in excess of 90°F (32°C); thunderstorms are common. Winter is short and mild.
General Information: There are no lifeguards; swim at your own risk. Insect repellent is recommended. Be sure to use a high-SPF sunscreen. Moor boats and seaplanes at designated sites only. There are no services or supplies on the island. Visitors must provide their own food, water, shelter and other supplies. Do not anchor in or otherwise damage coral.

EVERGLADES NATIONAL PARK

40001 State Road 9336, Homestead, FL 33034, tel: 305-247-6211.

Access: The eastern entrance is about 12 miles (19 km) southwest of Homestead via Route 9336. The western entrance at Everglades City is about

37 (60 km) miles southeast of Naples via Highway 41 and Route 29.

Seasons & Hours: The park is open daily, year-round; Main Visitor Center is open daily 8am–5pm; Royal Palm Visitor Center 8am–4pm; Flamingo Visitor Center 9am–5pm. Shark Valley and Gulf Coast visitor centers are open seasonally.

Entrance Fee: Yes.

Handicapped Access: Visitor centers, tram tours, several trails and campsites.

Activities: Scenic drive, tram tours, hiking, canoeing, wildlife-watching, fishing, interpretive programs.

Visitor Facilities: Visitor centers, marina, museum, environmental education center.

Camping: First-come, first-served.

Permits & Licenses: Florida saltwater and/or freshwater fishing license. Free backcountry camping permit.

Accommodations:

Flamingo Lodge★★, 1 Flamingo Lodge Highway, Flamingo, FL 33034, tel: 305-253-2241.

Additional lodging is available in Homestead, Florida City and Naples. Contact:

Greater Homestead/Florida City Chamber of Commerce, 43 N Krome Avenue Homestead, FL 33030, tel: 305-247-2332.

Naples Chamber of Commerce, 3620 Highway 41 North, Naples, FL 33940, tel: 813-262-6141.

Food & Supplies: A restaurant and marina are located at Flamingo. Additional services are available in Homestead, Florida City and Naples.

Weather: Summer is hot and very humid, with temperatures usually 80°–95°F (27°–35°C); thunderstorms are common. Winter is short and mild.

General Information: Insect repellent is highly recommended in the Everglades. Use a high-SPF sunscreen and wear a hat to avoid sunburn.

GULF ISLANDS NATIONAL SEASHORE

Florida District: 1801 Gulf Breeze Parkway, Gulf Breeze, FL 32561, tel: 904-934-2600.

Mississippi District: 3500 Park Road, Ocean Springs, MS 39564, tel: 601-875-0821.

Access: The Florida District is south of Pensacola via Highway 98 and Route 399. West Ship, East Ship, Horn and Petit Bois islands in the Mississippi District may be reached by boat from Gulfport or Biloxi (summer only).

Seasons & Hours: The park is open daily, year-round; Naval Live Oaks Visitor Center in Florida is open 8.30–4.30, extended hours in summer; Colmer Visitor Center in Mississippi is open daily 8am–5pm.

Entrance Fee: Yes, for some areas.

Handicapped Access: Visitor centers, some historic areas and campsites.

Activities: Hiking, swimming, boating, wildlife-watching, fishing, scuba diving, historic tours, interpretive programs.

Visitor Facilities: Most islands have visitor centers, boat dock, playground, bathhouses, museum, amphitheater.

Camping: First-come, first-served.

Permits & Licenses: Florida saltwater fishing license and/or Mississippi fishing license. Free backcountry camping permit.

Accommodations: None in the park. Lodging is available in Pensacola, Biloxi and Gulfport. Contact:

Pensacola Convention & Visitor Information Center, 1401 E Gregory Street, Pensacola, FL 32501, tel: 904-434-1234.

Mississippi Gulf Coast Chamber of Commerce, 1401 20th Avenue, Gulfport, MS 39501, tel: 601-863-2933.

Food & Supplies: Snack bars in the Florida District. Additional services are available in Pensacola, Biloxi and Gulfport.

Weather: Summer is hot and humid, with temperatures usually 75°–90°F (24°–32°C). Spring and fall are pleasant, 50°–75°F (10°–24°C). Winter is cool, 40°–65°F (4°–18°C).

General Information: Insect repellent is highly recommended. Use a high-SPF sunscreen and hat to avoid sunburn. Be careful of strong currents; never swim alone. Contact the park for a list of companies that rent boats and watersports gear.

For boat tour information in the Mississippi District, contact Ship Island Excursions, tel: 601-864-1014.

Georgia

CUMBERLAND ISLAND NATIONAL SEASHORE

PO Box 806, St Marys, GA 31558, tel: 912-882-4336.

Access: The island may be reached only by boat. A passenger ferry departs from St Marys about 8 miles (13 km) from Interstate 95 via Highway 40.

Seasons & Hours: The visitor center in St Marys is open daily 8.15am–4.30pm. Closed Christmas. Portions of the island are temporarily closed during the winter hunting season.

Entrance Fee: No.

Handicapped Access: Visitor center.

Activities: Hiking, swimming, camping, wildlife-watching, fishing, interpretive programs.

Visitor Facilities: Visitor center.

Camping: Reservations required.

Permits & Licenses: Camping permits.

Accommodations: Greyfield Inn offers the only rooms on the island. Contact: PO Box 900, Fernandina, FL 32035, tel: 904-261-6408.

Additional lodging is available in St Marys. Contact:

St Marys Tourism Council, PO Box 1291, St Marys, GA 31558, tel: 912-882-4000.

Food & Supplies: All food and supplies must be brought from the mainland.

Weather: Summer is hot and humid, with temperatures usually 80°–95°F (27°–35°C); thunderstorms are common. Winter is short and mild.

General Information: Insect repellent is highly recommended. Use a high-SPF sunscreen and wear a hat to avoid sunburn. There are no stores on the island, so bring all food and supplies. Visitation on the island is limited to 300 people per day, reservations are highly recommended. Contact the park for ferry and camping reservations, tel: 912-882-4335.

Kentucky

MAMMOTH CAVE NATIONAL PARK

Mammoth Cave, KY 42259, tel: 502-758-2328.

Access: The visitor center is 9 miles (14½ km) northwest of Park City via Highways 255 and 70.

Seasons & Hours: The visitor center is open daily 8am–5pm, extended hours in summer. Closed Christmas.

Entrance Fee: No; but there are fees for cave tours.

Handicapped Access: Visitor center, Heritage Trail, some campsites. A cave tour is available with assistance from volunteers or park rangers.

Activities: Cave tours, boat tour, hiking, camping, wildlife-watching, interpretive programs.
Visitor Facilities: Visitor center, post office, services and supplies.
Camping: First-come, first-served.
Permits & Licenses: Backcountry camping permits required.
Accommodations:
  Mammoth Cave Hotel★★, Mammoth Cave, KY 42259; tel: 502-758-2225.
  Additional lodging is available in Cave City, Park City, Bowling Green and surrounding towns. Contact:
  Cave City Tourist Commission, PO Box 518, Cave City, KY 42127, tel: 502-773-3131.
  Bowling Green Chamber of Commerce, PO Box 51, Bowling Green, KY 42102, tel: 502-781-3200.
Food & Supplies: There is a restaurant in the Mammoth Cave Hotel; supplies are available seasonally at the service center near the campground.
Weather: Summer is hot and humid, with temperatures usually 75°–95°F (24°–35°C). Winters are mild, with occasional snow. Cave temperature hovers around 54°F (12°C).
General Information: For cave tour reservations, contact contact Mistix, PO Box 85705, San Diego, CA 92186-5705, tel: 800-365-2267.

North Carolina

BLUE RIDGE PARKWAY

400 BB&T Building, One Pack Square, Asheville, NC 28801, tel: 704-271-4779.

Access: The parkway runs between Shenandoah National Park in Virginia and Great Smoky Mountains National Park in North Carolina. Several highways interstect the parkway, including Interstates 64 and 77 in Virginia, and 40 and 26 in North Carolina.
Seasons & Hours: The parkway is open daily, year-round. Some sections are closed by snow in winter. Visitor centers are open seasonally, hours vary.
Entrance Fee: No.
Handicapped Access: Most visitor centers.
Activities: Scenic drive, hiking, camping, fishing, horseback riding, historic sites, wildlife-watching, interpretive programs.

Visitor Facilities: Visitor centers, historic buildings, museum, arts and crafts centers.
Camping: First-come, first-served.
Permits & Licenses: Free backcountry camping permit.
Accommodations:
  Peaks of Otter, PO Box 489, Bedford, VA 24523, tel: 703-586-1081.
  Pisgah Inn, PO Box 749, Waynesville, NC 28786, tel: 704-235-8228.
  Additional lodging is available in towns along the parkway. Contact:
  North Carolina Division of Travel and Tourism, 430 N. Salisbury Street, Raleigh, NC 27611, tel: 919-733-4171.
  Virginia Division of Tourism, 901 E Byrd Street, Richmond, VA 23219, tel: 804-786-4484.
Food & Supplies: Several restaurants are on the parkway, including Peaks of Otter Restaurant (mile 86/138 km), Pisgah Inn (mile 409/658 km), Bluffs Coffee Shop (mile 241/388 km) and Mabry Mill (mile 176/283), Otter Creek (60/98 km) and Whetstone Ridge (mile 29/47 km). Additional services are available in surrounding towns and highways.
Weather: Temperatures vary depending on elevation. Summer temperatures are usually 55°–85°F (13°–29°C), cooler and breezier in higher elevations. Spring and fall are mild, with occasional showers and dense fog. Autumn foliage is spectacular. Snow and ice may close parkway in winter.
General Information: Keep your eyes on the road. Use pullouts and overlooks to view the landscape. The speed limit on the parkway is 45 mph (72 kmph), but traffic often moves slower. Use alternate routes for swifter point-to-point driving.

CAPE HATTERAS NATIONAL SEASHORE

Route 1, Box 675, Manteo, NC 27954, tel: 919-473-2111.

Access: The northern entrance is on the Outer Banks a few miles south of Nags Head. Ferries to the seashore depart from Swanquarter and Cedar Island.
Seasons & Hours: The park is open daily, year-round. Hatteras Island Visitor Center is open daily, 9am–5pm, extended hours in summer. Closed

Christmas. Other visitor centers are open seasonally; times vary.
Entrance Fee: No.
Handicapped Access: Visitor centers, designated campsites, and some nature trails with assistance.
Activities: Swimming, hiking, camping, biking, fishing, scuba diving, wildlife-watching, horseback riding, interpretive programs.
Visitor Facilities: Visitor centers, historic lighthouses, boat ramps, marina.
Camping: Reservations are available for Ocracoke Campground between Memorial Day and Labor Day. Contact:
  Mistix, PO Box 85705, San Diego, CA 92186-5705, tel: 800-365-2267.
  Other sites are run on a first-come, first-served.
Permits & Licenses: Freshwater fishing license.
Accommodations: Lodging is available in Manteo, Nags Head, Kill Devil Hills, Buxton, Ocracoke. Contact:
  Dare County Tourist Bureau, PO Box 399, Manteo, NC 27954, tel: 919-473-2138.
  Outer Banks Chamber of Commerce, PO Box 1757, Kill Devil Hills, NC 27948, tel: 919-441-8144.
Food & Supplies: Limited services are available at the Oregon Inlet Marina. Additional services are available in Manteo, Nags Head, Kill Devil Hills, Buxton and nearby villages.
Weather: Summer is hot and humid, with temperatures usually 75°–95°F (24°–35°C) and frequent afternoon thunderstorms. Winter is cold 35°–55°F (2°–13°C). Expect windy conditions in any season.
General Information: Ocean currents can be very strong. Lifeguards are not always available; never swim alone. Use a high-SPF sunscreen and wear a hat to avoid sunburn. Insect repellent is recommended for campers. For ferry information and reservations, call the North Carolina Ferry System, tel: 800-293-3779.

CAPE LOOKOUT NATIONAL SEASHORE

131 Charles Street, Harkers Island, NC 28531, tel: 919-728-2250.

Access: The seashore may be reached by ferry from Beaufort, Harkers Island, Davis, Atlantic and Ocracoke.

Seasons & Hours: The park is open daily, year-round. Harkers Island Visitor Center is open daily 8am–4.30pm. Closed Christmas and New Years Day.

Entrance Fee: No.

Handicapped Access: Visitor Center.

Activities: Hiking, camping, fishing, wildlife-watching, interpretive programs.

Visitor Facilities: Facilities are limited.

Camping: Primitive camping only.

Permits & Licenses: No.

Accommodations: None in the park. Lodging is available in Beaufort and Harkers Island and Morehead City. Contact:

> **Carteret County Tourism Development Bureau**, PO Box 1406, Morehead City, NC 28557, tel: 800-786-6962.

> **Outer Banks Chamber of Commerce**, PO Box 1757, Kill Devil Hills, NC 27948, tel: 919-441-8144.

Food & Supplies: Services are available in Beaufort, Morehead City and Harkers Island.

Weather: Summer is hot and humid, with temperatures usually 80°–95°F (27°–35°C) and frequent afternoon thunderstorms. Winter is a cold 35°–55°F (2°–13°C). Expect windy conditions in any season.

General Information: There are no roads and only limited facilities. Visitors should bring all essentials, including adequate food and water. Swimming is not recommended. Use a high-SPF sunscreen and wear a hat to avoid sunburn. Insect repellent is recommended.

For information and reservations on state ferries, call North Carolina Ferry System, tel: 800-293-3779. Additional ferries are managed by private concessionaires, tel: 919-728-2250.

Tennessee

BIG SOUTH FORK NATIONAL RIVER & RECREATION AREA

Route 3, Box 401, Oneida, TN 37841, tel: 615-569-9778.

Access: The recreation area is on the Tennessee-Kentucky border about 13 miles (21 km) west of Oneida, Tennessee, via Route 297.

Seasons & Hours: The park is open daily, year-round. The Bandy Creek Visitor Center is open daily 8am–4.30pm, extended hours in spring and summer. Closed Christmas

Entrance Fee: No.

Handicapped Access: Visitor center, some trails and campsites.

Activities: Hiking, swimming, boating, camping, horseback riding, fishing, wildlife-watching, historic exhibits, interpretive programs.

Visitor Facilities: Visitor centers, boat ramps, recreation sites, historic Blue Heron mining town.

Camping: First-come, first-served.

Permits & Licenses: Kentucky and/or Tennessee fishing and hunting licenses are required. Backcountry camping permits are recommended.

Accommodations:

> **Charit Creek Lodge**★★ (rustic lodge and cabins), 250 Apple Valley Road, Sevierville, TN 37862, tel: 615-429-5704.

> Additional lodging is available in Oneida and Jamestown 615-879-9948 in Tennessee and Whitley City in Kentucky. Contact:

> **Oneida Chamber of Commerce**, PO Box 4442, Oneida, TN 37841, tel: 615-569-6900.

> **Whitley City Chamber of Commerce**, PO Box 548, Whitley City, KY 42653, tel: 606-376-5004.

Food & Supplies: Services are available in Oneida and Jamestown in Tennessee and Whitley City in Kentucky.

Weather: Summer is hot and humid, with temperatures usually 75°–95°F (30°–35°C). Spring and fall are moderate, 65°–80°F (18°–27°C). Winter is mild, with occasional light snow.

General Information: The river is especially dangerous during periods of high water, but visitors should exercise caution at all times. Do not dive into the river. Never swim alone. Always wear a life jacket when boating. Local concessionaires rent canoes, tubes and other equipment; contact park headquarters for an up-to-date list.

GREAT SMOKY MOUNTAINS NATIONAL PARK

107 Park Headquarters Road, Gatlinburg, TN 37738, tel: 615-436-1200.

Access: The park is on the Tennessee–North Carolina border. The Sugarlands Visitor Center is 2 miles (3 km) south of Gatlinburg, Tennessee, via Highway 441 (Newfound Gap Road). The Oconaluftee Visitor Center is 2 miles (3 km) north of Cherokee, North Carolina, via Highway 441.

Seasons & Hours: The park is open daily, year-round. The Sugarlands and Oconaluftee visitor centers are open daily, year-round, hours vary seasonally. Closed Christmas. Cades Cove Visitor Center is open mid-March–November. New Found Gap Road may be closed by ice and snow in winter.

Entrance Fee: No.

Handicapped Access: Visitor centers, some campsites and some paved trails.

Activities: Scenic drive, hiking, swimming, camping, horseback riding, fishing, cross-country skiing, wildlife-watching, historic exhibits, interpretive programs.

Visitor Facilities: Visitor centers, historic villages, lookout tower.

Camping: Reservations are required May 15–October 31. Contact:

> **Mistix**, PO Box 85705, San Diego, CA 92186-5705, tel: 800-365-2267.

> Other sites are first-come, first-served.

Permits & Licenses: North Carolina and/or Tennessee fishing license. Backcountry camping permits are required.

Accommodations:

> **LeConte Lodge**★★ (rustic cabins), 250 Apple Valley Road, Sevierville, TN 37862, tel: 615-429-5704.

> **Wonderland Hotel**, Route 2, Box 205, Gatlinburg, TN 37738, tel: 615-436-5490.

> Additional lodging is available in Gatlinburg, Cherokee, Bryson City and surrounding towns. Contact:

> **Gatlinburg Visitor and Convention Bureau**, PO Box 527, Gatlinburg, TN 37738, tel: 615-430-4148.

> **Cherokee Visitor Center**, PO Box 460, Cherokee, NC 28719, tel: 704-497-9195.

> **Swain County Chamber of Commerce**, PO Box 509, Bryson City, NC 28713, tel: 704-488-3681.

Food & Supplies: Services are available in Gatlinburg, Cherokee, Bryson City and surrounding towns.

Weather: Temperatures may vary as much as 15°–20°F (–9°to –7°C) depending on elevation. Summer temperatures are usually 55°–85°F (13°–29°C), with sudden thunderstorms. Spring and fall are moderate, 45°–75°F (7°–24°C). Winter is moderate in

the valleys but very cold at higher elevations, with accumulations of snow.
General Information: Do not approach wildlife. Thin air at higher elevations can make hiking difficult. Insect repellent is recommended in summer. Stay on designated trails. Always use caution on slippery rocks near streams and waterfalls.

Virginia

SHENANDOAH NATIONAL PARK

Route 4, Box 348, Luray, VA 22835, tel: 703-999-2243.

Access: The park is about 85 miles (137 km) northwest of Richmond via Interstate 64 and 60 miles (97 km) from Washington, DC, via Interstate 66 and Highway 340.
Seasons & Hours: The park is open daily, year-round. Dickey Ridge and Byrd visitor centers are open daily March–early November, 9am–5pm.
Entrance Fee: Yes.
Handicapped Access: Visitor centers, some campsites and a paved trail.
Activities: Scenic drive, hiking, camping, horseback riding, biking, fishing, cross-country skiing, wildlife-watching, historic exhibits, interpretive programs.
Visitor Facilities: Visitor centers, historic buildings, amphitheater.
Camping: Reservations are available and recommended for Big Meadows Campground. Contact:
  Mistix, PO Box 85705, San Diego, CA 92186-5705, tel: 800-365-2267.
  Otherwise, first-come, first-served.
Permits & Licenses: Virginia fishing license. Backcountry camping permits are required.
Accommodations:
  Big Meadows Lodge★★, **Lewis Mountain Cabins**★ and **Skyland Lodge**★★–★★★ are managed by ARA Virginia Sky-Line Co., PO Box 727, Luray, VA 22835, tel: 703-743-5108 or 800-999-4714.
  Additional lodging is available in Front Royal, Luray, Sperryville, Waynesboro, Charlottesville and other towns near the park. Contact:
  Shenandoah Valley Travel Association, PO Box 1040, New Market, VA 22844, tel: 703-740-3132.
  Front Royal-Warren County Chamber of Commerce, 414 E Main

Street, Front Royal, VA 22630, tel: 703-635-3185.
  Page County Chamber of Commerce, 46 E Main Street, Luray, VA 22835, tel: 703-743-3915.
Food & Supplies: Several restaurants are located along Skyline Drive, including Big Meadows Lodge (mile 51/82 km), Panorama (mile 31œ/51 km) and Skyland Lodge (mile 42/67 km). Additional services are available in surrounding towns.
Weather: Temperatures may vary depending on elevation. Summer temperatures are usually 55°–85°F (13°–30°C), with sudden thunderstorms. Spring and fall are moderate, 45°–75°F (7°–24°C). Winter is mild in the valleys but cold, with occasional accumulations of snow and ice at higher elevations.
General Information: Keep your eyes on the road. Use pullouts and overlooks to view the landscape. The speed limit on Skyline Drive is 35 mph (56 kmph); use alternate routes for swifter point-to-point travel. Do not approach wildlife. Thin air at higher elevations can make hiking difficult. Use caution on slippery rocks near streams and waterfalls. Insect repellent is recommended in summer. Stay on designated trails.

Virgin Islands

BUCK ISLAND REEF NATIONAL MONUMENT

PO Box 160, Christiansted, St Croix, VI 00821, tel: 809-773-1460.

Access: The monument may be reached only by boat about 6 miles (10 km) from Christiansted.
Seasons & Hours: The monument is open daily, year-round.
Entrance Fee: No.
Handicapped Access: No.
Activities: Hiking, fishing, snorkeling, scuba diving, sailing, wildlife-watching.
Visitor Facilities: Picnic tables, grills, pavilion, restrooms, unloading dock, underwater trail.
Camping: No.
Permits & Licenses: No.
Accommodations: None in the park. Lodging is available on St Croix. Contact:
  Virgin Islands Tourism, PO Box 6400, St Thomas, VI 00804, tel:

809-774-8784 or 800-372-8784.
Food & Supplies: Available on St Croix.
Weather: Temperatures average 79°–85°F (26°–29°C) with little seasonal variation. High temperatures range in the 90°F (32°C), lows in the 60°F (16°C).
General Information: Never swim alone. Do not touch or stand on fragile coral formations. Insect repellent is recommended for hikers. Camping on the island is prohibited. Use a high-SPF sunscreen and wear a hat to avoid sunburn. Travelers returning to the US from the Virgin Islands are required to pass through Customs.

VIRGIN ISLANDS NATIONAL PARK

6310 Estate Nazareth, St Thomas, VI 00802, tel: 809-775-6238.

Access: The park is on the island of St John; access is by boat only. Ferries runs from Red Hook and Charlotte Amalie, St Thomas, and from West End and Road Town, Tortola, to the park gateway at Cruz Bay, St John.
Seasons & Hours: The park is open daily, year-round. Cruz Bay Visitor Center is open daily 8am–5pm.
Entrance Fee: No.
Handicapped Access: Cruz Bay Visitor Center. The ferry and Annaberg Plantation are accessible with assistance; contact park headquarters for details.
Activities: Scenic drive, hiking, camping, fishing, snorkeling, scuba diving, sailing, wildlife-watching, historic sites, interpretive programs.
Visitor Facilities: Visitor centers, historic sites, sports center.
Camping: Reservations are required. Contact:
  Cinnamon Bay Campground, St John, VI 00830, tel: 809-776-6330.
  Maho Bay Campground (privately-run), PO Box 310, St John, VI 00831, tel: 809-776-6226.
Permits & Licenses: No.
Accommodations: There are hotels and resorts for just about any budget on St John. Contact:
  Virgin Islands Tourism, PO Box 6400, St Thomas, VI 00804, tel: 809-774-8784 or 800-372-8784.
Food & Supplies: Restaurants and snack bars are located in Cruz Bay and Cinnamon Bay.
Weather: Temperatures average 79°F (26°C) with little seasonal variation. High temperatures range in the 90°F

(32°C), lows in the 60°F (16°C).

General Information: Remember to drive on the left. Never swim alone. Be especially careful in the big waves on the island's north shore. Do not touch or stand on fragile coral formations. Insect repellent is recommended for hikers and campers. Use a high-SPF sunscreen and wear a hat.

Travelers returning to the US from the Virgin Islands are required to pass through Customs.

Sailing, windsurfing, snorkeling and scuba diving lessons and excursions can be arranged by the Cinnamon Bay Water Sports Center, tel: 809-776-6330.

Historic & Archaeological Parks

The Northeast

Contact these parks directly for hours, seasons, access, road and weather conditions.

Connecticut

Weir Farm National Historic Site, 735 Nod Hill Road Wilton, CT 06897, tel: 203-834-1896. The home, studio and farm of American painter J. Alden Weir are preserved in a peaceful rural setting.

District of Columbia

Frederick Douglass National Historic Site, 1411 W Street SE, Washington, DC 20020, tel: 202-426-5961. This was the home of the influential black abolitionist from 1877–1895.

John F. Kennedy Center for the Performing Arts, National Park Service, 2700 F Street, NW, Washington, DC 20566, tel: 202-416-7910. Designed by architect Edward Durell Stone, the center is host to a variety of performances, including plays, concerts, ballets and operas.

Lyndon Baines Johnson Memorial Grove on the Potomac, c/o George Washington Memorial Parkway, Turkey Run Park, McLean, VA 22101, tel: 703-285-2598. A grove of white pines overlooking the Potomac River honors the memory of former president Lyndon B. Johnson.

Mary McLeod Bethune Council House National Historic Site, 1318 Vermont Avenue, NW, Washington, DC 20005, tel: 202-332-1233. The headquarters of the National Council of Negro Women, established in 1935, commemorates the distinguished educator who was its founder.

National Capital Parks, National Capital Region, 900 Ohio Drive SW, Washington, DC 20242, tel: 202-485-9880. More than 300 historic sites, monuments and memorials are scattered throughout the Washington DC area. Some of these sites include the Washington Monument, Vietnam Veterans Memorial, Thomas Jefferson Memorial, Lincoln Memorial and Ford's Theatre National Historic Site.

National Mall, c/o National Capital Region, 900 Ohio Drive SW, Washington, DC 20242, tel: 202-485-9880. An urban park stretching from the Capitol to the Washington Monument.

Rock Creek Park, 5200 Glover Road NW, Washington, DC 20015, tel: 202-426-6829. A large urban park with a variety of historical, natural and recreational facilities.

Sewall-Belmont House National Historic Site, 144 Constitution Avenue NE, Washington, DC 20002, tel: 202-546-3989. The headquarters of the National Women's Party commemorates Alice Paul, the organization's founder.

Theodore Roosevelt Island, c/o George Washington Memorial Parkway, Turkey Run Park, McLean, VA 22101, tel: 703-285-2598. A wooded island that features a statue of Theodore Roosevelt and dedicated to the 26th President's commitment to the nation's conservation.

White House, National Capital Region, 900 Ohio Drive SW, Washington, DC 20242, tel: 202-485-9880. The residence of US presidents since 1800.

Maine

Roosevelt Campobello International Park, c/o Executive Secretary Roosevelt Campobello International Park Commission, PO Box 97, Lubec, ME 04652, tel: 506-752-2922. Administered jointly by the United States and Canada, the island was the summer retreat of President Franklin D. Roosevelt until 1921.

Saint Croix Island International Historic Site, c/o Acadia National Park, PO Box 177, Bar Harbor, ME 04609, tel: 207-288-3338. Site on the current United States–Canadian border of an early attempt to establish a French settlement in 1604.

Maryland

Catoctin Mountain Park, 6602 Foxville Road, Thurmont, MD 21788, tel: 301-663-9330. A 5,770-acre (2,335-hectare) forest park on the eastern shoulder of the Appalachian Mountains. The presidential retreat at Camp David is located within the park but is off-limits to the public.

Chesapeake and Ohio Canal National Historical Park, PO Box 4, Sharpsburg, MD 21782, tel: 301-739-4206. Built in 1828–50, this 184-mile (296-km) canal runs along the Potomac River from Washington, DC, to Cumberland, Maryland.

Clara Barton National Historic Site, 5801 Oxford Road, Glen Echo, MD 20812, tel: 301-492-6246. The home of the founder, and also one-time headquarters, of the American Red Cross.

Fort McHenry National Monument and Historic Shrine, East Fort Avenue, Baltimore, MD 21230, tel: 410-962-4299. The attack on this fort during the War of 1812 inspired Francis Scott Key to write America's anthem *The Star-Spangled Banner*.

Fort Washington Park, c/o National Capital Region 900 Ohio Drive SW, Washington, DC 20242, tel: 202-485-9880. This fort was built in 1814 across the Potomac River from Mount Vernon.

Greenbelt Park, 6565 Greenbelt Road, Greenbelt, MD 20770, tel: 301-344-3948. A 1,175-acre (476-hectare) woodland park just outside of Washington, DC.

Hampton National Historic Site, 535 Hampton Lane Towson, MD 21286, tel: 410-962-0688. A lavish Georgian-style mansion built in the late 18th century.

Thomas Stone National Historic Site, c/o George Washington Birthplace National Monument, RR1, Box 717, Washington's Birthplace, VA 22443, tel: 804-224-1732. This site near Port Tobacco preserves Habre-de-Venture, a lovely Georgian mansion built in 1771 and home of Thomas Stone, one of the men who signed the Declaration of Independence.

Massachusetts

Adams National Historic Site, PO Box 531, Quincy, MA 02269-0531, tel: 617-773-1177. This was the home of two US presidents: John Adams and John Quincy Adams.

Boston African American National Historic Site, 46 Joy Street, Boston, MA 02114, tel: 617-742-5415. More than a dozen sites associated with antebellum black life are found along the 1½-mile (3-km) Black Heritage Trail.

Boston National Historical Park, Charlestown Navy Yard, Boston, MA 02129, tel: 617-242-5644. This park is made up of American Revolution-era sites scattered throughout the Boston area, including Bunker Hill, Old North Church, Paul Revere House, Faneuil Hall, Old State House and the USS Constitution.

Frederick Law Olmsted National Historic Site, 99 Warren Street, Brookline, MA 02146, tel: 617-566-1689. The home and workplace of the influential city planner, landscape architect and early conservationist.

John Fitzgerald Kennedy National Historic Site, 83 Beals Street, Brookline, MA 02146, tel: 617-566-7937. The park preserves the birthplace and boyhood home of the 35th President.

Longfellow National Historic Site, 105 Brattle Street, Cambridge, MA 02138, tel: 617-876-4491. The home of poet Henry Wadsworth Longfellow from 1837 to 1882.

Lowell National Historical Park, 246 Market Street, Lowell, MA 01852, tel: 508-459-1000. The park preserves the mills, canals and workers' houses of this early industrial town.

Minute Man National Historical Park, 174 Liberty Street, Concord, MA 01742, tel: 508-369-6944. Site of the opening skirmish, in 1775, of the American Revolution.

Salem Maritime National Historic Site, 174 Derby Street, Salem, MA 01970, tel: 508-745-1470. Several structures, including wharfs, warehouses and a custom house, date to the "China trade" of the late 18th and early 19th centuries.

Saugus Iron Works National Historic Site, 244 Central Street, Saugus, MA 01906, tel: 617-233-0050. The park preserves a blast furnace, forge, mill and other structures of the first major ironworks in North America, dating to the mid-17th century.

Springfield Armory National Historic Site, 1 Armory Square, Springfield, MA 01105-1299, tel: 413-734-8551. An important arms manufacturing site from 1794–1968.

New Hampshire

Saint-Gaudens National Historic Site, RR 3, Box 73 Cornish, NH 03745, tel: 603-675-2175. The home and studio of renowned late-19th- and early 20th-century sculptor Augustus Saint-Gaudens.

New Jersey

Edison National Historic Site, Mine Street and Lakeside Avenue, West Orange, NJ 07052, tel: 201-736-5050. Thomas Edison came up with some of his most famous inventions at this laboratory and home, occupied from 1887 to 1931.

Morristown National Historical Park, Washington Place, Morristown, NJ 07960, tel: 201-539-2085. This site was used as winter quarters by the Continental Army during the American Revolution in 1777 and 1779–80.

New York

Castle Clinton National Monument, Battery Park, New York, NY 10004, tel: 212-344-7220. Built in 1808–11, this historic structure at the tip of Manhattan served as a fort and later as an immigration center in the late 19th century.

Eleanor Roosevelt National Historic Site, 519 Albany Post Road, Hyde Park, NY 12538, tel: 914-229-7821. This park preserves Val-Kill, Eleanor Roosevelt's personal retreat.

Ellis Island, Liberty Island, New York, NY 10004, tel: 12-363-3201. America's museum-of-the-melting pot, the first stop for millions of immigrants arriving in the New World.

Federal Hall National Memorial, Manhattan Sites, National Park Service, 26 Wall Street, New York, NY 10005, tel: 212-264-8711. Built in 1842, this handsome structure in downtown Manhattan stands on the site where the Second Continental Congress convened in 1785 and George Washington was sworn in as President of the US in 1789.

Fort Stanwix National Monument, 112 E Park Street, Rome, NY 13440, tel: 315-336-2090. A reconstruction of the fort that was attacked by a British force from Canada in 1777.

Gateway National Recreation Area, Floyd Bennett Field, Building 69, Brooklyn, NY 11234, tel: 718-338-3575. The park includes a variety of historic structures, beaches and recreational facilities.

General Grant National Memorial, 122nd Street and Riverside Drive, New York, NY 10027, tel: 212-666-1640. Ulysses S. Grant and his wife are interred at this memorial on the west side of Manhattan.

Hamilton Grange National Memorial, 287 Convent Avenue, New York, NY 10031, tel: 212-283-5154. The home of Alexander Hamilton, the first US Secretary of the Treasury.

Franklin D. Roosevelt National Historic Site, 519 Albany Post Road, Hyde Park, NY 12538, tel: 914-229-7821. The park preserves Springwood, the home and birthplace of the 32nd president.

Martin Van Buren National Historic Site, PO Box 545, Kinderhook, NY 12106, tel: 518-758-9689. This is the retirement home of the eighth president of the US.

Sagamore Hill National Historic Site, 20 Sagamore Hill Road, Oyster Bay, NY 1171, tel: 516-922-4447. The park preserves the home of President Theodore Roosevelt from 1886 until his death in 1919.

Saint Paul's Church National Historic Site, 897 S Columbus Avenue, Mount Vernon, NY 10550, tel: 914-667-4116. An 18th-century church associated with the struggle over freedom of the press.

Saratoga National Historical Park, 648 Route 32, Stillwater, NY 12170, tel: 518-664-9821. This is the site of a critical American victory against the British in 1777 during the American Revolution.

Statue of Liberty National Monument, Liberty Island, New York, NY 10004, tel: 212-363-3201. Designed by Frederick Bartholdi, the famous 152-ft (46-meter) statue in New York Harbor was a gift from France to the United States in 1886.

Theodore Roosevelt Birthplace National Historic Site, 28 E 20th Street, New York, NY 10003, tel: 212-260-1616. A reconstruction of the house in which the 26th President was born.

Theodore Roosevelt Inaugural National Historic Site, 641 Delaware Avenue, Buffalo, NY 14202, tel: 716-884-0095. Roosevelt took the oath of office at this house after the assassination of President William McKinley.

Vanderbilt Mansion National Historic Site, Route 9, Albany Post Road, Hyde Park, NY 12538, tel: 914-229-7770. A lavish manison typical of the homes of the late 19th-century elite.

Women's Rights National Historical Park, PO Box 70, Seneca Falls, NY 13148, tel: 315-568-2991. This park preserves the Wesleyan Methodist Chapel, Elizabeth Cady Stanton home, McClintock House and other sites associated with the early women's rights movement.

Pennsylvania

Allegheny Portage Railroad National Historic Site, PO Box 189, Cresson, PA 16630, tel: 814-886-8176. Preserves traces of the first railroad to cross the Allegheny Mountains.

Edgar Allan Poe National Historic Site, c/o Independence National Historical Park, 313 Walnut Street, Philadelphia, PA 19106, tel: 215-597-8780. Poe lived at this site in 1843–44 when he wrote some of his best-known literary works.

Eisenhower National Historic Site, 97 Taneytown Road, Gettysburg, PA 17325, tel: 717-334-1124. The home of President Dwight D. Eisenhower and his wife, Mamie, during and after his term in office.

Fort Necessity National Battlefield, RD 2, Box 528 Farmington, PA 15437, tel: 412-329-5512. George Washington led a losing battle here in 1754 during the French and Indian War.

Friendship Hill National Historic Site, c/o Fort Necessity National Battlefield, RD 2, Box 528, Farmington, PA 15437, tel: 412-329-5512. This is the lovely old home of Albert Gallatin, Secretary of the Treasury under Presidents Jefferson and Madison.

Gloria Dei (Old Swedes') Church National Historic Site, Christopher Columbus Boulevard and Christian Street, Philadelphia, PA 19106, tel: 215-597-8974. An early Swedish church built around 1700.

Hopewell Furnace National Historic Site, 2 Mark Bird Lane, Elverson, PA 19520, tel: 610-582-8773. This is the site of an early iron-making village dating to 1771.

Independence National Historical Park, 313 Walnut Street, Philadelphia, PA 19106, tel: 215-597-8974. Set in the heart of Philadelphia, the park is the home of Independence Hall, the Liberty Bell, Carpenters Hall and other important 18th-century sites associated with American independence.

Johnstown Flood National Memorial, c/o Allegheny Portage Railroad National Historic Site, PO Box 189 Cresson, PA 16630, tel: 814-886-8176. This site commemorates the disastrous flood of 1889 that killed more than 2,000 people.

Steamtown National Historic Site, 150 S Washington Avenue, Scranton, PA 18503, tel: 717-340-5200. An early 20th-century steam rail yard is preserved here with locomotives, rail cars, a roundhouse and other structures.

Thaddeus Kosciuszko National Memorial, c/o Independence National Historical Park, 313 Walnut Street, Philadelphia, PA 19106, tel: 215-597-8974. The Polish hero of the American Revolution is commemorated at the Philadelphia house where Kosciuszko boarded.

Valley Forge National Historical Park, PO Box 23, Valley Forge, PA 19482, tel: 610-783-1077. The Continental Army wintered here in 1777–78 during the American Revolution. Original and reconstructed structures and occasional reenactments recall the events of the period.

The Midwest

Illinois

Lincoln Home National Historic Site, 413 S Eighth Street, Springfield, IL 62703, tel: 217-492-4150. Abraham Lincoln's home for 17 years before he became president.

Indiana

George Rogers Clark National Historical Park, 401 S Second Street, Vincennes, IN 47591, tel: 812-882-1776. This memorial commemorates the capture of Fort Sackville in 1779 by Lt Col. George Rogers Clark and the opening of the Old Northwest.

Lincoln Boyhood National Memorial, PO Box 1816, Lincoln City, IN 47552, tel: 812-937-4541. Lincoln spent his earliest years at this frontier farm.

Iowa

Effigy Mounds National Monument, 151 Highway 76, Harpers Ferry, IA 52146, tel: 319-873-3491. The park preserves extraordinary examples of ancient Indian burial mounds.

Herbert Hoover National Historic Site, PO Box 607, West Branch, IA 52358, tel: 319-643-2541. The site includes the birthplace, Quaker meetinghouse and grave of the 31st president.

Minnesota

Grand Portage National Monument, PO Box 668, Grand Marais, MN 55604, tel: 218-387-2788. This 709-acre (287-hectare) park preserves a 9-mile (15-km) portage and rendezvous point used by French voyageurs in the 17th and 18th centuries.

Pipestone National Monument, PO Box 727, Pipestone, MN 56164, tel: 507-825-5464. The park protects quarries used by Native Americans for centuries to obtain rock for making ceremonial pipes.

Missouri

George Washington Carver National Monument, PO Box 38, Diamond, MO 64840, tel: 417-325-4151. The birthplace and boyhood home of the black agricultural chemist whose experiments with different crops helped replenish the South's soil after the demise of cotton.

Harry S. Truman National Historic Site, 223 N Main Street, Independence, MO 64050, tel: 816-254-2720. The home of the 33rd president from 1919 until his death in 1972.

Jefferson National Expansion Memorial, 11 N 4th Street, St Louis, MO 63102, tel: 314-425-4465. Situated on the Mississippi riverfront, the park includes the 630-foot (192-meter) St Louis Arch (the "Gateway to the West"), as well as the Museum of Westward Expansion.

Ulysses S. Grant National Historic Site, c/o Jefferson National Expansion Memorial, 11 North 4th Street, St Louis, MO 63102, tel: 314-842-1867.

Grant lived at this home in the years before the Civil War.

Ohio

James A. Garfield National Historic Site, 8095 Mentor Avenue, Mentor, OH 44060, tel: 216-255-8722. This park interprets the life and career of the 20th president.

Mound City Group National Monument, 16062 State Route 104, Chillicothe, OH 45612, tel: 614-774-1125. The park preserves and interprets Hopewell culture burial mounds built from 200 BC–AD 500.

Perry's Victory and International Peace Memorial, PO Box 549, 93 Delaware Avennue, Put-in-Bay, OH 43456, tel: 419-285-2184. The park commemorates Commodore Oliver H. Perry's important naval victory during the War of 1812.

William Howard Taft National Historic Site, 2038 Auburn Avenue, Cincinnati, OH 45219, tel: 513-684-3262. This is the birthplace and boyhood home of President Taft.

The South

Alabama

Horshoe Bend National Military Park, 11288 Horshoe Bend Road, Daviston, AL 36256, tel: 205-234-7111. A major battle site of the Creek War of the early 1800s.

Russell Cave National Monument, 3729 County Road 98, Bridgeport, AL 35740, tel: 205-495-2672. Archaeological finds in this cave date from 7000 BC–AD 1650, chronicling an impressive succession of Native American cultures.

Tuskegee Institute National Historic Site, PO Drawer 10, Tuskegee Institute, AL 36087-0010, tel: 205-727-6390. Tuskegee is the college for black Americans founded by Booker T. Washington in 1881 and still active.

Arkansas

Arkansas Post National Memorial, Route 1, Box 16 Gillette, AR 72055, tel: 501-548-2207. The park commemorates the first permanent French settlement in the lower Mississippi Valley; the village was founded in 1686.

Fort Smith National Historic Site, PO Box 1406, Fort Smith, AR 72902, tel: 501-783-3961. One of the oldest

American forts in the Louisiana Territory, this site was dedicated to Indian affairs and establishing United States law on the frontier.

Florida

Castillo de San Marcos National Monument, 1 Castillo Drive, St Augustine, FL 32084, tel: 904-829-6506. Built in 1672, stately Castillo de San Marcos is the oldest masonry fort in the oldest permanent European settlement in the continental United States.

De Soto National Memorial, PO Box 15390, Bradenton, FL 34280, tel: 813-792-0458. Hernando de Soto landed here in 1539 during the first major European exploration of the southern United States.

Fort Caroline National Memorial, 12713 Fort Caroline Road, Jacksonville, FL 32225, tel: 904-641-7155. The fort stands near the site of a French Huguenot settlement dating to 1564–65.

Fort Matanzas National Monument, c/o Castillo de San Marcos National Monument, 1 Castillo Drive, St Augustine, FL 32084, tel: 904-471-0116. A Spanish fort built in 1740–42.

Timucuan Ecological and Historic Preserve, c/o Fort Caroline National Memorial, 12713 Fort Caroline Road, Jacksonville, FL 32225, tel: 904-641-7111. Traces of Native American occupation as far back as 2,000 years ago as well as colonial Spanish French and English artifacts have been uncovered at this ecologically significant site along the St Johns and Nassau rivers.

Georgia

Fort Frederica National Monument, Route 9, Box 286-C, St Simons Island, GA 31522, tel: 912-638-3639. Built in 1736–48 by British general James E. Oglethorpe to protect the region from Spanish incursion.

Fort Pulaski National Monument, PO Box 30757, Savannah, GA 31410, tel: 912-786-5787. A 19th-century masonry fort that was heavily bombarded during the Civil War.

Jimmy Carter National Historic Site, c/o Andersonville National Historic Site, Route 1, Box 800, Andersonville, GA 31711, tel: 912-924-0343. This park includes the boyhood home, high school, campaign headquarters and other sites associated with the 39th president.

Martin Luther King, Jr, National Historic Site, 522 Auburn Avenue NE, Atlanta, GA 30312, tel: 404-331-3920. The park includes the home, church and grave of the famed civil rights leader slain in Memphis.

Ocmulgee National Monument, 1207 Emery Highway, Macon, GA 31201, tel: 912-752-8257. This site preserves traces of several Indian cultures over a 10,000-year time span, including tools of Paleo-Indians, the huge temple mounds of the Mississippian culture, and artifacts of the once-powerful Creek Confederacy.

Kentucky

Abraham Lincoln Birthplace National Historic Site, 2995 Lincoln Farm Road, Hodgenville, KY 42748, tel: 502-358-3874. A 19th-century cabin similar to the one in which Abraham Lincoln was born stands at the site of his birthplace.

Cumberland Gap National Historical Park, PO Box 1848, Middleboro, KY 40965, tel: 606-248-2817. Daniel Boone explored this mountain pass, opening Kentucky to American settlement from the East.

Louisiana

Jean Lafitte National Historical Park and Preserve, 423 Canal Street, Suite 210, New Orleans, LA 70130, tel: 504-589-3882. The park protects historic and natural sites in and around New Orleans, including the site of the 1815 Battle of New Orleans, Acadian Cultural Center and wetlands south of the city.

Poverty Point National Monument, c/o Poverty Point State Commemorative Area, PO Box 276, Epps, LA 71237, tel: 318-926-5492. Remains of some of the most complex ancient Indian earthworks are preserved and interpreted at this park in northeastern Louisiana.

Mississippi

Natchez National Historical Park, PO Box 1208, Natchez, MS 39121, tel: 601-442-7047. Some of the best-preserved antebellum structures are found at this site, once occupied by French and Spanish colonists.

Natchez Trace Parkway, RR 1, NT-143, Tupelo, MS 38801, tel: 601-842-1572. A scenic drive of more than 400 miles (644 km) follows the old Indian trail from Nashville, Tennessee, to Natchez, Mississippi.

North Carolina

Carl Sandburg Home National Historic Site, 1928 Little River Road, Flat Rock, NC 28731, tel: 704-693-4178. This farm was poet Sandburg's last home.

Fort Raleigh National Historic Site, c/o Cape Hatteras National Seashore, Route 1, Box 675, Manteo, NC 27954, tel: 919-473-2111. The site of Sir Walter Raleigh's "Lost Colony," 1585–87.

Guilford Courthouse National Military Park, 2332 New Garden Road, Greensboro, NC 27410, tel: 910-288-1776. A crucial battle in the Revolutionery War was fought here, leading to the American victory at Yorktown.

Kings Mountain National Military Park, PO Box 40, Kings Mountain, NC 28086, tel: 704-936-7921. Site of a critical American victory during the American War for Independence.

Moores Creek National Battlefield, PO Box 69, Currie, NC 28435, tel: 910-283-5591. A major battle between Loyalists and Patriots took place here in 1776 during the American Revolution.

Wright Brothers National Memorial, c/o Cape Hatteras National Seashore, Route 1, Box 675, Manteo, NC 27954, tel: 919-473-2111. Wilbur and Orville Wright made the first sustained mechanized flight here in 1903.

South Carolina

Charles Pinckney National Historic Site, c/o Fort Sumter National Monument, 1214 Middle Street, Sullivans Island, SC 29482, tel: 803-883-3123. This site interprets the life and work of Charles Pinckney, a Revolutionary War veteran, framer of the Constitution and Governor of South Carolina.

Congaree Swamp National Monument, 200 Caroline Sims Road, Hopkins, SC 29061, tel: 803-776-4396. This park protects a 22,200-acre (8,984-hectare) alluvial floodplain with an ecological significant stand of hardwood forest.

Cowpens National Battlefield, PO Box 308, Chesnee, SC 29323, tel: 803-461-2828. Site of a decisive victory in 1781 in the American Revolution.

Ninety Six National Historic Site, PO Box 496, Ninety Six, SC 29666, tel: 803-543-4068. A colonial trading center, the park now preserves the remains of two villages, a plantation and ancient Indian sites.

Tennessee

Andrew Johnson National Historic Site, PO Box 1088, Greeneville, TN 37744, tel: 615-638-3551. The park includes the two homes and tailor shop of the 17th president.

Virginia

Arlington House, The Robert E. Lee Memorial, c/o George Washington Memorial Parkway, Turkey Run Park, McLean, VA 22101, tel: 703-285-2598. Lee's home is preserved at this site just across the Potomac River from Washington, DC.

Booker T. Washington National Monument, 12130 Booker T. Washington Highway, Hardy, VA 24101, tel: 703-721-2094. The birthplace and boyhood home of the influential Southern black leader.

Colonial National Historical Park, PO Box 210, Yorktown, VA 23690, tel: 804-898-3400. This extensive park takes in the sites of the first permanent English settlement on Jamestown island and the 1781 Battle of Yorktown.

George Washington Birthplace National Monument, RR1, Box 717, Washington's Birthplace, VA 22443, tel: 804-224-1732. A reconstructed mansion and landscaped grounds commemorates the birthplace of Washington, the first president of the United States.

George Washington Memorial Parkway, Turkey Run Park, McLean, VA 22101, tel: 703-285-2598. A scenic drive on the Potomac River from Mount Vernon to Great Falls.

Maggie L. Walker National Historic Site, c/o Richmond National Battlefield Park, 3215 E Broad Street, Richmond, VA 23223, tel: 804-226-1981. This site interprets the life and work of a leading member of Richmond's black community in the late 19th century.

Prince William Forest Park, PO Box 209, Triangle, VA 22172. tel: 703-221-7181. The park encompasses 18,571 forested acres (7,515 hectare) with hiking trails, campgrounds and other recreational facilities.

Wolf Trap Farm Park for the Performing Arts, 1551 Trap Road, Vienna, VA 22182, tel: 703-255-1800. This national park site dedicated to the performing arts is host to an active schedule of musical and other theatrical performances.

Puerto Rico

San Juan National Historic Site, 4 San Cristobal Norzagaray Street, Old San Juan, PR 00901, tel: tel: 809-729-6960. Construction of these old Spanish forts, including El Morro, San Cristobal and El Canuelo, was begun in the 16th century.

Virgin Islands

Christiansted National Historic Site, PO Box 160, Christiansted, St Croix, USVI 00821-0160, tel: 809-773-1460. The colonial period of the island is interpreted through a series of 18th- and 19th-century structures.

Salt River Bay National Historic Park and Ecological Preserve, PO Box 160, Christiansted, St Croix, USVI 00821-0160, tel: 809-773-1460. Established in 1992, the park contains archaeological evidence of all major prehistoric cultures in the Virgin Islands, and Christopher Columbus' only documented landing site in US territory.

Civil War Parks

Andersonville National Historic Site, Route 1, Box 800, Andersonville, GA 31711, tel: 912-924-0343. The site of a horrific Civil War prisoner-of-war camp, the park is dedicated to all POWs around the world.

Antietam National Battlefield, PO Box 158, Sharpsburg, MD 21782, tel: 301-432-5124. There were more than 23,000 casualties at this battle in 1862 during Robert E. Lee's first invasion of the North.

Appomattox Court House National Historical Park, PO Box 218, Appomattox, VA 24522, tel: 804-352-8987. General Robert E. Lee surrendered to General Ulysses S. Grant here in 1865.

Brices Cross Roads National Battlefield Site, c/o Natchez Trace Parkway, RR 1, NT-143, Tupelo, MS 38801, tel: 601-842-1572. The cavalry played a decisive role in this Confederate victory in 1864.

Chickamauga and Chattanooga National Military Park, PO Box 2128, Fort Oglethorpe, GA 30742, tel: 706-866-9241. Two major battles are chronicled at the park: a Confederate victory in September 1863 followed by a Union victory in November.

Ford's Theatre National Historic Site, c/o National Capital Parks, 900 Ohio Drive SW, Washington, DC 20242, tel: 202-426-6924. Abraham Lincoln was assassinated here in 1865 by John Wilkes Booth.

Fort Donelson National Battlefield, PO Box 434, Dover, TN 37058, tel: 615-232-5706. The Union Army's first major victory occurred here in 1862 under the command of Gen. Ulysses S. Grant.

Fort Sumter National Monument, 1214 Middle Street, Sullivans Island, SC 29482, tel: 803-883-3123. The first opening shots of the Civil War were fired here, in Charleston Harbor, in 1861.

Fredericksburg and Spotsylvania National Military Park, 120 Chatham Lane, Fredericksburg, VA 22405, tel: 703-786-2880. This historic 7,687-acre (3,111-hectare) park preserves portions of four major battlefields – Fredericksburg, Chancellorsville, the Wilderness and Spotsylvania Court House.

Gettysburg National Military Park, 97 Tawney Town Road, Gettysburg, PA 17325, tel: 717-334-1124. Union troops turned back the second Confederate invasion of the North in 1863 at this battle site, and Abraham Lincoln delivered his famous Gettysburg Address at the dedication of the National Cemetery.

Harpers Ferry National Historical Park, PO Box 65, Harpers Ferry, WV 25425, tel: 304-535-6223. Abolitionist John Brown's men raided the federal armory here in 1859 in an abortive attempt to start a slave revolt.

Kennesaw Mountain National Battlefield Park, 900 Kennesaw Mountain Drive, Kennesaw, GA 30144, tel: 404-427-4686. Union and Confederate

troops clashed here during the Atlanta Campaign in 1864.

Manassas National Battlefield Park, 6511 Sudley Road, Manassas, VA 22110, tel: 703-361-1339. General Thomas J. "Stonewall" Jackson played an important role in two Confederate victories here in 1861 and 1862.

Monocacy National Battlefield, c/o Antietam National Battlefield, PO Box 158, Sharpsburg, MD 21782, tel: 301-432-5124. General Jubal T. Early defeated Union troops here in 1864 during his drive toward the capital.

Petersburg National Battlefield, PO Box 549, Petersburg, VA 23804, tel: 804-732-3531. The Union Army tried to capture vital rail links at Petersburg in 1864–65.

Richmond National Battlefield Park, 3215 E Broad Street, Richmond, VA 23223, tel: 804-226-1981. The Union attempted to capture Ricmond at several battles – Cold Harbor, Drewry's Bluff, Gaines Mill, Malvern Hill, Beaver Dam Creek.

Shiloh National Military Park, Route 1, Box 9, Shiloh, TN 38376, tel: 901-689-5275. A decisive Union victory here in 1862 preceded the siege of Vicksburg.

Stones River National Battlefield, 3501 Old Nashville Highway, Murfreesboro, TN 37129, tel: 615-893-9501. The battlefield and cemetery at this 402-acre (163-hectare) park commemorate an important confrontation in 1862–63.

Tupelo National Battlefield, c/o Natchez Trace Parkway, RR 1, NT-143, Tupelo, MS 38801, tel: 601-842-1572. Confederate and Union forces clashed over a critical railroad link in 1864 at this Mississippi site, which is now a small park.

Vicksburg National Military Park, 3201 Clay Street, Vicksburg, MS 39180, tel: 601-636-0583. Reconstructed forts commemorate the siege of the city in 1863, ending in an important Union victory.

Wilson's Creek National Battlefield, Route 2, Box 75, Republic, MO 65738, tel: 417-732-2662. The first major battle west of the Mississippi River took place here in 1861.

Further Reading

General

The Edge of the Sea, by Rachel Carson. Boston: Houghton Mifflin Company, 1955.

A Fierce Green Fire: The American Environmental Movement, by Philip Shabecoff. New York: Hill and Wang, 1993.

The National Parks, by Freeman Tilden. New York: Alfred A. Knopf, 1968.

The National Parks: Shaping the System, by Barry Mackintosh. Washington, DC: National Parks Service, 1991.

The Quiet Crisis, by Stewart Udall, Salt Lake City: Peregrine Smith Books, 1988.

Romance of the National Parks, by Harlean James. New York: Arno Press, 1972.

A Sense of Wonder, by Rachel Carson. New York: Harper & Row, 1965.

Silent Spring, by Rachel Carson. Boston: Houghton Mifflin, 1962.

Walden and Other Writings, by Henry David Thoreau. New York: Bantam Books, 1962.

Parks & Wildlife

Biscayne: The Story Behind the Scenery, by L. Wayne Landrum. Las Vegas: KC Publications, 1990.

The Blue Ridge Parkway Directory. Asheville: Blue Ridge Parkway Association, 1994.

Cape Cod, by Henry David Thoreau. Princeton, NJ: Princeton University Press, 1993.

Cape Cod: The Story Behind the Scenery, by Glen Kaye. Las Vegas: KC Publications, 1980.

Easy Access to National Parks, by Wendy Roth and Michael Tompane. San Francisco: Sierra Club Books, 1992.

Everglades, by Connie Toops. Stillwater: Voyageur Press, 1989.

The Everglades: River of Grass, by Marjory Stoneman Douglas. St Simons Island, GA: Mockingbird Books, 1974.

Great Smoky Mountains, by Connie Toops. Stillwater: Voyageur Press, 1992.

Great Smoky Mountains National Park, by Rose Houk. Boston: Houghton

Mifflin Company, 1993.

Hiking the Big South Fork, by Brenda D. Coleman and Jo Anna Smith. Knoxville: University of Tennessee Press, 1993.

Isle Royale: Moods, Magic and Mystique, by Jeff Rennicke. Houghton, MI: Isle Royale Natural History Association, 1989.

The Maine Woods, by Henry David Thoreau. New York: Penguin Books, 1988.

Mountain Adventure, by Ron Fisher and Sam Abell. Washington, DC: National Geographic Society, 1988.

National Seashores: The Story Behind the Story, by Connie Toops. Las Vegas: KC Publications, 1987.

Other Insight Guides

The 190 books in the *Insight Guides* series cover every continent and include 28 titles devoted to the United States, from Alaska to Florida, from Seattle to Boston.

Two other titles are also relevant to the present volume:

Insight Guide: National Parks West is a companion guide to this volume. Ranging widely across the west, from Texas to North Dakota, from Colorado to California and then on to Washington state, the book also takes in the national parks of Alaska and Hawaii.

Insight Guide: Native America provides a unique blend of absorbing text about the Native Americans' culture and a detailed guide to Indian reservations,

historic sites, festivals and ceremonies, from the arid deserts of the Southwest to the lush woodlands of the East Coast.

Discovering nature: *Insight Guides* have always been ecologically aware and several "Discover Nature" titles in the series are written for those wishing to understand and appreciate nature and wildlife. They combine truly remarkable photography with an insightful and practical approach to travel.

Insight Guide: Amazon Wildlife brings together an impressive team of naturalists and top-class wildlife photographers to focus on the largest tropical rainforest on earth.

Insight Guide: East African Wildlife ranges across Kenya, Tanzania, Uganda and Ethiopia, combining essays on wildlife with a practical travel guide, from the sparkling waters of the Indian Ocean to the ice-encrusted peaks of the Mountains of the Moon.

Insight Guide: Indian Wildlife is a comprehensive guide to the wildlife parks of India, Nepal and Sri Lanka. It pro-

vides both a broad background to the region's wildlife and a practical guide to the art and practice of observing animals, birds and reptiles in their natural state.

Belcher/West Virginia Division of Tourism 64, 152–53
Arvilla Brewer 60–61, 216
Stephen Gorman 55, 58, 66, 132, 138, 172, 267
Robert Harrison 159, 160
Judith Jango-Cohen 57, 142, 281
Catherine Karnow 78
Lewis Kemper 35, 47, 124, 128, 129, 130, 131, 140, 284
Lyle Lawson 10–11, 30–31, 68–69, 72, 224–25, 230, 231, 233, 256, 257, 258–59, 260, 261, 263, 266
Bill Lea 2, 36–37, 38, 39, 44–45, 48, 50, 51, 59, 112–13, 125, 148, 201, 207, 210–11, 215, 217, 218, 219, 221, 222, 226, 227, 229, 235, 237, 265, 268–69, 275, 279, 304
Tom and Pat Leeson 18, 155, 179, 180, 185, 276–77, 287
Library of Congress 22–23, 25, 28, 29
Robert Llewellyn 52–53, 76–77, 85, 89, 108, 110–11, 116
Pat & Bob Momich/Toops Stock Photo 255
Steve Mulligan 139, 178
National Park Service 26, 27
Joseph Nettis 90, 91, 92, 93, 94, 95, 106
North Carolina Division of Tourism 65
Larry Rice 21, 73, 166, 173, 181, 194, 195, 196, 204, 283
Stephen Shaluta 9, 62, 63, 154, 158
D. Holden Bailey/Tom Stack & Associates (TSA) 292
Dominique Braud/TSA 170
David M. Dennis/TSA 42, 213
Steve Elmore/TSA 74–75, 83
John Gerlach/TSA 1, 40, 141, 174, 192R, 193L, 274
Kerry T. Givens/TSA 183
Victoria Hurst/TSA 147
Thomas Kitchin/TSA 175, 189, 223
Larry Lipsky/TSA 67, 278, 290, 295

Joe McDonald/TSA 171, 264
Timothy O'Keefe/TSA 294
Brian Parker/TSA 288–89, 299, 301, 303
Rod Planck/TSA 41, 169, 184, 192L, 193R
Bob Pool/TSA 87
Wendy Shattil/TSA 249
John Shaw/TSA 282
Robert C. Simpson/TSA Cover, 46
Richard P. Smith/TSA 182
Tom Stack/TSA 302
Richard Thom/TSA 164–65
Tom Till 14–15, 16–17, 32, 33, 43, 80–81, 82, 84, 86, 88, 97, 103, 105, 107, 109, 114–15, 127, 133, 134–35, 136, 144–45, 146, 186–87, 190, 197, 200, 203, 212, 253, 262, 270, 285, 300
Connie Toops 70, 71, 96, 99, 102, 137, 143, 161, 205, 206, 232, 234, 238–39, 242, 243, 244, 245, 246, 247, 271, 272, 286, 291, 293
Stephen Trimble 241, 248
Larry Ulrich 12–13, 34, 149, 151, 156, 157, 188, 191, 198–99, 240, 250–51, 252, 273, 296–97, 298
Art Wolfe 49, 176–77
George Wuerthner 54, 56, 104, 150

Maps Berndtson & Berndtson

Visual Consultant V. Barl

Index